# Training and Development

## Rosemary Harrison

Institute of Personnel Management

First published 1988
Reprinted, with minor amendments, 1989
© Institute of Personnel Management 1988, 1989

Typeset by The Design Team, Ascot, Berkshire
and printed in Great Britian by LR Printing Services Ltd. Crawley, West
Sussex

British Library Cataloguing Publication Data

Harrison, Rosemary
   Training and development.
   1. Personnel. Training — Manuals
   I. Title   II. Institute of Personnel Management
658.3'124

ISBN 0–85292–392–9

# Contents

## Chapter 3    Training and Development Responsibilities and Roles

## Chapter 4    The Integration of Learning and Work
## 1: The organization as a learning system

## Chapter 5    The Integration of Learning and Work
## 2: Auditing learning and developing effective learners

## PART TWO
## Managing Training in the Organization

### Chapter 6    Establishing the Training Purpose, Policy and Plan at Organizational Level

### Chapter 7    Organizing and Managing the Training Function

## Chapter 8 Assessing Needs at Operational Level: Job Training Analysis

## Chapter 9 Assessing Needs at Individual Level 1: Personnel specifications and records of performance

## Chapter 10 Assessing Needs at Individual Level 2: Trainability tests, assessment centres and self-assessment

Chapter 11    Assessing Needs at Individual Level
3: Appraisal of performance

Chapter 12    Designing the Learning Event
1: The learning task

Chapter 13    Designing the Learning Event
2: Applying 'principles of learning' to design tasks;
   practical issues affecting design

# List of Activities (A)
# and Practical Examples (E)

# List of Figures

# Acknowledgements

I would like to acknowledge five sources of inspiration in writing this book. Harry Barrington provided challenging comments on the first draft, and they had a fundamental influence on the final product. John Kenney and Margaret Reid's *Training Interventions* (1986) was always a major reference point, and is a primary text for any student or practitioner wanting to learn about training and development. Dr Alan Rutter, formerly Training Manager at Northumbrian Water and now a lecturer at Newcastle Polytechnic, gave unstintingly of his time and ideas in the many discussions between us about different topics in the book; without his help, Chapter 7 could not have been written. My 1987 Institute of Personnel Management part-time finalist students were a constant source of creativity, support and fun over the two years we spent together, and their splendid record of examination success was a well-deserved reward for their commitment to the subject.

Finally, my loving thanks to my husband and children, without whose patient understanding the whole project could never have been undertaken.

# Preface

The overall purpose of this book is to attempt to offer to students, tutors and novice practitioners, through the medium of a text interspersed with practical activities and illustrations, help in building up basic knowledge and skills and positive attitudes related to training and development in the workplace.

There are certain core skills — observation and reflection, analysis, creativity, decision-making and problem-solving, and evaluation — that are crucial to anyone with responsibility for promoting human resource development in the organization. If that person possesses these skills and has an understanding of major current training and development issues and of certain key strategies and techniques, then they should be able to operate effectively in a rapidly widening field of situations, acquiring more specialized abilities as necessary. The book therefore does not explicitly cover subjects like management and supervisory development, apprenticeship training, or any other special areas of need (all of which are in any case treated in great theoretical and practical detail in other texts). Instead this book tries to stimulate readers to develop practical 'activities' (most in the form of real-life case studies and consultancy projects) to which they are invited to respond both analytically and creatively.

On terminology: as a general point, every attempt has been made to avoid sexist language. In relation to organizational terminology, the word 'manager' refers to anyone who has managerial responsibilities, and therefore covers supervisory positions; terms like 'employees', 'people', or 'team' have been preferred to words like 'staff' or 'workers', whilst the words 'boss' and 'subordinate' do not appear, since they are inappropriate in a book which places so much stress on a joint approach to work planning, review, and diagnosis of needs, and on the right of everyone to development, whatever their formal status in the organization.

Since confusion often seems to exist about the meaning of terms like 'learning', 'training', 'education' and 'development', some explanations can be found in Chapters 1 and 4. It should, however, be pointed out here that the word 'training' is used throughout most of the book merely as a convenient shorthand for both planned instructional activities and all other developmental processes; also that the phrase 'learning event' encompasses not only structured training but the many other approaches through which people can acquire knowledge, skills and attitudes.

Finally, and most importantly, the book is concerned with *everyone* who holds responsibility for training and developing people in the organization, not just with personnel or training professionals. Wherever possible its terminology reflects this concern.

## PART ONE

# Human Resource Development in the Organization

CHAPTER 1

# An introduction to key issues*

## LEARNING OBJECTIVES

After reading this chapter you will

1 Understand what are the main themes of this book, and the rationale for its structure and content

2 Appreciate the difference and the interrelationship between development, education and training, both at national and organizational levels.

3 Understand what are some of the fundamental issues involved in human resource development strategy at national and organizational levels currently

4 Appreciate the tensions that are involved in human resource development, and the importance of a considered and informed approach to establishing policies and strategy in that area.

## The Main Themes of the Book

In 1985 a major report on training in British organizations, *A Challenge to Complacency* (Coopers and Lybrand), was published. The report offered evidence of a disturbingly low level of investment in training in both public and private sector organizations. The main reason for this widespread failure to perform a function which is so crucial to the achievement of organizational goals (see especially *Competence and Competition*. Institute of Manpower Studies,

*In this introductory chapter, unlike those that follow, there are neither activities nor case study illustrations.

1984) was seen by the authors to be a combination of complacent, ill-informed and sceptical attitudes to training at all organizational levels, including that of personnel practitioners themselves. If we accept this view (and the report's findings have been reinforced with too much evidence not to carry conviction), then developing more positive attitudes to training is a crucial task. The report made many suggestions about how to influence attitudes towards training but for the purpose of this book the following are particularly important:

• Exhortations and encouragements to invest in human resource development

• A more systematic approach to the organization of the training function, and greater expertise in training practitioners

• More rigorous costing and evaluation of training in order to demonstrate to managers its cost-benefit and cost-effectiveness to the organization.

• Case studies showing how training can contribute to the achievement of individual and corporate goals — and how failure to train can inhibit progress.

The book's focus, format and content are based on responding to these suggestions. It aims to produce or reinforce positive attitudes which should lead to a belief in the need for substantial investment in human resource development in organizations, and to offer help in building up necessary expertise.

Part One is concerned with everyone who has a responsibility for the development of people in the organization, highlighting the following: the themes of training and development as major contributors to organizational success; the political nature of developmental activity; the theory and reality of training responsibilities and roles in organizations and how to improve training's status; and the concept of the organization as a learing system, where everyone has a major part to play in continually realizing the potential of its individual members whilst simultaneously achieving operational goals.

Part Two is aimed more directly at the novice training practitioner, showing how to plan, organize and control training activities, with special emphasis on how to tackle the crucial areas of costing, assessment of needs, and the design and evaluation of learning events. It is relevant, however, to anyone with responsibility for managing learning processes and activities.

Throughout the book, case studies, almost all real life, offer examples of training successes and failures which are intended not only to help the reader develop the skills of the training 'consultant' (since all involved in human resource development should see themselves as consultants to their organization), but also to build up committed and informed attitudes to development of people.

## Fundamental Issues in Human Resource Development Strategy

The rest of this chapter is concerned to present an outline of seven of the most important issues confronting those responsible for formulating human resource development strategy both at national and organizational levels. They come in no order of priority, since all are, in their own way, of equal significance.

### Training and Development Expertise

In a situation where there is widespread complacency and ignorance about training, and few external pressures, whether cultural, legal or economic, on organizations to invest in it, much of the onus to demonstrate the value of an investment in development of people lies with the specialist practitioners. Yet *A Challenge to Complacency* (ibid), like other reports (eg Manpower Services Commission, April, 1987; Training Services Agency, 1977), showed too many practitioners to be apathetic, acquiescent in their generally low level of responsibility and their reactive, restricted role, as well as lacking in professional expertise. In the organizations where positive attitudes to human resource development did exist, they appeared to derive not so much from the efforts and credibility of training personnel, but from a situation where failure to train had an immediate and critical impact (eg service sectors with close customer-staff contact), or from a general ethos of caring for, developing and retaining staff.

### Human Resource Development Strategies

There are many strategies for achieving human resource development, but the rightful starting point is the corporate philosophy, or culture, relating to the value and place people should have within the organization. That culture sets the framework within which specific human resource development policies and strategies are formulated (see, for example, Benson, 1987; Fellbom, 1987; Harrison, 1988; Rothwell, 1984; Thomas, 1987; Upton, 1987). An organization's culture should, as at Marks and Spencer, be clearly reflected in all its personnel strategies that affect the development of people. These are:

**Organization Planning**, which determines the structure within which people will work, the roles and responsibilities they will carry, the tasks they will perform, and the extent of and limitations to their autonomy

**Human Resource Planning**, which determines how many people will be employed, how, when and where, and how they will be utilized

**Recruitment and Selection**, which open the door to particular opportunities for some and exclude others

**Leadership and Teamwork**, through which barriers to individual, group and organizational development are either broken down or erected

**Appraisal**, the process at the heart of development

**Learning** activities and opportunities, whether formally structured or a part of daily operations in the workplace

**Material Incentive Systems**, that either help to encourage people to develop or, as *A Challenge to Complacency* (ibid) observed, are so few in relation to areas like training that individual as well as organizational motivation to develop is low

**Measures to Protect People** against discrimination and in matters of health, safety and welfare, thus again either removing barriers to individual and organizational growth or putting such obstacles in their path that little can be achieved

**Termination Policies and Procedures** to ensure that, when people leave the organization, positive steps are taken to help them, facilitating their continued development rather than leaving them with little hope or aspirations.

These, then, are the major personnel strategies affecting human resource development in organizations. Most are referred to only briefly in this book hereafter, but they form the context within which all human learning and growth in organizations occur. It is, therefore, that context which must be examined first when learning initiatives are being planned: it will present opportunities, challenges and constraints within which those initiatives have to developed.

Overall human resource development strategy is thus the starting point. But there is also the matter of deciding on strategies for responding to the needs of particular sectors and special areas in the organization, and there are many possibilities other than or as well as formalized training: a team approach (with the training officer as a member); self-development with or without external courses; the use of internal courses; on the job learning; the use of a senior executive as a 'mentor'; external assistance, especially where the training department has low status in a company. Again, references to such strategies will be brief in the book (see, however, especially Chapters 4, 5 and 7), and it is therefore essential to emphasize at this point their nature and importance.

### The Interrelationship Between Development, Education and Training

So far in this Chapter terms like 'training' and 'human resource development' have been used almost as if they were synonymous. Throughout this book they will continue to be used rather loosely, usually as a convenient shorthand to indicate a variety of organizational learning activities. Yet the terms, together with that of 'education' do have quite distinct meanings, and it is important to have a clear understanding of those meanings at this stage.

Here are some dictionary definitions (Oxford, 1978):

**Develop:** to unfold more fully, bring out all that is potentially contained in.

**Educate:** to bring up so as to form habits, manners, intellectual and physical aptitudes.

**Train:** to instruct and discipline in or for some particular art, profession, occupation or practice; to make proficient by such instruction and practice.

We can see from these definitions why the overall term 'human resource development' (or its equivalent) is being used increasingly in organizations today in preference to the more limited term 'training'. Development is the all-important primary process, through which individual and organizational growth can through time achieve their fullest potential. Education is a major contributor to that developmental process, because it directly and continuously affects the formation not only of knowledge and abilities, but of character and of culture, aspirations and achievements. Training is the shorter-term, systematic process through which an individual is

helped to master defined tasks or areas of skill and knowledge to
pre-determined standards.

The need for an integration of these different kinds of learning
activity is highlighted in an area receiving increasing attention:
management development. In a major report (*The Making of
Managers,* 1987) Charles Handy called for organizations to produce
'a development charter' which would act as a guarantee of good
practice. His proposals reflected a concern for a marriage of
corporate and individual goals, and an integration of training,
education and development.

Reactions to the 'Charter Initiative' continue to be mixed, but an
increasing number of companies, including British Aerospace,
British Airways and GKN, have committed themselves to it, and the
Handy and Constable/McCormick Reports (1987) have stimulated a
wide-ranging debate about the education and development of
managers, especially with reference to the 'competencies' that make
them effective. However, for any organization to be fully flexible
and to achieve its objectives there must be a commitment to
establish good practice in the development not only of managers but
of the entire workforce; and there must be a full integration of
training, education and continuous development in the organization
if real growth at individual and organizational levels is to be achieved
and sustained.

## The Development of Core Transferable Skills as well as of Task-Specific Skills

Throughout this book the aim is to promote a strategy both of
continuous development and of relevant training and educational
initiatives. Continuous development, principally through the integration of learning and work so that both are achieved in the same
process, has as its major objective the achievement of operational
goals and the steady growth in ability to learn at every level, from the
individual to the organization as a whole. Whereas the main concern
in training is to help people acquire skills related to a particular task
or tasks, continuous development is primarily concerned with those
core problem-solving and decision-making skills to which the
Preface refers: Observation and reflection, Analysis, Creativity,
Decision-making/problem-solving and Evaluation.

## Directions in National Education and Training Strategy

However, this aim of achieving continuous development for and
within an organization is not a simple one. In fact it highlights
another major current issue: the extent to which policies ostensibly
aimed at 'continuous development', whether in the organization or
in the nation at large, are in reality mainly to do with training and

vocationally-oriented educational programmes: and whether they should be so.

It is not within the scope of this book or chapter to undertake a review of national education and training strategy. An excellent overview can be found in Kenney and Reid (1986), but so much is changing so rapidly that only reading of relevant journals and of the press can help to obtain an up to date picture. Suffice it to say that the overall purpose of White Papers from 'A new training initiative' (HMSO, 1981) to 'Training for Employment (HMSO, 1988), and of the related employment and educational legislation, projects and programmes, has been the active promotion of an integrated national education and training strategy based on the concept of lifelong and economically productive development for every individual, from school to retirement. The scope and range of initiatives can only be hinted at here:

### At Primary and Secondary Educational Level
Key initiatives include proposals for a national core curriculum and for testing at various age points; the Technical and Vocational Educational Initiative (TVEI); the Certificate of Pre-Vocational Education; the reform of the examination system in favour of continuous assessment as well as final examinations; a more comprehensive integration of the academic and the practical in all subjects; and records of achievement and profiling.

### Pre-Vocational Preparation
Amongst a very wide range of initiatives are the two-year Youth Training Scheme (YTS); a major emphasis on work-related non-advanced further education; intended reform of all apprenticeship systems; and review of all vocational qualifications. The increasing legislative and resource pressures on universities and polytechnics in order to make them more financially self-supporting and more 'responsive' to the economy's needs should also be noted under this heading.

### For Adults Both In and Out of Employment
Adult training, retraining and employability is the focus of the controversial 'Employment Training' programme, as well as of the proliferation of open learning ventures, the Open College, Training Access Points, and funding for a wide range of training projects.

Running through all this costly activity is a determination to reduce the gaps between education, employment, unemployment, and the needs of the economy, by producing a nation of young people and adults who will have the skills available in the right place at the right time to contribute fully to our economic goals. A laudable objective, and one to be echoed, surely, at the level of the individual organization. But it presupposes two things:

1 That there is valid and precise information about the skills that will be needed in order that the country's economic goals can be achieved both now and in the future. Yet, as many failed manpower planning exercises at national, regional and local level have shown, such precise quantification seems impossible. So surely the major need is for continuously developed, flexible people with an ability to learn and adjust to different demands, rather than for the trained people who have a mastery of only a limited number of job- or occupation-specific skills, vulnerable to change?

2 That the increasing scale of vocational preparation and the threatened decline in broad-based education from 14 years or earlier will not stunt the overall development of young people to the point where many will be capable of little beyond the confines of an occupation or set of skills into which they have been channelled at an early age, and in which they have been educated and trained.

To some at least this latter is a real and present danger. An employer, one of the winning entries in the 1988 LWT/*Observer* essay competition, writes:

> **Prevailing education policy blurs the distinction between education and training, but they are different. A good education develops the individual to the best of his or her abilities .... and imparts understanding on the basis of which new skills can be acquired. Training looks for performance in a specific skill; acquisition of future skills is not a requirement .... The school leavers of this decade will be the managers of the next .... Managers must be able to absorb complex, contradictory information, evaluate it, and draw conclusions. This process of assimilation, analysis and synthesis is the basis of all essay-based subjects within the arts .... A general arts and humanities education therefore furnishes school leavers with the ability to adapt to a range of work demands .... The need to equip them to survive in the job market should be reflected by widening their range of options, not narrowing them. (Cowie, 1988)**

In the *Daily Telegraph* (Walden, 1988) concern of a rather different kind was expressed by three leading Americans — Education Secretary Bill Bennett; Professor Alan Bloom, author of the best-seller *The Closing of the American Mind*; and the Librarian of Congress, Dr James Billington — who saw the push for vocational training rather than academic development resulting already in a weakening of ethical and cultural values and consciousness in their country.

Yet whatever the debate about the kind of relationship that should prevail between development, education and training, the push in Britain is towards an increasing vocational orientation. Between 1983 and 1997 the Government will have spent more than £1 billion on the largest ever investment in the British curriculum TVEI. Eventually this initiative which, through pilot courses in every local authority, is shifting the 14+ curriculum towards greater relevance for working life, will cover every school and every child in the country. One can see, in a single example, (Berliner, 1987) both the promise and the threat: at Sharnbrook Upper School in Bedfordshire, TVEI is completely integrated into the overall curriculum, and the school is now getting its best ever examination results, with the proportion of children staying after 16 having increased from 40% to 60%. All abilities are involved. But at that same school a youngster who did exceptionally well in his work experience at a local bank, training the staff in the use of word processors, was offered and accepted a job there, leaving school at 16. His school had assessed him as having university potential. Have his education and training led to his development, or to the stunting of his growth? Whilst recruitment to a bank at 16 has kept him from unemloyment, has that been at the cost of higher level skills and abilities that might otherwise have had the chance to grow, to the greater ultimate benefit both of himself and of society?

## Funding of Training Initiatives

So which direction does the organization take? Real human resource development, or training with education tied to its coat tails? The incentives, again, lead to the latter. In one sense there has probably never been so much funding available for training. The PICKUP guide, *Paying for Training* (1987) lists over 110 schemes to help employers, and one in four firms using the guide successfully sought funding for training under one of those schemes. Funding is also available from the EEC to run projects to update the skills of employees, especially in areas of emerging importance for business, or to develop training systems in new technologies using new methods. EEC funding is also available to set up training partnerships between the higher education sector and business and industry, either regionally or in key technologies.

Money is also being made available for initiatives in the tertiary education sector, especially those linked to new technology, and since the publication of the Handy and Constable and McCormick reports (1987), to the development of higher-level management education initiatives. Constable stresses the value of educational qualifications as a way of providing greater autonomy in career development for the individual, and of giving a breadth of awareness of the viewpoints of others in the organization, as well as providing specific competencies. So the role of education as a counterbalance to training and work experience is under active consideration in such quarters.

Money, on the other hand, is less freely available to support the recruitment, training and retention of those in whose hands so much of the educational task lies — teachers and lecturers. Money is also being withheld from those who refuse to conform with prescribed directions in education and training: the young person who does not want to join the YTS and loses unemployment benefit; students wishing to do degrees in those liberal, humanistic, or social science areas where courses are closing down because of their presumed lack of relevance to the needs of the economy; individuals wishing to pursue education courses or developmental activities of various kinds rather than being trained in skills which the organization but not they themselves see as more productive. And too often, training and development fail adequately to help those discriminated against so widely in society; not only ethnic minority groups and women, but also older people, the disabled, those whose sexual orientation does not conform to the norm. Where training, especially, should be used to break down barriers to opportunities within an organization, and to raise consciousness about discrimination so that attitudes begin to change, too often it stops short, and simply trains in procedures, doing the minimum necessary to avoid legal action.

### The Challenges of the 1990's: The European Market and Demographic Changes

Finally, as we move into the last decades of the twentieth century, human resource development in Britain faces two major challenges: the single European market, and the fact that by 1995 there will have been a drop of 25% in the number of 16- to 19-year olds in this country. Properly organized and sustained training and development will be essential if existing valued workers are to be retained in Britain, and if young people are to see in British organizations not only attractive financial rewards, but also meaningful long-term career structures and prospects. Comprehensive and high-quality management training and development is, in this context, of major importance, since inadequately skilled and poorly educated managers are unlikely to see the need for anything but a similarly low and narrow level of skills for all other employees.

## Will the Investment be Made?

After having recorded so many criticisms of the state of investment in training and development in this country, it is important to end on a positive note. Commenting on the 1987 National Training Awards, Keith Lathrope (1988) observed with disappointment that a large number of the 12,000 or so entries failed to specify clearly either the objectives of their training and development activities, or to produce bases for demonstrating the outcomes. However, he was greatly encouraged to find 'that so many organizations were able to attribute important benefits to the training, and detail the evidence in performance terms such as improved sales volume and revenue, service quality, productivity, product quality and improved profits and decreased costs. There were also examples of filling gaps in succession plans and overcoming skill shortages and improved performance of individuals'. There was evidence, too, of broader effects, notably the development of a 'learning climate' and greater willingness and ability to assist the learning of others. Among companies with a coherent strategic view of their future, training was being carried out on a systematic basis and was proving highly beneficial to their performance.

So here at last is not only 'clear evidence of a causal relationship between the enhancement of workforce skill and competence and improvement in overall performance of the organization' but also heartening signs of progress in training in the UK — in contrast, as Lathrope observes, 'to what has recently seemed to be a never-ending stream of reports telling us that we have got it all wrong'.

## CONCLUSION

Having read this chapter you should now:

1   Understand what are the main themes of this book, and the rationale for its structure and content

2   Appreciate the difference and the interrelationship between development, education and training, both at national and organizational levels

3   Understand what are some of the fundamental issues involved in human resource development strategy at national and organizational level currently

4   Appreciate the tensions that are involved in human resource development, and the importance of a considered and informed approach to establishing policies and strategy in that area.

The main learning points related to these objectives are:

1   ***The main themes of the book, and rationale for its structure and content***
In the belief that the major causes of the low level of investment in human resource development in British organizations today are attitudes of complacency and lack of expertise, the book aims to produce or reinforce positive attitudes about training and development in organizations, and to offer help in building up expertise in crucial areas.

2   ***Fundamental issues in human resource development strategy***
There are at least seven major issues to examine:

*Training and development expertise*
Several reports have shown that too many personnel and training practitioners are apathetic, acquiescent in their generally low level of responsibility and status and reactive role. They often lack expertise, especially in crucial areas like a systematic approach to training and development, cost-benefit analysis of training, and evaluation.

*Human resource development strategies*
The rightful starting point for the formulation of human resource development strategies is the organization's philosophy about the value and place of people in the business.
An organization's culture should be clearly reflected in, and should reinforce, all its policies that affect the development of people.
When deciding on strategies for responding to the needs of particular sectors, groups and special needs in the organization there are many possibilities other or as well as formalized training.

*The interrelationship between development, education and training*
**Development** is the primary process, through which individual and organizational growth can through time achieve their fullest potential.
**Education** is a major contributor to that developmental process, because it directly and continuously affects the formation not

only of knowledge and abilities, but of character and of culture, aspirations and achievements.

**Training** is the shorter-term, systematic process through which an individual is helped to master defined tasks or areas of skill and knowledge to pre-determined standards.

*The development of core transferable skills as well as of task-specific skills*
Throughout this book the aim is to promote a strategy of both continuous development *and* of relevant training and educational initiatives.

The primary skills with which a strategy of continuous development is concerned are core problem-solving and decision-making skills:

- Observation and reflection

- Analysis

- Creativity

- Decision-making/problem-solving

- Evaluation.

*Directions in national education and training strategy*
Another major current issue is the extent to which policies ostensibly aimed at 'continuous development', whether in the organization or in the nation at large, are in reality mainly to do with training and vocationally-orientated educational programmes; and whether they should be so.

*Funding of training initiatives*
Funding incentives currently favour training and related educational initiatives, rather than full human resource development. On the other hand, money is less readily available to pay and train those who are responsible for much of the educational task, and for those who do not wish to conform to prescribed directions in education and training.

*The challenges of the 1990's*
Two major challenges face human resource development in Britain in the last two decades of this century:

- THE SINGLE EUROPEAN MARKET

- THE DECLINE IN NUMBERS OF YOUNG PEOPLE AVAIL-
  ABLE FOR WORK

## CHAPTER 2

# The politics of training

## LEARNING OBJECTIVES

After reading this chapter and completing the various activities it contains, you should:

1 Understand what is meant by 'the politics of training'

2 Know how to analyse the context of an organization by reference to its primary culture, structure and power sources

3 Be able to diagnose the main political issues in a typical training situation and outline a strategy for dealing with them.

In any discussion about training, whether in a national or organizational context, it is essential to realize that what is at issue is political activity. Developing people consumes resources, and too often is not seen to use those resources in a way that makes a significant contribution to operational goals. Furthermore, where there is a specialist training function, whether a part of or distinct from the personnel function, it may have, at its head, someone who is at a relatively low level in the organization, and/or whose expertise and attitudes may fail to give them credibility in the eyes of those whose support they need: line managers, unions, the workforce, the Board. On the other hand, where human resource development is the responsibility solely of line managers, similar factors may conspire against achievement of effective results.

### The Politics of Training

Politics, or 'the art of achieving the possible', is what training is often all about. Those responsible for human resource development, looking at their own role, position, resources, skills and at the system in which they find themselves, must be able to assess what it is possible and necessary to achieve, and which of those possibilities to tackle first. Then an appropriate strategy must be adopted. It is indeed instructive to liken the management of training to a military activity, with a set of objectives, an overall way, or strategy, of achieving them, and short-term tactics to draw on in the face of different contingencies. After all, in many organizations today, training is under attack and starved of resources. Survival is increasingly difficult, and so political skill has emerged as being crucial to success, not just for the specialist but for all those in the organization who are responsible for the development of people or who see such development as a crucial managerial function.

So how can support for training be obtained? Industrial training boards are less influential now, and far fewer than they were; the law can, however, be a powerful ally, because legislation relating to employment is so full of training implications; the corporate plan, if there is one and if access to it can be obtained, will show areas of training needs; and managers and unions, if cultivated in the right way, can provide information on more than enough 'training problems' to tackle; many members of the organization will also be forthcoming about their own perceived needs, although many more will not, and some will lack the ability or information which would help them to diagnose those needs. But real, lasting support only comes with one thing: success. Choosing the areas of priority where training will make the most noticeable impact on the organization's effectiveness, then succeeding in those areas and ensuring the success is known about in order to build on it — all these activities are part of the 'politics of training'. In other words:

**Find out what they want, give it to them, and be seen to give it to them.**

But what about failure? We all make mistakes, big or small, and attempting to deny them outright rarely convinces. How does the skilled politician deal with failure?

---

## ACTIVITY

### Explaining Failure

How do you deal with your failure in a particular task or area of work when it has to be discussed with your manager, or with a powerful colleague, or admitted to those working for you? Please describe three or four of your typical methods.

## FEEDBACK NOTES

You have probably mentioned at least one of the following. There are so many ways of coping with failure that this is by no means an exhaustive list, just a few of the most common methods.

1  I admit the failure, and try to show that I have learnt from it and that it will not recur.

2  I try to cover up, blaming other people, events, problems, etc.

3  I minimize the seriousness of the failure, and try to show that there were compensating successes.

4  I try to show that it was not actually failure at all, but part of a plan, and the true benefits are shortly/in the longer term going to emerge. I deflect attention to the plan and its benefits, so that it becomes the focus of the discussion.

---

Political success is more often than not a matter of practising the last two tactics rather than either of the first two. Politics, after all, is the art of achieving the possible, and to be seen to fail too often and too badly is the one sure way of never achieving anything. However, it is important to remember that tactics relate to situations. Sometimes the general climate is such that honest admission of failure, together with convincing evidence that it will not recur, will be the best way of responding. However, in other types of situation or organization (and generally, too, the higher up the organization you are ) surviving failure will be much more difficult, and very compelling reasons will have to be found for discounting it and for people continuing to give you the support and resources you need. At the end of this chapter we will tackle a case study which will require you to look in some detail at this difficult area of dealing with failure. For the time being, let us note that:

**Politics is the art of achieving the possible, and of surviving. Strategies for both achieving and for survival are essential.**

## The Organizational Context of Training

So far, we have discussed politics in a general way, and have reached the conclusion that the essence of politics in training is to get support, to be seen to be successful, and to know how to survive failure. But we have also observed that politics are always rooted in a particular situation or organization. In other words:

**Success in politics involves understanding the context in which you have to operate and adapting to it.**

You will probably have met at least one manager who came to their present job with an excellent record of success, but somehow that success has not been repeated here. On analysis, some factor or factors in the two situations or 'contexts' will be different, and failure to identify and respond to that difference can be fatal.

So now we need to consider the particular context of training. We will examine three important aspects of context: Culture, Structure, Power.

There are, of course, many other factors which the training manager must consider when drawing up plans for training and development, and quite a wide range of them will receive further attention in Chapter 6. There are also other, more complex, ways of analysing the political reality of organizational life (eg Silverman, 1970). However, in this chapter use is made only of the simplest possible approach which is compatible with developing a practical understanding or organizational politics. It is in the culture, structure and power system of the organization that politics are embedded. If, therefore, we are unable to analyse these three aspects, we will have no real chance of success in handling the 'politics of training'.

### Organizational Cultures and Structures
First, cultures and structures. Try to give your own definitions of these terms. If you are familiar with organization theory, that should not be difficult, but if you are not, have a guess anyway: think about phrases like 'the culture of our country' or 'the structure of the family', because they contain some clues.

---

## ACTIVITY

### Culture and Structure

1  When we refer to the 'culture' of an organization, we mean in general terms: _____
   _____

2  When we refer to the 'structure' of an organization we mean in general terms: _____
   _____

---

## FEEDBACK NOTES

If you have anything similar to the following, then you are clearly familiar with what we are going to discuss. If you have not, then your queries should be answered in the next few pages.

When we refer to the '**culture**' of an organization we mean in general terms the set of norms, ideas and beliefs about how things ought to be done in the organization or in a particular part of it. Sometimes the word 'climate' is used instead.

When we refer to the '**structure**' of an organization we mean the network of roles and relationships whereby activities are allocated to different levels, parts and people of the organization. It refers to the way the organization is designed, or shaped. We can envisage structure as the 'skeleton' of an organization.

---

The culture of the organization is receiving a great deal of attention at present; it is difficult to pick up an article about organizational success without encountering the phrase, and writers on organizations as diverse as Xerox (Upton, 1987), Nabisco (Benson *et al.*, 1987), British Airways (Thomas, 1987), Levi Strauss (Carrier, 1986) and Woolworth (Rose and Newman, 1987) all emphasize the culture of those companies as central to their outstanding achievements.

Organization structure has, of course, for long been a focus of research and an acknowledged primary influence on organizational behaviour and performance. Child (1984) has written an exceptionally clear and practical book on how to analyse structure and how to select what is appropriate for the organization, and Mintzberg (1973) has developed one of the most widely-known and theoretically rigorous models for the analysis of structure.

However, culture and structure do not exist in isolation from one another. They are absolutely interrelated, and Harrison (1972) has developed a widely-used 'culture-structure' model, which is the subject of an illuminating chapter by Handy (1985, pp186–96). He observes that every organization has its own distinctive culture, which both gives rise to and in turn arises from (amongst other things) its particular structure. Many organizations, especially larger ones, contain more than one culture and structure, so that what Handy calls a 'differentiated' culture/structure system prevails. From these writers' work we can see that there are at least four main types of culture to be found amongst and often within organizations, each associated with a particular structure:

## 1 *The power culture and web structure*

This is the culture of centralized power. It is most often found in small entrepreneurial firms, and at the top of large, bureaucratic organizations. Control is exercised by one person, or by a small set of people, from whom rays of power and influence spread out, connected by functional or specialist strings. The structure to which such a culture gives rise is therefore web-like.

Essentially such organizations, or parts of them, are political. Decisions are taken largely on the outcome of the balance of power rather than according to set procedures or on purely rational grounds. People who succeed in this kind of organization are often those who want and can handle power, politically skilled, risk-takers rather than concerned with security. Since all key decisions are made only by one or a few people, such organizations move very quickly and react well to threats: they 'think on their feet'. Success means getting the results desired by the central power point: the methods tend to count for relatively little. Organizational life is highly competitive, and survival, even at the centre, is always difficult. In the end, the quality of those at the centre is their key to success and when a central figure goes, or is displaced, the whole balance of power in the system may change radically.

Those concerned with, or responsible for, human resource development in such a system have to produce the kinds of success desired by the central power source, and to relate training objectives and plans to needs recognized as important by that source: by no means an easy task.

## 2 *The role culture and pyramid structure*

This is the culture of bureaucracy. Its prevailing belief is that an organization should have its purpose and overall plan defined at the top, and then rely for its strength on a clearly defined hierarchy of functions or specialisms. Co-ordination of the many descending levels of departments is carried out at the top by a narrow band of senior management, advised by specialist functions. Rules and procedures govern every role and position in this pyramid hierarchy. They also govern communications and the conduct of disputes. Precedents dominate decision-making, and the whole organization tends to be security-oriented with a tendency to rigidity rather than to innovation. Role cultures and structures are slow to see and accept the need to change, and change itself is usually a lengthy and difficult process, with job definitions, rules, established methods of working and behaving pulling people back to the past rather than forward into the future. At the same time, the role structure is probably the most widely used way of organizing large numbers of people around a common goal, not only in work organizations but in states and religions: one has only to think of China, Germany, Russia, and the Catholic Church to see the enduring organizational power of the bureaucratic model, as well as the dangers inherent in its misuse.

For whoever carries responsibility for human resource development in such a system, the position to which he or she is allocated will be the major initial source of power. The higher the position, the more power to influence the system. However, even if the formal position is fairly low or peripheral, all is not lost: as the television series *Yes, Minister* so well illustrated, the person who knows their way round and through the rules, the files, the procedures and the whole political system can use them very successfully to achieve desired ends.

The greatest danger may well be that, in this inward-looking system, open-minded, objective and professional vision may become 'departmentalized'. How many managers have you met who have become absorbed in the goals and interests of their little empire, rather than striving for the benefit of the whole? And given the type of culture that prevails, is such behaviour surprising?

### 3 The task culture and net structure
*(also known as the 'organic' or 'matrix' type of system)*
Task cultures bring people together because there is a job or project to be done, irrespective of personal power or of formal position. The emphasis is on the team rather than the individual, because the culture is one of teams brought together to work on projects as they come in and who are then disbanded, with new teams formed as new projects arise. The structure can be pictured as a net, with some of the strands thicker and more permanent than the rest. Much of the power lies at the permanent knots of that net.

Task cultures and net structures are flexible and skilled, but Handy (1985) claims that they do not often produce economies of scale or depth of expertise, and that control, especially day-to-day control, needs special interpersonal and managerial skills. To be successful in such a structure, people need to be expert at their task, concerned with the project above all else, and ready to give it all the time, skill and effort that it requires. They must also be team-centred and able to cope with little supervision or control from above. Whoever is responsible for development of people in such a system will probably be concerned in the main with helping to build up teamwork and team skills (because expertise is often bought in rather than home-grown) and with the provision of training to meet specific needs as they arise; also with encouraging continuous development through the integration of learning with work, and through self-development.

Success will be a matter of being expert in tasks, but speed of reaction, flexibility, sensitivity and creativity are often more important than depth of expertise. Working in a task culture is challenging and stimulating, but few find it easy, because it requires constant effort to keep up to date in one's expertise; to move through a number of different teams as time goes on; and always to remain committed to the matter in hand, no matter how stressful the demands upon the individual.

When resources become limited in this kind of organization (or part of an organization, because most bureaucracies, for example, contain a number of task culture and net structures within the main system) and money and people have to be rationed, the norms of the culture come under challenge. Often there is a shift towards either a power or a role culture, and sometimes this can lead to a permanent change, and to a new structure. It is a possibility of which specialist functions should always be aware, and in the last few years many training managers have lost their departments, even their jobs, through lack of planning against such a contingency.

**4   *The person culture and galaxy structure***
This is not so much a type of organization, although some partnerships operate on this basis, as a way of describing those clusters of individuals one finds in most organizations, who see their job and the resources available to them mainly as a means of serving their own interests. Often these cultures exist where there is one person who has a unique contribution to make on the basis of specialist skills or knowledge, and so they become the 'star' around whom everything and everyone tend to revolve.

Anyone trying to promote general development of people in such a system can find it difficult to exercise significant influence. Often 'star' individuals not only need development themselves, but are also exercising a stifling effect on the development of their staff. But because they have unique skills, they can usually get other jobs without too much difficulty, or they may have protected tenure. In either case, they will probably fail to acknowledge any expertise as greater or more compelling than their own, and attempts at personal persuasion are unlikely to succeed. However, appealing to that expertise may be one way of at least using them to develop others; few can resist the plea to help those less gifted or knowledgeable than themselves by passing on some of their own immense fund of wisdom and experience, whether in a lecture, a more informal discussion, project work, or some other form of learning situation.

Another, and rather different, perspective is to see person cultures as those in which there is a strong belief in the need to respect individual values and interests and reduce to the minimum constraints on personal autonomy and development. The skill of management in such a culture is to continually hold in balance this belief, with its concern for appreciating and responding to individual needs and aspirations, with the responsibility of ensuring that work targets and commitment to organizational objectives are also achieved.

Now let's try something practical.

---

## ACTIVITY

### The Structure and Culture of My Organization

Take your own organization, or a department/section of it (or, if this is difficult for any reason, then some organization with which you are familiar) and analyse it in terms of its primary structure and culture. (Maximum recommended length: approximately 1,500 words)

Start your analysis with an introduction, of not more than two or three paragraphs, in which you briefly explain what your organization is and whether your chosen frame of reference is the whole organization (e.g. 'X' factory) or a particular branch, section, or department of it. You should also indicate how far your organization, or your chosen part of it, is considered to be 'successful', and any particular problems and/or opportunities it faces in operating.

Thereafter, pay particular attention to the following points, illustrating your analysis with practical examples and explanations wherever possible:

- The kind of culture and structure you think top management intends and believes to exist, and the kind of culture and structure you feel actually exists

- How far the culture and structure promote or reduce the organization's effectiveness and successful development

- The kind of people who get on in the system and the reasons for their success

- The kind of people who are unsuccessful in the system, and the reasons for their failure

- How far people's needs, aspirations and development are matters of real concern to the organization

- The pressures, tasks and opportunities facing human resource development because of the culture and structure of the organization.

## FEEDBACK NOTES

There are no feedback notes as such for this exercise, because the results will be different for each person who attempts it. However, if you are a student, tackling the Activity wholly or partly as a class exercise, then your tutor could split the class up into groups in order for group members to interchange information arising from their analyses. A full class session thereafter can then obtain from each group the most interesting outcomes from those group discussions.* The sorts of issues that can be examined include:

Where people come from the same, or similar, organizations, are their perceptions of the culture and structure in which they work the same, or different? Why? (For example, someone working in a personnel department in a local authority may be aware that the authority as a whole is rigid and bureaucratic, yet if their own department is organized more as a task structure where the management culture is one of teamwork, participative decision-making, and achieving a dynamic, pro-active role for the personnel function, then their daily perception of the organization will be very different from that of someone else working in a more centralized part of that same authority).

What about personnel and training staff in the various organizations? Have they leading roles in the organization? If not, why not? If they are effective, what are the reasons for this?

Specifically, how has political skill, or lack of it, affected the performance and achievements of personnel and training staff?

*There is an excellent questionnaire designed by Harrison (1972) and reproduced in Handy (1985, pp214–20), which offers an effective way of achieving practical insights into the culture and structure of an organization.

How far is development of people in the different organizations that have been analysed a major responsibility of the personnel department; and/or of a training specialist or department; or primarily the responsibility of line management?

What sorts of attitudes and policies are there about training and development in the various organizations, and how do these relate to the cultures and structures of those organizations?

---

In this section we have been looking at different sorts of cultures and structures between and within organizations, and we have seen that one easy and useful way to classify them is by using a fourfold system:

**There are at least four main types of culture, each with its typical associated structure. It is essential for anyone seeking to promote the development of people in an organization to identify the primary culture/s and structure/s to which they must relate, and to adapt their strategy accordingly.**

Culture and structure are two of the three factors relating to the political context of training with which this chapter is concerned. The third factor is power.

## Power in Organizations

**Power is a property that exists in any organization...Politics is the way power is put into action.**
*(Torrington and Weightman, 1985)*

It is essential for anyone trying to promote the development of people in an organization to understand the basis of power in that organization, and how to acquire and use power in order to achieve their objectives.

There are innumerable studies of power in organizations, and one of the most compelling is the social action analysis contained in Silverman's complex but fascinating book (1970), to which reference has already been made. French and Raven (1959) and Handy (1985) offer particularly absorbing discussions of power and influence in organizations. With acknowledgement to their work, I am going to list six types of power, and ask you to explain each one, if possible, as a way of opening up our discussion.

## ACTIVITY

### Types of Power in Organizations
Here are 6 types of power commonly met in organizations. Please
write what you think each means.

Physical power

Resource power

Position power

Expert power

Personal power

Negative power

---

## FEEDBACK NOTES

Now let's check on definitions (see Handy, 1985, pp120−29).

*Physical power* means the kind of power that derives from
physical strength, appearance or presence. Often, in fact, someone's mere presence in a workplace is enough to galvanize
everyone into action. So when we think about physical power, we
should consider not just the effect actual power can have, but also
the ways in which the potential of such power can influence
people.

*Resource power* means control of resources valued by those you
wish to influence. The resources can be anything: money,
promotion, a bigger carpet in the office. What matters is that they
are wanted, valued. Many of those who are responsible for
developing others have few direct resources of their own, and so
one of their first tasks must be to discover who hold the resources
that they need, and how to obtain those resources.

*Position power* We have already seen the importance of position
as a source of power in a role culture, and the implications for
those trying to develop people in such a system.

***Expert power*** in one's field is, as we have seen, highly valued in a task culture, although less reliable as a power source in a role culture (where the expert can quite quickly be cut down to size by rules and procedures, time lags, and the many convoluted decision-making mechanisms).

***Personal power*** deriving solely from the individual's character and personality, is a type of power seen at its most obvious, probably, in power cultures, where it is often used to reinforce all the other power sources of the person or group at the centre. However, it is an important quality for someone like a training practitioner to possess if working in a task culture, where interactions are often difficult and sensitive to manage. And when confronted with a person culture, personal power may be the only way of influencing the 'stars'.

***Negative power*** We can all withdraw effort and commitment. Sometimes the results are not as we had hoped: unless we are in a job or have a skill that is vital, and is difficult to replace, then withdrawal of effort may have no real impact even when a large number of people join together in the withdrawal. However, developing people depends for its success on getting the full commitment and enthusiasm of everyone, from the manager who provides, or withholds, crucial information about the learning needs of staff, to the individual placed in a learning situation but not necessarily motivated to learn from it, especially if he or she sees no meaningful rewards at the end of the process. Inability to understand and deal with the exercise of negative power is a major weakness in anyone responsible for developing learning in the organization.

---

This simple method of analysis enables anyone engaged in developing people to acquire a basic understanding of the main types and sources of power confronting or available to her in the organization, and from that analysis she can then consider how best and most appropriately to use the power she has; how, perhaps, to develop a wider power base; and how to improve interactions with others.

**There are many power sources in an organization. It is important to identify the type of power possessed by oneself and by others. Knowing how to use and relate to different types of power is a major political skill.**

Now let's try a case study, to put some of these ideas into practice. Please read the case study carefully, and then answer the questions on it. It can either be tackled as a self-learning activity, or as course work (if you are a student) or as a class activity with students and tutor agreeing on how it should be done. It tends to stimulate a lot of thought and discussion, because although it is a fictional study it nevertheless describes situations with which many people, even if they are not in a training function, are very familiar.

---

**ACTIVITY**

**CASE STUDY: The Management Training Problem**

You are a training officer, aged 26, working in the Personnel Department of a large private sector service organization in the Midlands. You were recruited three years ago, after working for two years with an industrial training board, mainly in an administrative capacity, dealing with Youth Training Scheme (YTS) paperwork. You have a polytechnic degree in business studies, and in your present post you are mainly involved in YTS operations (your organization is a managing agent). You have no formal personnel or training qualifications, although you would like to acquire some. There are several other personnel staff, one of whom is a training officer specializing in technical training.

Your boss, the Personnel Director, is a middle-aged man, Roger Mason, IPM-qualified, and considered by top management to be effective. He has been with the organization for fifteen years. He is not so highly regarded by many other staff in the organization, who see the personnel function as a very bureaucratic department, absorbed in paperwork and procedures rather than offering real help to anyone. Mason's main interest and workload lie in industrial relations. He is currently heavily involved in drawing up an equal opportunity policy for the organization. He has always tended to 'manage by exception', only worrying when things go wrong. Staff are reluctant to ask him, or each other, for help, as they are afraid that this may be construed as a sign of incompetence on their part, and most stick rigidly to their job descriptions. You do not much like working in the department, but are hoping that once you have a little more experience you will get another post and move on. You intend to specialize in training.

Just after you joined the organization, Mason told you to 'do something about educating our junior and middle managers'. He said top management felt that the performance of these groups, and of supervisors below them, was not always as good as it could be (although he gave you no specific evidence on this score). Furthermore, the younger people at least, many of whom were in technical functions, would be moving up in the next few years, and it was felt that they needed a greater awareness of what general management involved. Mason would like some courses to be organized, although nothing too expensive.

You knew little about management training, but it seemed to you that education was a very important part of people's development: it broadened their minds and gave them new knowledge and techniques. You therefore suggested that about six managers at various levels and from different departments in the organization should be sent on a Diploma of Management Studies (DMS) course at the local polytechnic each year. The two-year part-time course involved attendance one afternoon and evening a week, with subjects like Organizational Behaviour, Quantitative Methods, Management Practice, Finance and Marketing. Students also had to tackle a work-based project in their second year.

Mason liked the idea, particularly as it did not involve his department in anything more than calling for nominees and organizing their attendance. Subsequently sixteen managers have gone on the DMS, at the rate of around five a year. All were chosen by Mason from nominations made by the superior officers of the staff concerned. He did not explain the criteria either of the nominations or of his selections to you.

This year Mason has been asked by top management for some information about the management programme to go into the Annual Report. Last week he came to you in a panic, asking you to provide the information for him in two weeks time.

You have therefore been going round departments talking to all those who have been through the courses, or are still studying on them. The courses seem popular with the staff from departments like management services, sales and marketing — all of whom tend to be in their twenties or thirties, and with degrees or equivalent qualifications. They find the course content intellectually stimulating, and some are able to apply newly-learnt techniques to their jobs, although the majority find that there is no real support for or interest in this in their departments. However, the remark made by one of them to you typifies the general feelings of this group:

> I won't be here for ever, so I'll be able to use the learning in the next job I get. In the meantime, it's certainly made me more aware of the deficiencies of this place — especially how out of date my boss is! Pity you couldn't persuade him to do one of these courses!

The nine staff from this group who have gone through the DMS, or are currently studying for it, have all done well in course work and final examinations, and have particularly enjoyed the project work.

Unfortunately the seven staff from technical departments are neither so satisfied nor so successful. Their average age is mid-thirties to mid-forties, and all have technical qualifications, one a degree. Some of them have supervisory responsibilities, others do not. All find the course hard, some because so much of the content is completely outside their experience and the others because, to quote one:

> **We've been doing our jobs perfectly well up to now: why are we being pushed onto these college courses? We're not going to get more pay or promotion, and there's nothing new in any of it except that Organizational Behaviour stuff — and that's just common sense, anyway — a lot of jargon, but that's all it really is.**

One of the technical staff dropped out after two months and although three others passed the examinations last year, one did not, and has to resit this year. Most feel that on balance the DMS is pointless for them. It does not help them with their daily problems, and they resent the fact that whilst 'whizz kids from sales and marketing have got it made' they themselves cannot even get cover when they are away each week, and they already have such a mass of work to do that piling up 'all this homework business' was just an impossible burden.

You have had a preliminary chat with Mason about these reactions, and he is rather concerned, especially about the technical people and their managers, with whom he has never had particularly good relationships. He has asked you to see him tomorrow to discuss the situation, and to decide what should be said about the programme in his Annual Report. Your discussion will need to be handled with considerable political skill. Why? What are the main political issues? Outline how you propose to deal with the discussion, and what you hope and intend to get out of it.

---

## FEEDBACK NOTES

The training officer will have to explain the failures in the programme to his Personnel Manager not only in a way that will leave his own credibility intact but in a way that will help the Manager, in turn, to present a positive rather than a negative picture in his Annual Report.

## Clarify objectives

The training officer's major concern should be that, in future, needs for training are accurately assessed, and training objectives and plans are agreed and understood, and have the commitment of management, supervisors and shop floor staff. The design of training should in future motivate and help learners to gain from training. He will also want to leave the meeting with the active support of his Manager.

## Put failure into context and look for successes

His best strategy will probably be to stress the benefits that have arisen from the programme so far (and there are quite a number), and, whilst admitting failures, to put them into context. The programme has, after all, run for three years, so some failures are inevitable. Furthermore, major activities such as this not infrequently uncover problems that were probably always there, and could have come to the surface at any time: for example the gap between older and younger staff, and between different specialists and generalists. These are essentially organizational problems, which must be viewed in that wider context. What rewards does the organization offer its older managers and supervisors for the effort required of them in going through a tough examination course, for example? How far does its salary and career structure support such initiatives? What explanation was offered to staff initially about their enrolment on the DMS? Why is there inadequate support for many of the staff when they try to put their new learning into practice?

## Get support for training (from learners and managers)

Having looked at the successes of the programme, and emphasized the need for a wider perspective on some of the problems which have come to light during the three years, the training officer can then, perhaps, suggest that at this stage joint discussions, even joint planning and design, between training, managerial and supervisory staff would be a positive way forward. Other, more work-related, developmental initiatives may be relevant now, rather than just concentrating on educational courses, and the ideas of the staff and their managers should be very valuable here. Such activities would also help older staff, and those in technical positions, for whom more work-based activities would seem relevant and motivating. Involving their managers in more discussions would also be a way of getting those managers more interested in the whole idea of developing their staff, and thus of reducing the problems of transfer of learning that some staff experienced when they tried to apply learning from the DMS course to their jobs.

### Consider culture, structure and power factors

This sort of training situation is very common in a large bureaucratic organization like this one, with a culture in the personnel department that does not encourage a systematic or creative approach to human resource development, nor one which stesses its relationship to corporate objectives. Of course, in reality the training officer should have queried the need for the focus on managerial training and development in the first place. What was the evidence that there were deficiencies here? Or that training was the best response to those deficiencies? And of course he should have looked at other ways of responding to the Personnel Manager's instructions: what about training and development through work-based activities, rather than, or as well as, an educational programme? And there should have been careful monitoring of the selection and progress of staff on the DMS, together with evaluation at the end of each course. And what about pre-course briefing, and post-course de-briefing for the staff?

In other words, there are very many things the training officer should have done, but obviously inexperience and his junior position in the Personnel Department help to explain why he did not do them. No doubt by now he is well aware of his deficiencies. For the discussion, however, he should avoid too much breast-beating, or he may find himself being made a scapegoat by his boss, rather than being able to do anything constructive about the situation. He should aim instead to agree with his boss on establishing positive links between training and line management staff, and on developing simple but effective procedures for the diagnosis of learning needs, and for selection and monitoring of staff on training and development programmes. He should also point to the value of trying to take a wider perspective on human resource development in the organization.

---

That was quite a complex case study, involving considerable knowledge of training and development in order to deal with all of its problems. However, our interest in it was related to political issues, so don't worry if you missed some of the more specialized points that I have covered in the feedback notes — it is the general political strategy that is the important point to consider:

- Clarify your objectives

- Consider culture, structure, and power factors

- Put failure into context and look for successes

- Get support

## CONCLUSION

Having read this chapter and completed the various activities it contains, you should now:

1  Understand what is meant by 'the politics of training'

2  Know how to analyse the context of an organization by reference to its primary culture, structure, and power sources

3  Be able to diagnose the main political issues in a typical training situation, and outline a strategy for dealing with them.

The main learning points related to these objectives are:

*1  The politics of training*
Politics is the art of achieving the possible and of surviving. Strategies for both achieving and for survival are essential. Success in politics involves understanding the context in which you have to operate and adapting to it.

*2  The organizational context of training*
There are three major aspects to the context of training:

Culture

Structure

Power

*Culture* means the set of norms, ideas, beliefs about 'how things ought to be done' in the organization.

*Structure* means the network of roles and relationships whereby activities are allocated to different levels, parts and people of the organization.

Culture-structure theory offers a practical and effective way of analysing and understanding much about the context of training.

There are at least 4 main types of culture and structure:

- Power culture and web structure

- Role culture and structure

- Task culture and net structure

- Person culture and galaxy structure.

It is essential for anyone seeking to promote the development of people in an organization to identify the primary culture/s and structure/s to which they must relate, and to adapt their strategy accordingly.

There are at least 6 major sources of power in organizations:

- Physical

- Resource

- Position

- Expert

- Personal

- Negative.

It is important to identify the type of power possessed by oneself and by others. Knowing how to use and relate to different types of power is a major political skill.

A general strategy for political success in training is:

- Clarify your objectives

- Consider culture, structure, and power factors

- Put failure into context and look for successes

- Get support.

## REVIEW ACTIVITY

Finally, here are some questions which you can either tackle as essays (if you are a student): discuss with colleagues or fellow-students: or simply think about now that you have completed this chapter.

- What do you understand by the phrase 'the politics of training'? Illustrate your answer with specific examples.

- How can training officers increase support for their activities?

## CHAPTER 3

# Training and development responsibilities and roles

## LEARNING OBJECTIVES

After reading this chapter and completing the various activities it contains, you should:

1 Understand what are the main levels of responsibility for training and development in organizations, and what tasks these should involve

2 Understand the main types of training roles, and the main influences on the development of particular roles in an organization

3 Understand the implications for training and development responsibilities and roles in the widespread failure in British organizations to make a significant investment in human resource development

4 Be able to produce an appropriate strategy for improving the status of training in a particular organizational context.

Throughout this chapter it is particularly important to remember that the word 'training' is used simply as a convenient shorthand for *any* responsibilities and activities that help people to develop in an organization. Likewise when reference is made to those with training responsibilities, this encompasses line managers as well as personnel or training specialists unless stated otherwise.

### Organizational Responsibilities for Training and Development

At an Industrial Society conference in 1987, Mecca Leisure's Personnel Services Director, Ewan Park, said that training and development was not just the responsibility of training departments.

It was a team effort involving everyone: individual employees, managers, and the personnel department. In fact, at least four levels of responsibility can be identified for most organizations:

Top management

Line management

Specialist staff

The individual

**Top management**
Here lies the responsibility for harnessing human resource development to the corporate goals of the organization, and for ensuring that learning needs at individual, departmental and overall organizational levels are identified; that a purpose, policy and plan for human resource development are established in the organization; that adequate resources are made available for the operation of the plan; and that this investment is carefully evaluated.

**Line management**
Line managers, by definition, carry the fundamental responsibility for ensuring that their people are helped to perform their jobs effectively and efficiently, and have the kind of learning opportunities through which their abilities and potential can be developed. This responsibility means that managers, whether alone or with the help of specialist staff, must:

1  Identify the learning needs of their people, in relation to present work, individual aspirations, and future demands

2  Prioritize and plan how to meet needs, within constraints of available resources

3  Ensure that those plans are carried out, and that they are monitored and evaluated

4  Ensure that effective transfer of learning occurs so that work and people benefit as quickly as possible from learning experiences.

**Specialist staff**
An organization may have a department which carries a defined responsibility for training and development. Sometimes the person-

nel function carries it out, or delegates that work to training specialists; sometimes training departments are established, either within or independent of the personnel department; sometimes training is part of some other area of activity. No matter how human resource development is organized in a specialist department, however, the fundamental task remains the same. It has been described as follows:

> **Primarily, it is to ensure that all managers are aware of their responsibility for training and, secondly, to assist them in discharging their responsibility when appropriate.**
>
> *(Singer, 1977, p17)*

Singer then points out that the training specialist must be both pro-active and re-active:

> **In the pro-active capacity he or she should seek to ensure that training responsibility is taken seriously by all managers, and by the organization as a whole. In the re-active capacity he provides a centre of excellence about learning more about how to do training in particular circumstances.**
>
> *(Ibid)*

Thus if there is a training manager, he must ensure that, whatever the area of training and development for which he/she is responsible, organizational objectives are served, and must also help managers to do this by providing an expert service.

### The individual

As a member of the organizational team, every individual has a responsibility to consider what are their own learning needs, in relation to their daily work, forthcoming changes, and their career aspirations. Self-directed learning and self-development are increasingly important for everyone, whether in or out of employment, and if the organization offers no opportunities for individual development, then these may be the only ways in which he or she can realize their potential.

Individuals should also take an active role in articulating their needs, and should seek to make a positive contribution to the formulation of training policy and plans, in order for the planning, execution and evaluation of their development to become a genuinely two-way process. Only thus can they hope to influence those who carry training roles (especially, of course, their own managers at whatever level), and so put pressure on the organization to achieve a marriage rather than a divorce of individual and corporate developmental goals.

(For further discussion of the individual's responsibility for their learning, and how they can develop skills that will help them here, see Chapters 10 and 11).

## Types of Training Roles

What do we mean by 'role'? The Oxford dictionary (1975) says:

**Role: Actor's part; One's part or function**

This is a useful way of thinking about 'role' because of the emphasis on playing a part, on relating in a particular way to others, as well as on tasks to be performed. It is also illuminating because it contains the concept of dynamism: every actor differs in his or her interpretation of a given part, and makes of it something unqiue as well as fulfilling its formal requirements. These related ideas of a given and a developed role are emphasized in much of the research about training roles published in recent years. However, it is not the purpose of this chapter to survey the very considerable literature on training roles. An excellent summary and discussion can in any case be found in Kenney and Reid (1986). What will be outlined here is probably the most widely known explanation of training roles. Pettigrew, Jones and Reason (1981,1982) have identified five training roles, using categories which are not mutually exclusive. The roles can be held by specialists or by line managers: the descriptions are to do with what they involve, not who carries them out.

### The change agent

Concerned with the definition of organizational problems and helping others to resolve these through changing the organizational culture. Kenney and Reid (1986) see this as a difficult and not always a legitimate role for training. Many, however, view it as one of increasing relevance, if training is to justify its claim to be a board-level function.

### The provider

Reacts to requests for training help in appropriate ways, but does not take a more proactive part in organizational life. Supports the existing structure and culture of the organization by conforming to its expectations and requirements.

### The passive provider

Again, concerned with the maintenance and not with the changing of the organization, but differs from the 'provider' role because of lack of expertise (especially of political skills) in putting across and developing even that role with conviction. Therefore a very low level of activity and of influence in the organization.

**The training manager**
Focuses on the managerial aspect of training, being primarily concerned with its planning, organization, direction and control, especially in relation to the organization of training departments or sections.

**The role in transition**
A role for training that is in the process of changing from that of 'provider' to that of 'change agent'. The work therefore currently includes elements of both sorts of activity.

**The Reality of Training and Development in Organizations**
So far we have looked at text book explanations of training responsibilities and roles. However, training takes place in the real world, and here, as was observed in Chapter 1, the picture is depressing. Despite many indicators of the value of training as an investment for every organization, helping to improve its profitability, reduce its costs, increase the commitment and motivation of its people and release their potential, perceptions of that value remain low.

In 1984 the report *Competence and Competition* (Institute of Manpower Studies) highlighted both the major investment our international competitors make in training, in order to boost company development and enhance longer term competitive performance, and the very poor training record of most British organizations. As we have described in Chapter 1, the report, *A Challenge to Complacency* (Coopers and Lybrand, 1985), showed how widespread was the apathy. Few organizations showed real commitment to training, which was rarely a board level matter.

In view of this lack of support for training at the top of organizations, it is not surprising that the same report revealed that in most companies training responsibility was devolved to two main levels only: branch or division managers, supported by personnel and training functions. Line management, however, is so often under pressure to achieve short-term objectives to do with profitability or reduction of 'costs' that again real support for human resource development — other than the most basic forms of training — is fairly rare. This, coupled with the fact that in few organizations is there an awareness of how work and learning can be integrated in order to achieve continuous development of people in a cheap, effective and stimulating manner (see Chapters 4 and 5), means that people are one of the most under-utilized resources organizations possess.

At the specialist level, the report's authors found that training managers and departments had a relatively low status, with limited and reactive roles and tasks, and with a general lack of expertise in crucial areas like planning and organizing training, cost-benefit analysis and evaluation.

For individuals, there are often no incentives to press for training, since the rewards, material or otherwise, in most organizations are so few. For some, training and other forms of development might help master a new job or responsibility; or (especially in the public sector) influence a promotion decision; or open up wider career opportunities, often outside the present organization in which they work. But for most, especially given the fact that career progression is so rarely dependent upon training and qualifications at all levels (as it is in Germany), individuals in British organizations are often, like management, apathetic or complacent in their attitudes to training, and therefore rarely put pressure on the organization to provide developmental opportunities.

An illustration of the typical effects of such a low level of responsibility and such limited tasks for training in the organization is given by Alan Fowler:

**The traditional emphasis in local government training on the acquisition of professional qualifications creates a danger that training might be seen to too great an extent as an end in itself. Perhaps the biggest challenge for the training officer, at local authority level, is to develop ways of monitoring work performance, in order to assess not only where training is needed but also to ensure that, when (resources) are put into training, there is an identifiable return in terms of raised standards of quality and performance. This can only be done 'at the coal-face'. The training officer who spends his time running courses in the training centre, or booking staff on to external courses and quizzing them on their return...is not merely doing only half his job. He runs the risk of being totally non-productive — because he is not assessing the impact of training in the work situation...*The best training officers at local level are those who make their reputations not by running eye-catching courses but by assisting managers to create the type of learning environment at the workplace which stimulates the effective self-development of every member of staff — including the manager himself.* (Italics mine)** *(Fowler, 1980).*

We can see clearly from this example that the inevitable result of apathy and complacency, coupled with a lack of belief in the real value of training as an investment, is the delegation of training responsibility to a level in the organization where there is either lack of expertise or of energy and commitment to question or seek to prove its worth. Training activities are limited in scope and meaning, and the training role becomes purely reactive, usually no more than that of 'passive provider'.

We can summarize, therefore, by observing that:

**Research indicates that there is little real support for training as a board level responsibility, or as a major contributor to corporate goals, in the majority of British organizations, whether in the public or private sector. Support at other levels is also weak. The fundamental cause appears to be one of attitudes, notably at the top of those organizations.**

**The training role is usually that of passive provider, whilst training managers and departments tend to have low-level status, and to be confined to reactive training activities.**

**Widespread neglect of training and development in organizations, together with lack of awareness of the value of integrating work and learning as a cheap, stimulating and effective way of continuously developing both, means that people are one of the most under-utilized resources most organizations possess.**

## Major Influences on Training Responsibilities and Roles

If there is such a striking discrepancy between the theory and practice of training responsibilities and roles in the organization, why is this? Let us at this point try to define the major influences that operate to produce 'training reality'.

We can start by remembering our initial definition of 'role':

**Role: actor's part; one's part or function.**

It has already been observed (see page 39) that when an actor plays a part, it is the interplay of their given role and the way they develop it that explains the uniqueness of their performance. Relating this concept to training, we can say that:

**Formal and informal factors influence the parts, or roles, that**

people play, and so also influence training and development roles in a particular organizational context.

## ACTIVITY

### Factors Influencing Training Roles

Please describe, by reference to Pettigrew's categorization system (see page 45), the role held by whoever carries the main operational responsibility for the function of training and development in your own organization, or in some organization with which you are familiar. (It may, for example, be a Personnel Director or Manager, or a Training Manager or Officer, or a designated line manager. If you work in a split-site organization, it may be someone at Headquarters who decides on policy which line managers then have to carry out). Produce a list of the main factors, formal and informal, which you think influence that person's role.

## FEEDBACK NOTES

There are a great many different factors that influence training responsibilities and roles, so only some of the main ones are listed here.

### The Environment of the Organization

This refers to the outer world of the organization, and all the opportunities and constraints, threats and challenges, that it poses. Training responsibilities and roles in an organization which is fighting for survival in increasingly competitive markets will, for example, be very different from those in a large, stable bureaucracy where the pace of change in the outer world is relatively slow, and where training may largely be a matter of continuing to carry out long-established routines.

Another aspect is the political environment. In the 1960's the biggest source of change for training in organizations was the advent of industrial training boards. Immediately there was an increase in the amount and kind of training tasks that had to be performed in most organizations. This often led to an expanded and higher-level role for training. In the early 1980's, the political decision to abolish most training boards had the opposite effect, with a widespread return to low-level training tasks and responsibilities, and passive, reactive functions. But in the early 1980's we also saw an unprecedented degree of central government intervention in education and training, and this continues to represent a source of opportunity and challenge, as well as of pressure, that no-one with training responsibilities can afford to ignore. (See Chapter 1)

## Organizational Goal and Tasks
The overall goal of an organization and its tasks and level of achievement of these tasks are crucial determinants of an organization's primary training needs. They should therefore have a fundamental influence on determining what training activities, responsibilities and roles are to be performed.

## Organizational Structure
Here, we must consider the effects of the organization's structure on the training and development roles and tasks. Sometimes, and almost always in large-scale organizations, there will be what Handy (1985) calls a 'differentiated' structure, with elements of bureaucracy in the routinized areas of activity, but with, say, more of a team-centred, matrix structure in areas requiring flexibility and innovative activity. As we have seen in Chapter 2, the structure and culture in which those with training responsibilities have to operate have major effects not only on training roles but also on choice of training strategies.

One very important structural issue is the place and operation of the personnel function in the organization. As Mumford (1971) points out, 'the historical development of the personnel function ...may or may not have included training.' He goes on to observe that a similar and important factor will be 'the number of other specialists such as work study, O & M, medical services, already reporting to a manager'.

## Organizational Technology
This refers to the way in which work and work processes are organized, the type of technology used, and, in particular, the technology available for training. As we shall see in Chapter 14, there are many important changes taking place in training technology, especially with the growing focus on computer-based training, and these too affect training roles.

## The Workforce
Its size, behavioural patterns, performance, occupational structure and learning needs are all important factors.

To produce this list, I have made use of the well-known analytical model of the organization as a system, with key interrelated elements producing a particular type and level of output and of interaction with the environment. (See Figure 1)

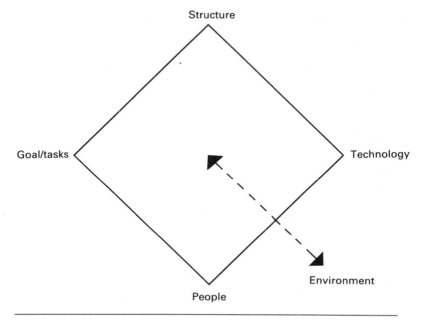

**Figure 1: The organization as a system**

There is one more factor, however, which is crucial in determining the place of training in an organization:

## The Political System
This is a term used to indicate a variety of factors that in reality exercise major influences on training responsibilities and roles. For example:

### Culture and attitudes
This refers to the prevailing system of beliefs about, and attitudes towards, training in the organization. We have already seen that Britain's poor training record seems more to do with attitudes than with any other single factor. Yet where attitudes are positive, the investment in training can be dramatic (Coopers and Lybrand, 1985). A striking example of this is to be found in John Laing Construction, where it is policy to 'grow our own' from shop floor to director level, and where, due to the paternalistic vision of the firm's founder, his absolute belief in the right of everyone to be developed, and his insistence that the firm as much as the individual benefited from such development for the firm, there is a continuing and heavy investment in development of people. It is all the more remarkable

in an industry where such investment is rare, and where there are a variety of economic reasons which often make failure to invest a plausible business decision.

### Commitment to training

It is essential to examine the type of commitment to training by personnel at various levels of the organization, and especially the personal views of top and line management. There must be an analysis, less of what people say than of what they do. *A Challenge to Complacency* (1985) found that whilst most managers gave lip service to training, their actions belied these statements: they did little if anything to give it real support.

### Evaluations of training

This leads to the importance of discovering what key people in the organization see as the value of whatever training is done. What views have they on the need or otherwise for changes in the organization's approach to, or activities in, training? On what solid information are these views based? What criteria are being used in the evaluations? *A Challenge to Complacency* (1985) found that although most managers expressed themselves satisfied with the training investment in the organization, most had no significant knowledge of exactly what training was being done, what it cost, or what were its results and benefits. Neither did training personnel take a lead in providing such information, or appear to see any need to do so.

### Training expertise and interactions

Roles and relationships do not remain static. Anyone with training responsibilities is in constant interaction with others in the organization. These interactions, together with the expertise shown by those with training responsibilities, will either help or hinder the development of status for training. As Mumford (1971) observes in relation to the training manager, they 'may be a skilled practitioner or an exhausted manager put out to graze'. The inept, unskilled manager has little chance of improving the role of training in the organization, and may indeed find that, as a consequence of repeated failure to seize opportunities and to prove the value of training, the role becomes further reduced. Likewise the influential line manager who shows colleagues and team how little he or she values training and development will often foster a climate of scepticism that will be hard for anyone else to change.

At the end of this section we can therefore say that:

There are six major influences on training responsibilities and roles in the organization: the environment, goal and tasks, structure, technology and workforce of the organization, and its political system.

The elements of the political system that have a direct influence on the training role are: culture, commitment to training, evaluations of training, and training expertise and interactions.

---

**How to Improve the Status of Training in the Organization**

What, then, is to be done, both to ensure that training responsibilities at all levels are accepted and carried out, and that meaningful and more proactive training roles are widespread rather than rare in organizations?

There are no easy answers. However, in our analysis of the main influences on training we have developed a model which can help to supply starting points whereby ultimately the status and role of training in a particular organization can be improved. Whoever is responsible for training and development should first carefully consider their organization, or particular part of it, by reference to its:

Environment

Goal/tasks

Structure

Technology

Workforce

Political system

They must then consider what are the main threats, opportunities, and learning needs that become evident from their analysis. Careful consideration of the environment, for example, may reveal important changes in the make up of the labour market, or in legislation, or opportunities in new technology; and it will almost certainly show unexpected, often very cheap, sources of help for particular learning needs. There are many such areas of opportunity, for example, in the secondary education sector. Yet in how many organizations is the world of work still too far apart from the local school? It only takes a little research to increase awareness of such opportunities, and relate them creatively to organizational situation.

Looking at the ever-important political system of the organization, a simple training activity for a manager hitherto an opponent of any investment in training may establish more positive interactions, and win support for training from that manager and those he or she influences. This might be perhaps a costing of turnover in new recruits and the offer of a cheap but effective induction course, with evaluation of its costs and benefits.

Thus in order for human resource development to become a dynamic function in the organization, the task must be approached systematically but also creatively. There must be analysis of the key learning needs related to present efficiency and effectiveness, and to the future, and agreement on how these should be prioritized and tackled in different organizational areas and situations. The training practitioner should develop particularly strong links with managers and unions, and show that she is a fully professional, expert member of the management team, with a vital contribution to make to the organization's goals.

There are three particularly crucial areas of skill for the training manager or anyone responsible for training in the organization, and these must be mastered if attitudes to training are to be changed, and if training is to make its maximum impact on performance:

### A systematic approach

This does not mean that developmental initiatives (such as many of those considered in Chapters 4 and 5) should never be spontaneous, or that there should be a rigid and bureaucratic approach to training; neither is it to deny that often a learning event may itself trigger off new needs for further learning that would have been impossible to predict before that event. It simply means that in order to determine as precisely as possible what are the minimum resources the organization should invest for the development of its workforce, an accurate assessment should be made of known and agreed training needs at all levels. A training plan can then be formulated which can guide the organization in its investment of resources, in the operation of training and development, and in their evaluation. Within the context of the individual manager's department, the same systematic approach should be carried out, leading at the least to an awareness of what needs exist at that level, and therefore enabling the manager to put forward a reasoned argument for the resources to meet those needs.

### Financial expertise

It is essential to be able to spell out clearly and meaningfully what training and development are costing the organization; what are the benefits of this investment; what are the costs of not training. Without this information, there is no possibility of making valid decisions about whether to increase or reduce expenditure, or to alter training in order to achieve a better balance of costs and benefits.

**Evaluation**
This must be systematic, expressed in a language that managers can understand, and must, again, deal in detail with cost-effectiveness; the benefits flowing from training and development; and any areas where improvements or changes are needed.

These three areas are dealt with in detail in Part Two of this book, and in the case studies about Northumbrian Water and Mansells (Chapters 6 and 7) you will find examples of training which has achieved its high level and status in those organizations largely through the efforts of expert practitioners who, in their different ways, analysed the influencing factors on training and took a proactive stance which not only gave training increasing credibility and support, but enabled it to make a fundamental contribution to the success of the business. Note in each case the high priority given to a systematic approach, skilful financial management, and relatively simple but effective evaluation of training. In the 'retail store's appraisal project' (Chapters 12 and 13) and in 'the local authority evaluation project' (Chapter 15) you will find examples of organizations where the commitment of senior management, and the general culture of the organization, together with the shared expertise of managers and a consultant, resulted not only in a major continuing role for training, but also in the growth of widespread attitudes of support for investment in human resource development throughout those organizations.

In Chapters 4 and 5, as we explore the meaning of the organization as a 'learning system' we will see how by building concepts of learning into the everyday language of the organization, attitudes to training and development should begin to change. Attitudes, after all, are shaped by experience, and as experiences change so therefore will the attitudes related to them.

In organizations where training is a central part of business activity, the level of training expertise is high, and has often been a determining factor in the development of the function. The culture of the organization also supports and promotes that development. So changing the status of training in the organization is to do on the one hand with expert practitioners and line managers who, if not themselves expert, are committed and know where to look for training help; and on the other, with building up an organizational culture which places a real value on attracting and retaining motivated and skilful people, and therefore is prepared to make a substantial investment in human resource development.

Here is a final Activity about changing the status of training in your organization, or one with which you are or have been familiar.

## ACTIVITY

### Improving the Status of Training in the Organization

Using theory covered in the early part of this chapter, define the levels at which training and development responsibilities are mainly exercised, and the role that training and development generally has in the organization.

Then produce an analysis *either* demonstrating that training is a high-level and fully effective function in the organization, contributing significantly to organizational goals; *or* concluding with recommendations aimed at ensuring that in future training responsibilities will be carried out effectively at top management, line management, specialist (if any) and individual levels; and that training will assume its most appropriate role in that organization.

## FEEDBACK NOTES

It is impossible to give meaningful feedback on an exercise which will produce a different response from every individual. Suffice it to say that any analysis should relate to that checklist of influencing factors:

Environment

Goal/tasks

Structure

Technology

Workforce

Political system

and should examine how far training and development are currently performed in a skilled, proactive manner, with special reference to the need for a systematic approach, financial expertise, and evaluation; or point out where improvements are needed. Recommendations and actions should reflect these concerns, and should be practical, cost-effective and politically sensitive.

## CONCLUSION

Having read this chapter and completed the various activities in it, you should now:

1  Understand what are the main levels of responsibility for training and development in organizations, and what tasks these should involve

2  Understand the main types of training roles, and the main influences on the development of particular roles in an organization

3  Understand the implications for training and development responsibilities and roles in the widespread failure in British organizations to make a significant investment in human resource development

4  Be able to produce an appropriate strategy for improving the status of training in a particular organizational context.

The main learning points related to these objectives are:

1  *Organizational responsibilities for training and development*
   At least 4 levels of responsibility for training and development can be identified in most organizations:

   • Top management

   • Line management

   • Specialist staff

   • The individual

The task of a training manager (Singer, 1977) is primarily to ensure that all managers are aware of their responsibility for training, and then to assist them in discharging their responsibilities.

**2   Types of training roles**
A role can be defined as:
ACTOR'S PART; ONE'S PART OR FUNCTION
This emphasizes interactions with others, tasks to be performed, and the concept of dynamism.

Research has identified at least 5 types of training roles, although they are not mutually exclusive:

- The change agent

- The provider

- The passive provider

- The training manager

- The role in transition

**3   The reality of training and development in organizations**
Research indicates that there is little real support for training as a board level responsibility, or as a major contributor to corporate goals, in the majority of British organizations, whether in the public or private sector. Support at other levels is also weak. The fundamental cause appears to be one of attitudes, notably at the top of those organizations.

The training role is usually that of passive provider, whilst training managers and departments tend to have low-level position and status, and to be confined to reactive training activities.

Widespread neglect of training and development in organizations, together with lack of awareness of the value of integrating work and learning as a cheap, stimulating and effective way of continuously developing both, means that people are one of the most under-utilized resources most organizations possess.

**4   Major influences on training responsibilities and roles**
Formal and informal factors influence training and development roles in a particular organizational context. 6 main factors relate to the organization's:

- Environment

- Goal/tasks

- Structure

- Technology

- Workforce

- Political system

In the political system, the 4 key elements affecting the status of training are:

- Culture and attitudes

- Commitment to training

- Evaluations of training

- Training expertise and interactions

**5   *How to improve the status of training in the organization***
In order for training and development to become a dynamic function in the organization, the task must be approached systematically but also creatively. There should be analysis of the 6 main factors that influence training and development responsibilities and roles, and any recommendations or actions should be practical, cost-effective, and politically sensitive.
There are 3 particularly crucial areas of skill:

- A systematic approach

- Financial expertise

- Evaluation

---

## REVIEW ACTIVITY

Finally, here are some questions which you either tackle as essays (if you are a student); discuss with fellow-students or colleagues: or simply think about now that you have completed this chapter:

- Find out (e.g. from your library, your Training Agency area office, local schools and colleges, or personal contacts) THREE practical ways in which the training function in your organization has benefited or could benefit from local pre-vocational education developments or schemes. Prepare a brief report for your manager or personnel/training department presenting your findings and their implications for future training policy or initiatives.

- Analyse by reference to practical examples, preferably taken from your own organization, the difference between 'proactive' and 'reactive' training and development roles.

## CHAPTER 4

# The integration of learning and work 1: The organization as a learning system

## LEARNING OBJECTIVES

After reading this chapter and completing the various activities it contains, you should:

1 Understand two major theories about the nature of the learning process, and appreciate their practical relationship to the organization of learning in the workplace

2 Appreciate the value of integrating work and learning, and the importance of a process of continuous development of people, operational tasks, and the organization

3 Understand how the organization can be seen and managed as a 'learning system', where organizational and individual growth can be achieved continuously in parallel.

### The Learning Process, in Theory and in Practice

Organizations, and the people within them, develop by learning. But what, exactly, does 'learning' mean? Try to produce your own definition, in no more than one or two sentences, in the space below, by thinking about what has happened when you have 'learnt' something.

_____

## ACTIVITY

Learning is  _____

_____

_____

## FEEDBACK NOTES

One well-known definition is:

**Learning is a relatively permanent change in behaviour that occurs as a result of practice or experience.**
*(Bass and Vaughan, 1967)*

In other words, we have learnt something when we have acquired new or changed knowledge, skills, or attitudes that stay with us, becoming part of our regular behaviour or performance; and that 'relatively permanent change in behaviour' is brought about by practising something we have been taught, or that we teach ourselves or experience, until it has been fully absorbed.

---

Thinking about learning in this way leads to two major theories which feature throughout this book because they have important practical implications for the development of people and of organizations. All we need at this stage is an introduction to these theories, and an appreciation of how they relate to one another, and to the wider context of organizational learning.

### Kolb's Theory (1974)

First of all, learning can be viewed as a circular and perpetual process, whose key stages are: experience; observation of and reflection on that experience; analysis of the key learning points arising from it; and the consequent planning and trying out of new or changed behaviour. Often people go through this cycle almost instinctively, sometimes so skilfully that they produce increasingly successful behaviour in situations which initially caused them problems; but often, too, they make mistakes at one or more stages of the cycle so that the ultimate skills, knowledge or attitudes acquired do not lead to any improvement. This concept of the learning process is shown in Figure 2.

Let's look at this theory more closely. When was the last time you felt you *really* learnt something? Take yourself back to that occasion, and try relating it to Kolb's concept of the learning process. Here is an everyday example:

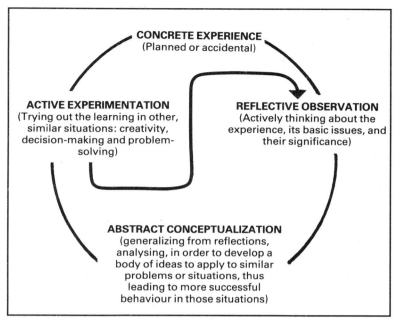

**Figure 2:    The learning process** *(Based on Kolb, Rubin and McIntyre, 1974)*

## CASE STUDY: Mary and Her Manager

Mary came out of her manager's room groaning inwardly. He had called her in half an hour ago, without warning, and she had walked into another veiled dressing down, and the usual failure to put across her defence in a convincing way, or to change his view of the event. Why did he always manage to throw her like this? She knew that their personalities were so different that the relationship was always going to be difficult, but there had to be some way of getting things onto a better footing. What could she do?

When she got into her office she sat down and REFLECTED for quite a long time, not only about her most recent EXPERIENCE with him, but about all the other times when meetings or discussions between the two of them had gone badly. Then, as she thought it all through, she OBSERVED that it didn't happen the same way every time. Sometimes things went well: when she knew a meeting was coming up, and she could prepare for it very thoroughly in advance, getting all her facts together, and anticipating every major criticism that could be made of her line of logic, until her arguments, proposals or conclusions were virtually watertight. On those occasions, because she had thought it through so carefully, her own emotions tended to take a back seat, and the discussion with her manager became much more objective — she could cope with most of his endless questioning because she had played devil's advocate herself beforehand. But, she REFLECTED, when she didn't know beforehand what the meeting was to be about, she began to panic as soon as she got into the room. She felt no match for his dry, legalistic probing, his apparently sarcastic comments, or for the rapid instructions and follow-up questions he would often throw at her. His formality and sharpness always made her feel that he was looking for failure, and expected it to occur.

Slowly, she began to ANALYSE. She started to relate her observations to some of her knowledge about personality and behaviour (she was studying for the Institute of Personnel Management examinations!), and she began to see in her own behaviour all the signs of stress and destructive relief of tension that she had read about in her text books. So, what did the books say about constructive responses? What principles did they advocate, and what could she think up herself? She happened to have a copy of *20 Ways to Manage Better* (Leigh, 1984) in her bookcase, and opening it, she found a chapter on 'Coping with failure' that suddenly seemed to pull all her experiences together. Gradually she began to see a pattern in her successful meetings which conformed with the positive suggestions and principles she was reading about. A strategy was developing in her mind for coping better with those unexpected times when she had to go in for a new brief, or for a reprimand over some error she had made. She decided to make herself try the new strategy on the very next occasion, and see if it worked: she would EXPERIMENT, in order to overcome her problems with her manager. Of course, it wouldn't work perfectly at first, but every new EXPERIENCE of such meetings that she encountered from now on represented opportunities for her to EVALUATE and perhaps again alter her strategy, until at last she had learnt how to overcome her problems.

Mary, in this learning process, had been using those core learning skills to which we have made regular reference in this book so far. They are crucial in any problem-solving situation:

Observation/reflection

Analysis

Creativity

Decision-making/problem-solving

Evaluation

I wonder whether that example is familiar to you? It is a factual one, and I am glad to say that Mary did succeed eventually, and by that circular learning process, repeated several times round, she did develop a new way of dealing with those awkward unexpected meetings, and now has a much better relationship with her boss. I hope that, in reading her story, you have also gained a better understanding of Kolb's (1974) learning theory, and begun to see how very practical and useful it is.

This continuous learning process should not be dismissed simply as an interesting aspect of daily life, or left to the individual to manage and possibly but not inevitably benefit from. If those with a responsibility for the development of people in the organization can 'manage' a variety of everyday work situations, as well as planned training activities, in ways that will foster the key skills involved in the learning cycle then those skills can be transferred to an ever-widening range of organizational problems and situations. Not only individual but organizational performance will thus be developed. It is those 5 skills with which this book is primarily concerned, since they are core to the success of anyone with a responsibility for human resource development in an organization.

Perspectives on the learning process which emphasize experience as the well-spring of learning lead to a focus on 4 important practical issues:

### The organization as a learning system
The organization is full of a rich variety of experiences and tasks which, carefully managed, can promote the kind of learning which will lead to the achievement of organizational as well as individual goals.

### Integration of learning with work
Integrating learning with work in order to promote both individual and organizational performance is as valuable a strategy as the creation of special training activities. It can also be a cheaper and more effective one.

### Continuous development in the workplace
There are great individual and organizational benefits to be derived from a strategy of continuous rather than sporadic development of people at work, notably in the contribution it can make to building up a flexible and motivated workforce with relevant skills for whatever tasks come to hand.

### Development as a fundamental management responsibility
It has already been emphasized in the previous chapter that every

manager has a primary responsibility for developing people. This point is reiterated here, and it becomes very clear that although personnel and training specialists should act as resources and facilitators, they must not and cannot take over that essential managerial function.

Now let us look at a practical example of the way in which a real-life organizational problem was used as a learning vehicle leading to the continuous development of a group of people.

---

**CASE STUDY: The Colour Television Project** (Barrington, *Personnel Review*, Vol. 15, No. 1, 1986)

'When colour TV was first introduced on a major scale, it was appreciated that a new dimension was being added to advertising commercials. Six months before the actual start date, a senior marketing manager (in the organization in which I then served) was charged with collecting — from places such as film studios, colleges of art, and advertising agencies — as much know-how about colour as he could assimilate.

After one month, he had to present his findings to a collective meeting of marketing management. That meeting raised a large number of unanswered questions, and he and several others were charged with further investigations. Another meeting a month later produced more sharing of experience, more unanswered questions, more commitment to get answers, and so on. By the fourth month, discussions were tending to accept certain questions as 'only answerable via experience' and creative decisions were beginning to be taken on how the experience should be managed.

This was the learning system in action, members defining their needs and researching to collect data which was then shared with colleagues to produce decisions on change, all in the service of operational ends. Learning was integrated with work, and both the work and the people were developed via the one process...'

In this case study we can see how a number of individuals gradually developed into a continuous learning group, achieving, as they tackled an operational task, a steady improvement in skills of reflection, analysis, creativity and decision-making which not only helped them to deal effectively with the immediate work project, but which could then be applied to future projects.

Of course other strategies could have been used, and often are in similar situations: a specialist could have been brought in to tackle the whole colour TV project, and would no doubt have done the job effectively and in a much shorter time: but no one else would have developed much from such a strategy. Or the team could have been trained in the appropriate skills and knowledge, so that necessary learning would have been acquired and could then be applied to that and any future similar task: but that would have been a lengthy and expensive approach. The strategy actually adopted was cheap, effective, and achieved work and learning targets, as well as the development of a work team.

---

From this case study, then, we can see that there are many benefits in allowing time at work to be spent in this kind of learning activity, using operational tasks as the learning material.

So, to sum up:

- Learning can be viewed as a circular process where the key stages are experience, reflection, theorizing and experimentation. The key skills involved are those of observation, analysis, creativity, decision-making/problem-solving and evaluation.

- Integrating learning with work both achieves work targets and develops people simultaneously.

**Stimulus-Response Theory**
Our second major theory about learning seems at first sight very different. It sees the mastery of the learning process in relation to 4 key factors:

Drive

Stimulus

Response

Reinforcement
(*see* for example, Gagne, 1965).

*Drive*
For learning to occur there must first of all be a basic need which makes someone want to learn, and which acts as the continued spur to that activity: in other words, there must be a *drive*, or motivation, to learn.

### *Stimulus*

A stimulus is a message which makes an impact on our senses because it relates to one or more of our primary or secondary drives. For learning to occur, people must be stimulated by the learning situation: methods of learning must be used which make a level of impact sufficient to enable and encourage the person to learn in that situation.

### *Response and Reinforcement*

In every learning situation the learner must acquire appropriate responses, ie skills, knowledge, attitudes, which will lead to improved performance and/or development of potential. These responses must be reinforced by practice and feedback of various kinds until they are fully learnt, whilst unproductive responses must be identified before they become habitual.

This may seem an instrumental and grosssly over-simplified explanation of human learning. One is reminded of animal psychology and the so-called 'law of effect', and pictures come to mind of the dog, cat or pigeon being 'trained' to perform in desired ways by a process of instruction, reward and punishment. It also seems at odds with Kolb's experience-based and learner-led theory.

But the differences are only apparent, not real. Let us think more carefully about Stimulus-Response theory. What it *actually* stresses is the importance of the following:

### Awareness of learning needs

If learning, whether pre-planned or arising out of everyday experience, is to succeed, people must want and see a need to learn. They must recognize what their learning needs are in order to choose, respond to, and benefit from the most appropriate learning experiences.

### Objectives and planning in the learning process

Setting objectives for learning, be they generalized or highly specific, and planning for that learning to take place in a given period of time, be it tightly or loosely defined, are always important parts of any learning process. However, according to the situation they may be the responsibility of the individual learner, or of the group manager, or of a personnel or training specialist. Furthermore, objective-setting and planning do not lead inevitably to the structured training situation: nor do they mean that the learning experiences have to be dominated by a 'trainer', using only passive skills on the part of the learners. There are an increasing number of organizations now where strategies such as quality circles, briefing groups and team building activities are built in as part of a planned overall development programme. Indeed, such strategies may themselves constitute virtually the whole of that programme (this is especially true of management development).

### Appropriate learning strategies
Those responsible for helping people and organizations to learn must think carefully about systems and methods that will have appeal for the particular learners and situations concerned. In the case study about colour television, it was clearly sensible to go for a learning approach that focused on getting the job in hand done at the same time: integrating learning with work was highly appropriate and cost-effective. However, there are many other situations where important learning needs may require a carefully planned training programme or a series of well-designed developmental activities, through which specified learning objectives can be achieved by designated learners over a set period of time.

### Avoiding a false distinction between active and passive learning skills
Even where, for good reasons, education or training takes place within a clearly defined structure, the learners often have to use those key learning skills of observation and reflection, analysis, creativity, decision-making and evaluation in a wide range of active and experience-based situations. However, the skills of absorbing and being able to reproduce given information or actions are crucial to many learning tasks too. We are not talking about intrinsically opposed skills here, but simply about different types of skills, relevant to different learning situations and tasks.

### Reinforcement of learning
There is always a need for practice and feedback throughout the learning process, however these may be provided, in order that learners can quickly and confidently acquire new learning, and test it out in their practical situations. Kolb's theory emphasizes this when it shows the stage of experimentation leading into further experience, which then generates the possibility of review, analysis and modification or repetition of the new learning.

So there is no essential contradiction between the two approaches to the learning process that we have been examining in this chapter. Taken together, they offer valuable insights about the learning process and its relationship to individual and organizational growth:

### Needs, objectives and planning are major keys to learning
Needs, whether of the organization or of the individual, dictate the

learning objectives. Once these are clear, then it is possible to plan what experiences (i.e. jobs, responsibilities, areas of activity, training programmes) ought to be undertaken, or sought, and by whom. Of course simply being part of a work-centred, natural learning experience may often allow participants to gain a perception of new needs and therefore of new learning objectives; but the principle remains unchanged: needs lead to objectives which in turn help to give direction and meaning to the learning process.

**Appraisal of performance, both at organizational and individual levels, is essential to the planning and success of learning**
The way in which experiences are tackled, or, given the apparent ability and potential of people, seem likely to be tackled, will show what further experiences are required. Thus analysis of the learning experience must be carried out at organizational and individual levels if relevant strategies are to be developed. (Appraisal of individual performance is covered extensively in later chapters of this book.)

**Careful consideration must be given to learning strategies**
Strategies must suit the learners and their needs.

**Throughout the learning process there must be stimulation and reinforcement of learning**
At each stage of learning, there may be problems. Perhaps the wrong kind of experiences are being provided, or focused on; perhaps the learners lack time, encouragement or skill to reflect on and therefore learn from experience (whether it is a work project or some part of a structured training or educational programme); perhaps they lack or are not being helped to develop analytical skills which will enable them to provide an accurate diagnosis when this is called for. Whoever is responsible for the learning process, be it the individual or someone acting as the manager of a learning event, must know how to apply the right kind of stimulation, practice and feedback at the crucial stages of learning (see Chapter 5 for more practical guidelines on the development of learning styles and skills).

**Managing the Organization as a Continuous Learning System**
In this final section we will look at the overall management of the organization as a continuous learning system.

In organizational life, everyday experience is probably the most fundamental influence on people's learning, whether of attitudes, skills or knowledge, and this experience consists not simply of the work that people do, but of the way they interact with others in the organization, and the behaviour, attitudes and values of those people. It consists, in fact, of their entire work environment. Three practical points arise from this consideration of the influences on people's learning in the organization:

### Everyday experience should be carefully examined, because of its effects on learning

We should be aware, whether as employees, managers or training specialists, of the kind of experiences offered in the daily work environment, and of the learning that is occurring because of them. Some of that learning will have a positive effect on performance, but much of it may have adverse effects: for a variety of reasons people may be acquiring attitudes that conflict with work objectives, and they may be developing serious errors or gaps in knowledge and skills.

### Everyday experience should be used as a source of learning

In this chapter we have already given examples of the kind of initiatives which can lead to the integration of learning with work, ranging from self-directed and individualized learning ('Mary and her Manager') to group learning such as that contained in the Colour TV Case Study or that promoted by briefing groups, quality circles, and various kinds of team-building activities. For more detailed information on all these initiatives, you will find helpful reading contained in the 'Further Useful Reading' section at the end of this book.

### The organization should therefore be viewed and managed as a continuous learning system

But how, exactly, can this be done? Kolb (1974) says that learning should be an explicit organizational objective, 'pursued as consciously and deliberately as profit or productivity'. He stresses that there must be 'a climate seeing the value of such an approach ... developed in the organization'.

So it seems as if we are back to the problem of changing attitudes and culture: a lot more difficult than it is often made to seem. And continuous development is basically about an attitude, a way of looking at the relationship between people, work, and organizational development. However, it can, and must, be pursued as consciously as any planned training activity. It is to help in the task of managing the organization as a continuous learning system that the Institute of Personnel Management has published its very practical *Code of Continuous Development* (1987). Please now turn to Appendix 1 and read through the Code to see what people at different levels of an organization should do in order to achieve the following:

**Self-directed, lifelong learning by means of policies which will allow and facilitate such learning at work, and through the medium of work itself.**

There are 7 areas of activity, all explained clearly in the Code:

Policies

Responsibilities and roles

The identification of learning opportunities and needs

Learner involvement

The provision of learning resources

Benefits

Results.

In the following chapter we will see how organization learning can be audited, and how people can be helped to become effective learners.

## CONCLUSION

Having read this chapter and completed the various activities it contains, you should now:

1   Understand two major theories about the nature of the learning process, and appreciate their practical relationship to the organization of learning in the workplace

2   Appreciate the value of integrating work and learning, and the importance of a process of continuous development of people, operational tasks, and the organization

3   Understand how the organization can be seen and managed as a 'learning system', where organizational and individual growth can be achieved continuously in parallel.

The main learning points related to these objectives are:

## 1 The learning process, in theory and practice

**Learning has been defined as 'a relatively permanent change in behaviour that occurs as a result of practice or experience'.**
*(Bass and Vaughan, 1967)*

There are two major theories about learning which have important practical implications for development of people and of organizations. First of all, learning can be viewed as a circular and perpetual process (Kolb, 1974), whose key stages are:

- Experience

- Reflection

- Conceptualization

- Experimentation

The key skills involved are those of:

- Observation/reflection

- Analysis

- Creativity

- Decision-making/problem-solving

- Evaluation.

This perspective on the learning process, with its emphasis on experience as the well-spring of learning, leads to a focus on 4 important practical issues:

- The organization as a learning system

- Integration of learning with work

- Continuous development in the workplace

- Development as a fundamental management responsibility.

The integration of learning with work, using operational tasks as learning material, both achieves work targets and develops people simultaneously.

The second major theory about learning stresses 4 key factors:

- Drive

- Stimulus

- Response

- Reinforcement.

Both theories stress 4 points:

- Needs, objectives and planning are major keys to learning

- Appraisal of performance, both at organization and individual levels, is essential to the planning and success of learning

- Careful consideration must be given to learning strategies

- Throughout the learning process there must be stimulation and reinforcement of learning.

2  **Managing the organization as a continuous learning system**
In organizational life everyday experience is probably the most fundamental influence on people's learning, whether of attitudes, skills or knowledge. This leads to 3 practical points:

- Everyday experience should be carefully examined, because of its effects on learning

- Everyday experience should be used as a source of learning

- The organization should therefore be viewed and managed as a continuous learning system.

It is to help people in the task of managing the organization as a continuous learning system that the Institute of Personnel Management has published its *Code of Continuous Development* (1987), see Appendix 1.

The Code highlights 7 areas of activity:

- Policies

- Responsibilities and roles

- The identification of learning opportunities and needs

- Learner involvement

- The provision of learning resources

- Benefits

- Results.

---

## REVIEW ACTIVITY

Finally, here are some questions which you can either tackle as essays (if you are a student): discuss with fellow-students or colleagues: or simply think about now that you have completed this chapter:

- How would you explain 'continuous development' to a manager in order to motivate him or her to have a greater commitment to the process in their workplace?

- What is 'continuous development'? What is its relevance to the UK's training problems?

- What are the main elements of the Institute of Personnel Management's 'continuous development' philosophy? Which, if any, are already accepted within your organization? What further developments would you propose?

# The integration of learning and work 2: Auditing learning and developing effective learners

## LEARNING OBJECTIVES

After reading this chapter and completing the various activities it contains, you should:

1   Understand the importance of auditing learning in the organization, and know how in general terms this can be done

2   Be able to analyse your own and others' learning styles and skills

3   Understand how effective learners can be developed in the organization.

### Auditing Learning in the Organization

In order to make best use of the organization as a learning system, those responsible should carefully examine the current situation, analysing needs and achievements; in other words, carry out a 'learning audit'. The sort of questions to ask are the following:

### What learning is going on here?

How do people learn their jobs, tasks, and attitudes? Who and what helps or hinders them in that learning process? Are the right kinds of practice and experience offered, so that effective and permanent changes to behaviour and performance occur? What are people's views about their own learning?

### What planned development is going on here?

How, and by whom and what, are people being developed, and to what ends. If any formal development programmes exist, are they tailored to meet the combined needs of individuals and of the organization? What opportunities are there for self-development, and for 'learning to learn', and how far are people equipped to understand, identify and benefit from such opportunities? Again, what are the views of the people themselves on these points?

**What aims and policy exist?**
What, if any, learning and development aims and policy exist here? Are they understood and communicated to everyone? Or are the growth of commitment, abilities and potential left to chance, or at the most to *ad hoc* interventions — a course here, a pep talk or word of criticism there?

**What organizational growth is being achieved?**
Is organizational performance and growth being stimulated by the kind of learning being pursued? (For example, Chapter 4 explained how planned integration of work and learning promotes individual learning, teambuilding, and operational effectiveness. What are the costs of learning? (See Chapter 7.)

Implicit in these questions is the view of the organization as a learning system that we examined in the previous chapter, and we saw there how important is the task of managing that system: there needs to be 'management of learning resources' as distinct from simply 'management of training resources' (ie of those resources which are used in planned training activities — see Chapter 7). An explanation of how a more systematic, planned approach can be adopted to the assessment of needs is given in Chapter 6. Here, we are simply looking at the general concept of a 'learning audit' and the main issues with which it is concerned, no matter how informal or formalized the audit itself may have to be.

Once we have some kind of overview of the organization as a learning system, we can then think more constructively about how people could best be helped to become effective learners in that system, able to obtain the greatest advantage from every potential learning experience.

## Developing Effective Learners

**The importance of helping individuals to develop continuously at and through work**
It is important to examine more closely the value of continuous development for and to each member of that organization, and how they can be helped to become fully effective learners.

Careful attention to the development of every individual at work is as important as it is to the development of children at school, of students at college or university, and of all of us as we move through life. Every human being, even the most severely retarded or disadvantaged, benefits immeasurably from undergoing continuous experiences which help them to acquire new learning and to develop their abilities. People are the most expensive resource an organization possesses, so making sure that they are properly equipped to perform well, and continuously developed so that all their abilities and potential can be discovered and fully utilized to their own and their organization's benefit in due course, is not just a praiseworthy social act: it is sound economic sense. This leads to the realization that:

### *All organizations today need adaptable workers*
Everyone in an organization should be able to move into new areas of work, and learn and practice new skills, if organizations are to survive and develop, and if people are to have any real chance of continuous employment throughout their working lives.

### *Every manager should help their people to develop their abilities and achieve growth and the realization of potential*
Someone who is always 'growing' in their work is more likely to be flexible when there is a need to acquire new skills or jobs, and more likely to adapt easily to change, and to see change itself as a challenge rather than a threat, than someone who has only been trained for the job they do.

## Learning Styles and Skills
But in order to develop, people need the right kind of learning styles and learning skills. In Chapter 4 we examined the core learning skills that relate to learning based on everyday experience. But people also have styles of learning, which influence not only how they learn in a particular situation, but also how they manage, solve problems, and make decisions in their work.

Honey and Mumford (1986), using Kolb's (1974) ideas as a theoretical base, have done major research which has indicated that predominant learning styles tend to fall into one of the following four categories, related to the four different learning processes described by Kolb. I reproduce their definitions below:

### *Activists*
Activists involve themselves fully...in new experiences. They enjoy the here and now and are happy to be dominated by immediate experiences. They are open-minded, not sceptical, and this tends to make them enthusiastic about anything new...they revel in short-term crisis fire fighting. They often tackle problems by brainstorming...(They tend to be) bored with implementation and longer-term consolidation.

### *Reflectors*
The thorough collection and analysis of data about experiences and events is what counts so they tend to postpone reaching definitive

conclusions for as long as possible...They prefer to take a back seat in meetings...(and) enjoy observing other people in action....When they act it is as part of a wide picture which includes the past as well as the present, and others' observations as well as their own.

### Theorists
They tend to be detached, analytical and dedicated to rational objectivity rather than anything subjective or ambiguous. Their approach to problems is consistently logical...They prefer to maximize certainty and feel uncomfortable with subjective judgements, lateral thinking and anything flippant.

### Pragmatists
Pragmatists are keen on trying out ideas, theories and techniques to see if they work in practice...They don't like 'beating around the bush' and tend to be impatient with ruminating and open-ended discussions. They are essentially practical, down to earth people who like making practical decisions and solving problems...Their philosophy is...'If it *works* it's good'.

(*Honey and Mumford, 1986*)

In any organization there will be a mix of activists, reflectors, pragmatists and theorists: people whose way of learning and approach to problems and decision-making is primarily even if not completely characterized by the forms of behaviour described under those headings. What is important is to identify the different learning styles and approaches, so that there can be a matching of styles to needs, and so that those dominated by one style more than any other can improve their effectiveness by developing a wider range of styles to suit their present and future roles and tasks. For example, there is no point in allowing situations or decisions calling for an essentially practical approach to be dominated by theorists; nor for a problem which must be sorted out in a totally logical, systematic way to be handled exclusively by pragmatists. Likewise when a specialist in, say, engineering design wants to move into a managerial position, he or she must develop an approach to that new job that will balance out what may be a natural tendency to reflect and theorize with the ability, when needed, to be pragmatic.

At this point, why not try to find out what kind of learner you are yourself: Honey and Mumford's questionnaire can be found in their book (1986). It has been used by many managers and others, and the authors say that it is generally felt to have a high degree of validity, although they recommend that you should try it twice in a two or three-week period, rather than just once, to get a fairly reliable set of scores. Of course, the questionnaire is meant to be a thought-provoking mechanism rather than a stringently scientific measuring instrument, so do bear that in mind when you have scored up your results.

Interestingly, Honey and Mumford, who have looked at the primary styles of various occupational groups, find that trainers tend to have high 'activist' tendencies. (They do stress, however, that the samples are not large enough to be sure that this conclusion was generally valid.) Herein, perhaps, lies the explanation of the successes and failures of those training personnel who are strong on innovation and lateral thinking, infectiously enthusiastic and gregarious, loving the limelight and generating an atmosphere of excitement and challenge; but poor at evaluating what they do and learning from it; poor at relating what they do to a body of theory to see if that might help them to do it better, or at ensuring that those theories they teach are valid in the practical context; poor at analysing how far what they do is in fact logical; and poor at making sure there is a transfer of training at the end of the learning event, so that training actually works in the real-life situation, and at changing it if it does not. If you recognize the type, it all helps to show that theory produced from experience (Kolb's and Honey's theories) and related to other situations (Honey and Mumford's research) can indeed produce valuable insights and learning.

### Developing the Learners
Now let us relate Kolb's learning theory, and our ideas about learning styles and skills, to learners in our own organization. Consider the following statements:

> **Our cyclical economy and the speed of technical change suggest that 'learning to learn' is the central training problem of our time.**
>
> *(Kenney et al, 1979)*

> **Every manager, every trainer, every supervisor, every experienced worker has a responsibility for guiding and helping others to learn from everyday experience.**
>
> *(Manpower Services Commission, 1980)*

> **People can become self-directed learners, understanding their learning styles and developing the skills needed for effective learning. Thus they can manage their own learning processes instead of relying on the system, or hoping they will learn naturally.**
>
> *(Mumford, 1981)*

What underlies all these statements is an awareness that, if people are to learn continuously, and to take advantage of the rich resources offered by the organization as a learning system, they must have relevant learning ability. How can this ability be fostered? How, for example, can those responsible for human resource development in a large organization, with several thousand people in its workforce, hope to develop people as learners? As with any other complex task, we must simplify it by reducing it to its essentials.

The Institute of Personnel Management's *Code of Continuous Development* (1987, see Appendix 1) explains how people can be helped, and can help themselves, to become effective learners. However, it is appropriate here to go into rather more detail about what the training specialist or anyone with responsibility for development of people in the organization can do to help. Six major activities seem essential:

## Self-development
Clearly, whoever is trying to help people become effective learners must themselves have an adequate mastery of each of the four major types of learning skill, and so one of their first tasks should be to identify what kind of learner they are themselves at present (using Honey and Mumford's learning inventory (1986), which takes about 20 minutes to complete and to score; or Kolb's (1974), which takes rather less time, and offers a very interesting alternative. If both are used, illuminating comparisons can be drawn from the two sets of scores). They then need to work out an action plan to improve those learning skills which will enable them to function effectively along all four dimensions rather than just one or two (Honey and Mumford's book gives detailed guidance and examples to help here).

## Promote self-directed learning
Self-directed learning and self-development are crucial activities for all who need to learn continuously, and so those helping to develop people in organizations must then explain and promote these processes. The appraisal interview offers a major opportunity for this, and will be examined in some detail in Chapter 11. However, since it is increasingly important for people to play an active part in their own development, how can this process of self-directed learning be carried out? Basically by individuals identifying their own needs related to their present work, to any changes likely to occur to it in the future, and to their career aspirations; and then by following the advice given by Mumford (1981) in an extremely stimulating article on management self-development:

Review how far their learning opportunities are inhibited or encouraged by their own learning style (do past learning experiences indicate that they are dominated by one style of learning?): or by their manager, or by the organizational culture and structure in which they work

Assess how far and with what effect the organization relies on structured learning experiences such as courses or specially-constructed learning projects

Review their core learning skills of observation and reflection, analysis, creativity and decision-making, and evaluation, and consider how to use them more effectively

Review the work and other experiences in which they are involved in terms of the kind of learning opportunities they offer

Look for potential helpers in the self-development process: colleagues, specialists, manager, mentor, spouse

Draw up learning objectives and a plan of action

Set aside some time each day (or each week) to answer the question 'What did you learn today?'
                    (*Mumford, Personnel Management*, August 1981)

(More information on self-assessment follows in Chapter 10.)

**Promote a climate of awareness about continuous development**
Trainers must be continually on the look out for everyday opportunities which can be converted into conscious learning experiences for various groups or individuals. Personnel and training staff especially should have discussions with managers and other key personnel in the organization, over coffee or lunch, after meetings, during talks about people's training needs, even, possibly, at specially arranged 'Continuous Development' seminars. They can in all these simple ways begin to build up an awareness in the organization about what continuous development means, and how it can be achieved through the integration of work with learning as well as through the more elaborate and expensive formalized learning events.

**Design training events which will develop learning styles and skills**
If training is to be fully accessible to all who need it, then it should be designed in such a way as not only to avoid the discriminatory

barriers forbidden by law, but also to accommodate whenever necessary a range of learning styles, rather than appeal to only one type of learner. But training must also help learners to acquire or develop those styles most suited to the tasks they have to carry out; a training manager's course, for example, should promote all four types of learning style, in order to produce at the end of the day people who are *not* predominately activists but have a balance of skills across the four categories, thus enabling them to function effectively in the *different* situations in which training experts have to operate.

### Seek to reduce organizational barriers to the development of appropriate learning styles and skills

Trainers should likewise promote an awareness that healthy organizations should recognize and encourage diversity of learning approaches, and should appreciate their relationship to behaviour and performance. If, for example, the preferred mode of learning in a particular organization is by experience, and no time or support beyond basic skills training is available for those wishing to learn also by different methods (for example, by an educational course or programme) then the implications of such a policy need to be articulated very clearly by whoever is responsible for training and development of personnel. The workforce will no doubt become actively involved in their jobs, and in the short-term at least time and money will be saved; sooner or later, too, most people will reach an adequate level of performance. However, lack of development of reflective, analytical and pragmatic abilities other than those needed to master the job in hand will in the end lead to a lack of innovative skills and of flexible and forward-looking managers, and to an emphasis on past practice rather than on new ways of doing things.

Cuthbert (1984) describes how one of the first things done by Formica at a time when it needed to build up a high quality and adaptive workforce, was to train and develop teams and place emphasis on reflection by managers of the ways in which they managed; on observation of the human processes set in motion by different sorts of management style and organization structure; on acquisition of a wider band of knowledge about leadership and teamwork; and on experimentation with different approaches until work behaviour and performance showed real improvement. It was an extremely successful programme, incorporating all four of Kolb's learning 'modes' (1974).

### Influence appraisers to consider learning styles when examining performance, or in selection situations

Finally, anyone trying to help people become more skilled learners should seek to influence those involved in all forms of appraisal processes including selection, transfer, promotion and termination of employment (an easier task if there is appraisal training in the organization, and/or if personnel and training are closely integrated functions). Criteria should be developed which relate to the learning, problem-solving and decision-making styles and skills needed, and these criteria should help to guide appraisals. In this way not only should judgements and decisions become more valid but, in the process of discussing this extra dimension, there should be an improvement in managers' understanding of how central a part learning style and skills play in people's behaviour and performance at work.

Is this an unrealistic objective? No. Honey and Mumford's *Learning Styles Inventory* (1986) has already been used:

- To select salesmen for the computer industry

- To select graduate management trainees

- To put together compatible project teams

- To aid career counselling and guidance

- As part of an in-company annual appraisal system

- As part of a market research survey.

Now, let's apply the learning in this chapter to a practical task about which you can then reflect, in order to produce a set of concepts that you can apply to similar tasks in the future. This is a task that faced me in November 1986.

---

## ACTIVITY

### CASE STUDY: Continuous Development for IPM Students

You are the Employee Development tutor on a Stage 2 part-time IPM course, with 25 part-time students who know very little about continuous development, either in theory or in practice. Their average age is 28, and they come from both private and public sector organizations. You are running a two-day non-residential workshop at a local hotel, and you and they have agreed that its learning objectives will be as follows:

**Overall purpose**

To understand what continuous development (CD) is, in order to assess its benefits for individuals and organizations, and to be able to apply it in a practical situation. The major immediate need to which it relates is to help students tackle any CD question on their examination paper next May.

**Specific learning objectives**

By the end of the workshop each student should:

1 Know the CD philosophy with special reference to the IPM's *Continuous Development Code*

2 Know about the main theories relating to CD

3 Know about the main elements of CD

4 Understand what distinguishes CD from other forms of learning and development

5 Be able to draw up a CD programme relating to his or her individual needs

6 Be able to draw up a CD programme for an organization

7 Be able to critically evaluate CD theory and practice.

## ACTIVITY TASK:

Please design a Programme for the 2-day workshop. Hours are approximately 9.00 am to 5.00 pm each day. (If you are a student, you could do this Activity as a class-based exercise, or as an individual assignment.)

---

## FEEDBACK NOTES

There are many ways of designing such a workshop, and reflection and analysis with colleagues or co-students and tutors will undoubtedly prove the most effective way of producing something worthwhile. My own students designed a workshop which incorporated a major CONCRETE EXPERIENCE (they chose as their main task to split into groups, each of which had to design a CD programme for a particular organization or department of their choice), and included provision of opportunities for REFLECTION, OBSERVATION, periods when the students would be able to learn about CD THEORY and then relate that to their practical task, and opportunities to EXPERIMENT with what they were learning in a practical way before going back to home and/or workplace and taking part in further EXPERIENCE which would help the learning to be fully transferred.

Since continuous development was a major area of our syllabus, it represented a real work task. By jointly designing it (in class two weeks beforehand), then after the workshop evaluating it at our next class meeting, and relating the whole experience to learning theory and to theory on the design of training, we were all involved in a continuous learning experience where work and learning were integrated, and the work task became the learning material.

It proved to be an extremely effective workshop at all those levels, and the longer-term effects on the students were quite striking. Students who completed diaries for a few months after the workshop, charting the progress of self-directed and work-based learning plans to improve their learning styles, gained insights into those styles, and the ways in which these affected their behaviour and reactions to situations at work. In some cases there were marked and very productive behavioural and work changes. One very shy young female student began to make herself speak out with her views on many occasions at work when before she would have stayed silent (usually in group meetings, or discussions with her boss); to her surprise she found that people listened to her and that she influenced their views; and so she became increasingly involved in different levels of decison-making. Her new-found confidence and greater assertiveness also extended into her private life. All the changes were, for her, major signs of the emergence of a more active personality, still enjoying reflecting and observing, but now much more interested in and able to tackle everyday experiences in a positive way so that she could learn from, and grow through, them.

Finally, of those 25 students, 20 took the IPM final examinations in May 1987 and achieved outstanding results in Employee Development, where, compared with a national pass rate of 60%, 85% of the group passed including two who obtained distinction (and distinctions are rare!). The three who failed got marginal grades, and so could hope for better results in the resit examinations. Whilst our pass rate for the other subjects was high in comparison to the national average, this was a remarkable set of results. There were, of course, many possible reasons for it, but the students and I felt that the workshop and its consequential learning was, for all of us, some sort of turning point: motivation and interest in learning seemed then to take a leap forward, and the students showed an increasing determination and ability in mastering whatever learning problems faced them, and in consciously developing more than one primary learning style in order to further their various learning objectives. Understanding your own learning processes is not easy, but once you become interested in doing so, the first step towards continuous development has taken place.

---

## CONCLUSION

Having read this chapter and completed the various activities it contains, you should now:

1  understand the importance of auditing learning in the organization, and know how in general terms this can be done

2  be able to analyse your own and others' learning styles and skills

3  understand how effective learners can be developed in the organization.

The main learning points related to these objectives are:

### 1  Auditing learning in the organization
Those with responsibilities for development of people in an organization should find out:

- What learning is going on

- What planned development is going on

- What aims and policy exist

- What organizational growth is being achieved

The reason for these questions is to establish what is happening about learning in the organization, the sorts of resources being devoted to it, and the results being achieved.

### 2  Developing effective learners
It is important to help individuals to develop continuously at and through work because

- All organizations today need flexible, adaptable workers

- Every manager should help their people to develop their abilities and achieve growth and the realization of potential.

**Learning styles and skills**
In order to develop, people need the right kind of learning styles and learning skills. Honey and Mumford (1986) describe 4 types of learners:

- Activists

- Reflectors

- Theorists

- Pragmatists.

**Developing the learners**
The Institute of Personnel Management's *Code of Continuous Development* (1987, see Appendix 1) explains how people can be helped, and can help themselves, to become effective learners.

There are at least 6 major ways in which anyone with responsibility for development of people in the organization can help with the development of learning styles and skills:

- Self-development

- Promote self-directed learning

- Promote a climate of awareness about continuous development

- Design training events to develop learning styles and skills

- Seek to reduce organizational barriers to the development of appropriate learning styles and skills

- Influence appraisers to consider learning styles when examining performance, or in selection situations.

## REVIEW ACTIVITY

Finally, here are some questions which you can either tackle as essays (if you are a student): discuss with follow-students or colleagues: or simply think about now that you have completed this chapter:

- Indicate with examples how the training department can encourage line management to make fuller use of learning opportunities in normal organizational activities.

- What have been the formative experiences that have shaped you own attitudes, skills and knowledge in relation to your present or last job? How, in retrospect, could you have been helped to learn more effectively form everyday work experience?

# Managing Training in the Organization

## CHAPTER 6

# Establishing the training purpose, policy and plan at organizational level

## LEARNING OBJECTIVES

After reading this chapter and completing the various activities it contains, you should:

1 Understand the difference between a purpose, policy and plan for training in an organization

2 Be able to choose an appropriate strategy for assessing an organization's training needs and developing a training plan

3 Know how to draw up an organization's training plan.

In this chapter the main focus is on drawing up an organization-wide policy and plan for training and development, and although it refers to a training manager carrying out this task, it is intended to offer practical guidelines to anyone who, in the particular organization, may hold such a responsibility: a personnel professional, a senior or middle-level manager, etc. In the same way, although its concern is with an organizational policy and plan, its basic principles and approaches are just as relevant within a more limited frame of reference, for example a section, sector or department.

### Establishing a Purpose, Policy and Plan for Training

## ACTIVITY

### CASE STUDY: The New Training Manager (Part 1)

You have been appointed as an organization's first Training Manager (any type of organization of your choice, with a workforce of about five hundred people, an office and a secretary/clerk shared with the Personnel Manager). You report directly to the Personnel Manager, who, at 37, is six years older than you, and has been with the organization for ten years. She is one of the organization's senior officers, and you have been told at your interview that within certain obvious parameters she will be giving you a free hand to establish and run training and development as you see fit. You will be expected to advise on the purpose of training in the organization, and to draw up policy guidelines for approval by the top management team. You will then be expected to develop a detailed training plan for the organization, and establish and hold responsibility for a training budget.

It is your first day. You are due to have a meeting with the Personnel Manager at mid-day, and the primary aim is to agree on how you will carry out your first task: drawing up a training purpose, policy and plan for the organization. What sorts of issues and questions will you raise in order to help you tackle that task?

---

## FEEDBACK NOTES

Of course there are innumerable issues and questions that you could list. Those shown below, however, cover those which need to be raised most immediately:

How soon must the training plan be drawn up, and what staff resources will you have (if any) to help you?

### Environment
Is the organization stable, or exposed to external pressures, threats, changes? How are these likely to affect the training function?

What training links, if any, exist with people and institutions outside the organization?

eg  Consultants

    Providers of external courses (both training and educational)

    Training Board advisors

    The Training Services Commission and other training bodies

    Other local training officers/managers

Careers officers

Local schools.

If any direct use is made of them, why, and with what results? Does anyone measure their effectiveness?

## Goal and tasks

What has been the overall purpose of training and development in the organization up to now?

What are thought to be the major training tasks facing the organization now, and in the period of the corporate plan (if there is one)? Why?

What, if any, are the kind of training and development tasks currently carried out in the organization? Specifically, what is done in the following areas:

Assessment of needs

Analysis of jobs/tasks

Appraisal of people

Specification of training objectives

Allocation of resources

Recruitment, selection and continuous assessment of learners

Design of training events

Operation of training events

Evaluation of learning, training and development?

## Structure

What is the overall structure of the organization: is it primarily a power, role, task or person structure?

Does anyone have any formal responsibilities for training at top, line management and specialist levels of the organization?

What is intended to be the precise nature of the organizational links between yourself and other parts of the organization, especially Personnel?

What formal or informal procedures, related to training and development tasks and activities, currently exist in the organization?

To what extent would you be able to change current procedures?

By whom are training activities recorded and evaluated?

When staff are sent on training programmes or external activities, what is the nature and extent of the Personnel function's responsibility for those staff?

What is you own formal role and what are your prescribed responsibilities?

Are you to be given a free hand in organizing training? What is the exact nature of your authority and discretion here?

## Technology

What kind of 'training technology' exists, or is available? What are the main media and methods of training and development that you could use, on and off the job?

Is there any possibility of using open learning, computer-assisted learning, etc? (NB: Information on media and methods is given in Chapter 14).

## Workforce

What is the occupational structure of the workforce?

What are felt to be the main current and future training and development needs of different sectors of the workforce?

## Political System

What is the general climate of opinion about training in the organization?

Which managers and other key personnel in the organization particularly support training and development activities? Who, on the other hand, have no interest in them, or are likely to oppose various initiatives?

How is training generally evaluated in the organization? What criteria are used?

Are there, or is it likely that there will be, any problems in trying to involve line managers in the diagnosis of training needs and in other aspects of training and development?


Thus we have established which issues to raise and what questions to ask by reference to the checklist we developed in Chapter 3 (page 43):


Environment

Goal and tasks

Structure

Technology

Workforce

Political system

I am sure there are many other issues you have thought of, and many other specific questions. In order to develop an organizational purpose, policy and plan for training, a very wide-ranging set of questions have to be asked. They cover not only the immediately obvious ones relating to training needs, but also issues about the external and organizational environment in which training will have to take place; the role and level of training in the organization, and how far the brief in relation to policy formulation and training planning is rigid or flexible; many other important structural issues; and, of course, those major political issues which will go far to determine what support the person responsible for drawing up the training policy and plan can expect as they try to find out what needs really exist, and how they can best and most feasibly be met (incidentally, a major 'political' factor in this case study will be the Personnel Manager's personality, her perceptions of the training function, and her reactions to the new training practitioner).

So in the first meeting with their Personnel Manager (or whoever it may be to whom the training manager has to report, because of course in many organizations training is a quite separate function or department from personnel, and in some there may not even be a personnel function) a training manager must not only try to obtain certain crucial facts about training needs. They must also try to build up a mental picture of the organization, establishing where there are constraints, problems and opportunities. As we saw in Chapters 2 and 3, training and development are very political activities, and anyone moving into a new training role must be aware that a strategy failing to take that political dimension fully into account cannot succeed.

---

So far, we have looked at the planning of training in a generalized way. Now, we need to examine in more detail the various practical stages it involves.

## The Training Purpose and Policy
All organizations need to have, in some form, a purpose, policy and plan for training.

### The purpose of training

must clearly express the overall reason why the organization is investing in training.

### The training policy

must give the guidelines to be followed in the organization's training activities; it sets the scene for the training PLAN which can then be drawn up. The policy must clarify the allocation of overall responsibilities for training, and matters such as the main types of training to be done, and the resources the organization is prepared to provide to ensure that training is carried out.

### The training plan

must explain in detail what will be done in order to realize the training PURPOSE and POLICY in a practical way. It should include content and objectives of training, location and methods, timing and sequence, allocation of specific responsibilities for each area of training, and how training will be evaluated.

So we can state that:

**Training purpose and policy establish the framework within which the training plan can be drawn up.**

At this point our training manager may be faced with a dilemma: how can an organization be clear about the purpose of training, and the policy it should adopt towards training, until training needs have been identified and assessed? Yet a full-scale assessment of needs could take months. What, in the meantime, is to be done about purpose and policy to act as guidelines for the activities of the training function? As in so many areas of training and development, a pragmatic approach will provide the answer: if there is already a purpose and policy statement (or its informal equivalent) in existence, then initially the training manager should discuss it with management and, if relevant, union representatives, and should make any amendments that are generally agreed to be necessary. A systematic assessment of needs can then follow, with further changes to the statement of purpose and policy being made if necessary. If there is not a purpose and policy statement, then a reasonably accurate although generalized estimate of overall needs can be obtained by the senior management team (and again, as relevant, by union representatives), in order to draw up a provisional statement. A fuller assessment of needs can then, as already described, lead to a final and formal purpose and policy statement in due course.

It may be the case however, that because of the situation in the organization a formalized purpose, policy and even plan may not be able to be drawn up at all. Training may have to be a matter of responding immediately to major problems, usually in order to help the organization survive. In this case, a 'problem-centred' strategy can be used, as described later in this chapter, where purpose and policy are informally agreed,' even if not written down, and where planning is on a rolling and short-term basis instead of over a fixed and relatively long period of time.

Whichever strategy is adopted, discussion and agreement with management and other interested parties over the exact purpose and policy for training is a first priority.

Four major categories of possible training need in the organization should always be considered; those relating to:

- Staff newly appointed from outside the organization

- Newly promoted staff

- Existing staff

- Staff facing change.

Since Chapters 9, 10 and 11 deal in detail with the analysis of individual needs, there will be no further discussion of these four categories in this chapter.

Now, here is an Activity to reinforce what has been learnt so far about the purpose and policy for training in an organization.

---

## ACTIVITY

Here is a training policy statement. Please read it carefully, and then answer the question at the end.

### Statement of Training and Education Policy: Northern Rock Building Society, Gosforth, Tyne and Wear

1    The Society's policy is to provide training for all staff in order that they can perform their individual jobs effectively, and in doing so, ensure that the Society achieves its objectives.

1.1 Education and professional qualifications are a vital part of training and development. Education by broadening awareness of the working environment helps to develop individual performance.

1.2 Training is a vehicle through which new skills can be acquired and existing skills developed, to allow individual members of staff to give maximum contribution to benefit the Society.

2   The Personnel and Training Services Controller is responsible for ensuring that training and education activity is directed towards the achievement of overall Society business objectives.

2.1 Day to day management of all training and education activity is the responsibility of the Training Manager.

2.3 Each line manager has the lead responsibility for the development of their staff and for assessing their training and education needs. This is supplemented by an annual evaluation of Society-wide needs by the Training Manager.

2.4 Coaching in immediate work processes and tasks and for inducting new staff into the Society is the responsibility of the appropriate line manager, supported by staff of the Training Department.

2.5 The development of the annual training programme and subsequent budget submission is initiated by the Training Manager for review by the Personnel and Training Services Controller.

2.6 Course content and presentation is developed by Training Officers, in association with the Training Manager. Attendance on external conferences and courses has to be specifically approved by the Training Manager, in line with overall budgetary provision.

3   Control of the training and education budget is the responsibility of the Personnel and Training Services' Controller, who reports twice yearly to Executive Committee.

3.2 The total cost of training and education will be contained within the relevant budget, as agreed on an annual basis.

4    There are no exclusions to the types of training the Society is prepared to offer to assist in the achievement of corporate and operational plans. No individual will be excluded from receiving training on the grounds of age, sex, colour, grade or any other criteria which could be deemed as discriminatory or divisive.

4.1  In practice, most of the training carried out in the Society will be on the job training and a major role of the Training Department is to provide support to the Managers in their role as trainers. This support goes well beyond simply running training courses, and includes assistance with formulating training plans, advice on training methods, and provision of equipment and facilities.

4.2  The Training Department is available for advice, assistance and support to Managers to enable them to fulfil their responsibility regarding  training.

4.3  In addition, advice and practical help on all matters relating to training and education is readily available from the Training Department.

5    All training requests reflect needs and will be treated sympathetically.

5.1  The training resources are dependant on several factors, for example budgetary constraints, and the training priorities necessary to fulfil the Society's objectives. Consequently there may be occasions when a training request may be postponed or refused due to other priorities. In these circumstances the Training Manager is the final arbiter.

5.2  The Society has the right to insist upon the training of individuals whenever this is necessary to ensure the achievement of Society objectives.

5.3  Each member of staff has access to the Society's training facilities by direct communication to the Training Department via their immediate supervisor or through any existing or future formal training request system.

6    The mechanics for implementing training and education policy, and the actual working details of that policy are contained in the following pages of the Training and Education section of the Procedures  Manual.

August  1987.

(Extract from 'Statement of Training and Education Policy', included by permission of Northern Rock Building Society, Gosforth, Tyne and Wear. The original statement has been slightly altered and shortened to suit the purposes of this exercise)

Which paragraph/s in the Northern Rock statement represents the PURPOSE of training and education at the Society, and which paragraph/s represents the POLICY? Please give a brief explanation for your answer.

---

## FEEDBACK NOTES

In the Northern Rock statement, paragraph 1 (1.1 to 1.2) represents the 'PURPOSE' of training and education, because it explains in general terms why the Society is investing in those functions and the benefits it expects will be forthcoming from that investment.

Paragraphs 2 to 6 define the Society's 'POLICY' in training and education. They define the rights, roles and responsibilities of everyone in the organization in relation to training and education; the resources that will be devoted to it; the kinds of training and education, in general terms, that will be carried out; how and by whom assessment of needs will be undertaken; and how requests for training and education will be dealt with. They therefore clearly establish practical guidelines for training and education, which can subsequently be translated into detailed plans for each department and sector of the Society.

The statement is extremely comprehensive and informative, and is clearly an excellent guide to all Northern Rock personnel. Others you may come across may not be so detailed, but remember that essentially all that they need to clarify is the following:

**The purpose of training**
**The policy to be pursued to achieve that purpose**

---

### The training plan
Once purpose and policy have been agreed, even if only informally, then training plans covering each area of need, preferably in the form of a master training plan for the whole organization, can be drawn up. Singer (1977, p31) is helpful here, observing that for each area, the plan should show:

- The content of training

- The performance standards to be achieved

- Where and how training will be given

- Who is responsible for making arrangements and for the training

- The timing and sequence, bearing in mind priorities

- The method to be used in assessing results.

### Strategies for Assessing an Organization's Training Needs and Developing a Training Plan

Strategy has been described as the art of directing and planning. When we refer to 'training strategy' we usually mean two things:

> **The overall approach chosen to assess training needs and the particular ways in which training will be carried out in the organization — eg on the job, off the job, buying in training, using outside courses or activities etc.**

In relation to the overall approach chosen to assess training needs, there are two main strategies that can be adopted:

> **The total, or comprehensive, strategy**
> **The problem-centred strategy**

Each, as will be seen, also leads to agreement on which *specific* training strategies will be adopted in the organization.

These two strategies are not in opposition to one another, nor are they at extreme ends of any kind of continuum. They are simply approaches which are the same in their general principles, but in their detailed operation fit different kinds of situation. The comprehensive, 'management by objectives' strategy starts with an analysis of the corporate plan and ends with the formulation of an organization-wide training plan containing unit and individual plans for training and development. Ultimately, these will contribute to operational ('business') success in the forthcoming year (a year is usually the planning period for this kind of strategy). It is a strategy relevant for organizations where the environment is relatively stable, and where longer-term training plans can be developed with an acceptable chance that they will continue to be relevant. The organizations must also have the time and resources. For organizations like these, typified by Northumbrian Water, as I shall shortly show, the 'total' strategy is appropriate and effective. On the other hand, for organizations which are either in an unpredictable, competitive environment and/or lack the resources for the 'total' strategy, something more selective and immediate in its payback is needed. Organizations like these need training to help them deal with their immediate and pressing problems. For them, the 'problem-centred' strategy, as already indicated in the previous section, is essential. Such an organization is 'Mansells' (not its real name), and it too will be described in this chapter.

Both strategies are systematic; it is the timescale and scope of assessment and planning that are the major differentiating factors. With the 'total' strategy, the timescale is usually at least a year with perhaps several months available to collect all the initial information and go through the various stages needed in order to produce from it a comprehensive, detailed and fully costed training plan covering the whole organization. With the 'problem-centred' strategy, the timescale of the training plan itself may only be a few weeks or months, so the gap between assessment of needs and responding to them has to be minimal. The plan, such as it is, may barely appear on paper, and must be completely flexible, to accommodate an ever-changing situation. It will deal with immediate needs rather than attempting a thorough assessment of every sector of the organization. Let us now look at each strategy in detail, to explain exactly how they are carried out.

## The 'total' strategy

---

### CASE STUDY: Northumbrian Water's Strategy for Drawing up a Training Plan (By permission of Northumbrian Water)

Northumbrian Water (then called Northumbria Water Authority) was set up in 1974. Since then it has gone through a variety of changes, with a workforce which peaked at 2,500 in 1979 and had decreased to 1,500 in 1987. With a policy of virtually no external recruitment since 1979, the training function was asked not to do less training, but to help develop highly committed people within the contracting workforce who could do more work, and be more flexible, than before. Northumbrian Water (NW) employs many varied professional groups, the majority engineers and chemists, and within the manual and clerical workforce too there are many different occupational groups. As part of its policy of contraction to a core of highly effective and adaptive personnel, there is a special focus on management development and training, with particular attention paid to identifying people's aptitudes, attitudes and potential related to the management development programme (to which further reference will be made in Chapter 11). The Chief Executive has an absolute commitment to this programme, and this sets the tone of the 'culture' relating to development in the organization as a whole: an example of the way in which, as noted in Chapters 1 and 3, that overall philosophy about people has such a direct influence on training's role and status in the organization.

1979–1987 were critical years. Before then, the training function had been viewed by most people at NW as rather peripheral, an administrative function mainly concerned with arranging for staff to go on a variety of Water Council courses in order to become technically proficient in their jobs. From 1979, however, training became viewed increasingly positively as an aid to organizational performance, and as a means to the end of developing a slimmer, more flexible as well as more skilled workforce at all levels. With the 'total' strategy, the key stages leading to the formulation of a detailed organizational training plan are:

Establish the PURPOSE of training in the organization

Establish the POLICY for training in the organization

Establish the PLAN for training in the organization.

With NW, the PURPOSE of training, the overall reason for its existence, can be described as follows:

## Purpose of Training

The overall purpose of training at NW is to contribute to continuous improvement and profitability by helping to develop, within a contracting workforce, people who can do more, and have the skills, attitudes and commitment to respond flexibly to whatever changes may occur, whether internal or external.

With such an overall purpose, the POLICY for training — ie the routes which have to be followed in order for the PURPOSE to be achieved — is as follows:

## Policy for Training

The following categories of training should be carried out in the order of priority indicated, in each financial year:

A    training to meet health and safety legislation, other relevant
     legislation, and further education programmes which are recog-
     nized as part of NW's employee development programme

B    training to ensure that specialist knowledge necessary to NW is
     retained

C    training needed for people who are to be seconded to another
     job or rotated through jobs as part of the NW's development
     programme

D    training directed to improve the job performance of people in
     their present job within the forthcoming year

E    training which is desirable but not essential, and can be
     undertaken at any time if it is not possible to carry it out within
     the forthcoming year.

With this PURPOSE and POLICY in mind, the training manager has to
produce NW's TRAINING PLAN. This is a detailed and fully costed
documentation of all training to be carried out in the forthcoming
year. For each training event, the plan describes the need for each
trainee, and the means by which it is to be met, in terms of the
resources to be deployed (ie training organization, methods and
cost). In other words, the plan gives to training a strategy in our
second sense of the word: the ways in which training needs will be
met. Those needs themselves are, at source, related to present
performance data on employees and to the demands of the future
business plans of NW. Training events are prioritized for action,
using the same categories as those listed in the policy statement.
The plan progresses through stages of refinement and scrutiny, from
its embryo form to a statement of company intent which is then
communicated to all parties involved in the training programme. In
order to achieve this result by the beginning of each financial year,
planning will have been under way for three to four months,
involving some 100 managers, four personnel officers, and the
training manager in its consultative processes.
     Eight steps in the evolution of the training PLAN at NW can be
distinguished:

## STEP 1  The Training Need
The first step, which at NW currently takes place in early December
each year, is to study the organization and annual plans for the
organization. The training manager and personnel officers then
discuss with every manager the training and development needs for

their department. At this stage, they will be aware of any impending organizational changes, new technology initiatives, new plant and machinery and any new staff coming into the organization. In establishing training needs they will rely upon the manager's interpretation of events as well as upon corporate strategy.

### STEP 2   Possible Solutions

During this phase of the discussion, the degree to which training can contribute to meeting departmental needs must be assessed. Performance targets and outputs of the department are examined, and help to give objectivity to the discussions. At the individual level NW operates a systematic and generally effective scheme of appraisal for all its managers and other senior people, and so information about management training needs comes mainly from the results of appraisal interviews. Where the appraisal system is not yet operative, information will come from the managers' views, performance records, career plans, potential reviews, etc.

Quite often problems which are perceived initially by managers to have a training and development solution turn out to be problems needing some other solution, and vice versa — and this is an absolutely critical stage in these discussions. It is essential to be clear as to the real nature of a problem: if performance is poor, for example, it may be because of no or inadequate training, but it could as easily be because of poor motivation, ineffective management, faulty equipment, and so on.

Thus in this second step the training manager and personnel officers have detailed talks with every manager to ensure that all the departmental and individual needs raised are indeed best, and most cost-effectively, met by a training response, and that those needs are jointly defined and agreed, using a prioritization system which has been laid down in the POLICY for training.

### STEP 3   Select Training Events

At this point it is important to discuss options for training, with a view to being as cost-efficient as possible. Initially the possibility of on the job events is explored to achieve the required learning, rather than looking at external courses of action as a priority. This strategy has led to a very significant overall shift at NW in recent years, from a reliance on external courses to a major emphasis on in-house training, much of it done by consultants tailoring their training to suit the specific needs of the organization's employees, as well as by NW's own people taking over more training (for example, in appraisal skills and team building) once they have acquired the necessary skills.

### STEP 4    Create Training Plan

Next, the training manager constructs his first draft of the annual training plan, which identifies each department's and each individual's training needs and the relevant courses of action which have been agreed with the managers of those departments and individuals.

### STEP 5    Establish Priorities

The budgeting process conducted by the training manager starts at this point, when, within the training plan, he classifies training needs and events on an A to E scale according to priorities established in the overall TRAINING POLICY of the Authority.

### STEP 6    Apply Budgetary Constraints

After training has been categorized, the training manager then makes an estimate of the costs involved in the initial draft of his training plan, including the options which were discussed with managers. Costing is done using current prices (an inflationary factor is later added, as calculated by the accountants), examining both direct and indirect costs of training. (See Chapter 7 for an explanation of indirect, or 'hidden', training costs.)

At NW managers are required to submit departmental budgets for the coming financial year in late January. Total budget figures are then allocated before the beginning of the financial year to enable managers to allocate resources appropriately, based on their January submissions. Once the training manager receives his budget allocation, adjustments to the plan are quite straightforward, as the plan itself has been built up on a pyramid of costs (ie all 'A' events costing £x, all 'B' events costing £y, etc). Reappraisal of the options available may result, for example, in the use of more internal training, or in dropping some category E training. In the latter event, subsequent reassessment of the original need will be carried out, to see whether or not training is still appropriate.

### STEP 7    Communicate Results

Once the training plan has been fully costed and agreed by the Board, a copy of the relevant sections is given to each manager as an *aide memoire* and plan for each department. This then becomes an essential tool of reference for the review meetings the training manager holds with managers throughout the forthcoming year.

### STEP 8    Monitor and Evaluate Training

A continuous appraisal of progress and budgetary control is maintained by the training department with management and those who go on training and development programmes. The monitoring of costs in comparison with budget is not a difficult task, since the training plan has been costed specifically to events, to departments and to clear categories of course fees, travel and subsistence expenses, and fees paid to external consultants and trainers. Monitoring is, however, vital, for two reasons:

It enables a tight control to be exercised over on-going training, so that if at any point costs are exceeded, appropriate action can be taken, whereas if costs should be below those estimated, then there is flexibility either to include any hitherto deferred 'E' category training, or to do additional training to meet some unexpected contingency

It enables the training manager to build up his 'value for money' statement which is included in his annual report on the training plan: this includes statements related to parameters like:

- number of 'person days' of training, compared with last year

- overall expenditure on training, compared with last year

- number of 'person days' of training carried out in-house, compared with last year

- the unit cost for provision of training per 'person day'.

This 'value for money' section is essential to demonstrate the acccountability of the training function in the language of performance ratios, well understood by all managers. It is a vital factor in the corporate acceptance of and regard for training. Every line manager is expected to use this language, and the training manager should be no exception. He or she too is responsible for a managerial function which must be able to justify itself by reference to financial criteria, although hopefully not by short-term profitability ratios alone.

To this 'value for money' section one more dimension is added: ratings from 0 to 5 relating to managers' and learners' views of the failure or success of training events. This data is extracted from a system of training evaluation involving the learner and manager before, during and after any external training courses with a duration of two days or more. For internal courses a special assessment form is devised to analyse trainees' reactions to the training. Employees who are undertaking further educational courses are individually counselled by the training manager at least annually to review progress and highlight any problems.

Thus the eight steps involved in the 'total' strategy for drawing up an organizational training plan are:

AGREE THE TRAINING NEEDS

CONSIDER POSSIBLE SOLUTIONS

SELECT TRAINING EVENTS

CREATE THE TRAINING PLAN

ESTABLISH PRIORITIES

APPLY BUDGETARY CONSTRAINTS

COMMUNICATE RESULTS

MONITOR AND EVALUATE TRAINING.

So far we have been looking at a strategy to develop a training plan for the kind of organization that is operating in a fairly predictable, stable environment, and/or has the time and resources to carry out a detailed, across the board assessment of training needs in order to produce a comprehensive plan of training for that organization in the forthcoming year: the 'total' strategy. However, when life is unpredictable for an organization, and/or when there is not the time or resources to carry out such a time-consuming and exhaustive analysis, what approach can then be used to ensure that, nonetheless, training remains an essential part of business activity, and makes a major contribution to survival and success? Let us now look at the 'problem-centred' strategy, and see what that involves.

## The 'Problem-Centred' Strategy

More and more firms in the private sector, and most particularly firms in declining or rapidly changing industries, find themselves unable to plan ahead with any degree of certainty. Some, even if they have detailed business plans covering the next twelve months or so, may be reluctant to divulge certain parts of them to the personnel or training department. So what can be done in order to produce relevant training for the organization? The most effective planning strategy is the 'problem-centred' one. This is best described by examining the case of the Training Manager at 'Mansells'. (In the following case study, a few details that might enable the organization concerned to be identified have had to be altered. However, in every other respect this is a factual account).

---

## CASE STUDY: Mansells, Birmingham (Part 1)

In the mid-sixties Mansells employed around 10,000 people producing high voltage switchgear primarily for the home market. Because of a sudden reduction in anticipated power requirements in the UK, the firm had to start trying to sell the bulk of its output overseas. By 1974, because of the continued dearth of home orders and fierce competition overseas, redundancies began. By 1986 the total workforce was only 1,200, the site reduced in size, and the training department, once very large, and with a generous budget and many forms of specialized training, consisted only of one full-time person, the training manager. There was no centralized training budget, unit managers held their own training budgets, and would only spend on training what they considered was relevant to their immediate needs. The training manager's main problem was to keep training alive. His approach was (as it remains) entirely problem-centred. He was out and about in the firm all the time, developing the kind of relationship with managers and unions whereby they asked him for guidance when they had needs that they thought training could resolve (and he would tell them that training was not the best solution for a particular need if he thought that this was the case). He sought to develop a relationship, too, whereby he could diplomatically suggest to them that training should be done in certain areas where they had not already perceived a need for it. He thus assumed a proactive as well as a reactive role.

The status of training was never higher, and as the firm's economic situation began to stabilize, more money was again put into the training function. In late 1987 two training officers were appointed, mainly to do job training analysis at shop floor level, and to design training based on accurate and comprehensive knowledge of the level and type of skills needed in order to ensure fully effective and efficient performance. But specialized training is only part of the story. The training manager believes there is a need for human resource development to be as work-related as possible, and therefore for a continuous integration of work and learning in the workplace (see Chapters 4 and 5). He has successfully promoted the development of team briefing meetings at supervisory level and of quality circles throughout the firm. He plays an important role himself in these initiatives, and is seen as a core member of the

work team in all the situations in which he offers advice or other
forms of resources.

He is a very busy manager, and considers that the cutback in the
training function, and the approach to planning training which is
based on seeking out and responding to those most critical
problems for which training is the best response, has ensured that
all training is now:

**a means to an end which is identifiable and agreed between
himself and all the interested parties**

**fully cost-effective, because he has to justify his charges to the
last pence before a unit will agree to pay out money: the
training has to prove itself, and is then valued**

**seen to be an essential function, not an optional or peripheral
activity**

**a genuinely collaborative activity**

**takes in all relevant forms of continuous development, not
just 'training packages', thus leading to organizational as well
as individual growth.**

There is no formalized purpose or policy for training at Mansells, but
it is clear that implicitly both exist:

**Purpose**
Human resource development is a continuous and collaborative
activity, encouraging flexibility, and a positive attitude towards
change. It must help people to think of and carry out ways of
doing things better, and to develop systems to suit the changed
times.

(This purpose is being achieved because generally, within a much
reduced workforce, there has been a very significant breakdown in
demarcation barriers, with people at all levels doing all kinds of jobs
instead of just single tasks, and collaborating in the promotion of a
variety of initiatives to improve performance and methods.)

**Policy**
to ensure that continuous human resource development is a basic
line management responsibility, with the training manager acting
as a catalyst and resource for managers;

to focus especially on key groups, on whom the survival of the company directly depends: supervisors, managers, high fliers whose retention and development is crucial to the future of the company, and all shop floor and office people;

to prioritize training, but to preserve flexibility in order to cope with unexpected contingencies;

to develop contacts with any people and institutions who can provide effective and cost-efficient training — polytechnics, schools, business schools, etc;

to monitor and record training events with a minimum of paperwork, but ensuring that information is up to date and accessible, thereby leading to appropriate action.

Since long-term training planning can only be at a minimum, there is no formalized TRAINING PLAN, other than papers that from time to time have to be drawn up for training board or for budgetary purposes. But the training manager and line managers know at all times exactly what has been done, needs to be done, and can be done, and at what cost, if training is to make its full contribution to the business — and that is the measure of a good training function.

---

In this illustration the same eight steps as are used in the 'total' approach have been taken in order to develop the organization's training plan. The only difference is in the detail of how they are done. The main factors that call for differences are the emergency nature of the exercise, and the very short time-lag that can be afforded between initial definition of the problem and the final training event.

Here is how the eight steps can be applied, using the problem-centred approach, by whoever is responsible for training.

### STEP 1   The Training Need

The training manager should discuss with managers on a continuing basis what are the most urgent problems they face. She should then clearly define with them what the problems really are, and which would seem to call for training as an appropriate remedy. Agreement should be reached in specific terms on training objectives and on precisely how training can help to reduce or overcome the problems. At regular intervals (determined by the length of the business planning cycle) the training manager must check on the business plans and any other information available about future changes, to see if training is needed to be fed into those.

### STEP 2   Possible Solutions

Here, again as with the 'total' approach, the training manager must analyse whether this particular problem is one that training not only can deal with, but can deal with more cost-effectively than any other process. To quote:

> **Within the limits of overall company policy, the training manager is free to consider whether changing the organization, the equipment, or the job itself, or changing the people concerned by selection, would ease the problem, before the expensive, uncertain process of training is embarked on.**
>
> *(Gane, 1972)*

### STEP 3   Select Training Events

Here, agreement must be reached on who is to be trained, how many of them, when and where they will need training, and how they will be trained. Training can be done in any cost-effective, feasible and agreed way of achieving the necessary learning, and does not need to include a 'course'.

### STEP 4   Create Training Plan

Other than training done to meet certain major future needs, which will usually be planned and agreed some time in advance, (for example, retraining to cope with redundancies or redeployment of workers, or to prepare key workers to operate new technology) the training plan will be informal rather than heavily documented. Training manager and relevant line managers will simply note the number and names of the trainees, the objectives, the type, location and timing of the training, and its cost (which will often, as at Mansells, have to be met from the departmental managers' business budgets).

### STEP 5   Establish Priorities

Although training, with the problem-centred approach, is done on a rolling basis rather than on the basis of an annual plan, attention must still be paid to overall priorities. Planning probably no more than a few weeks ahead, the training manager must still ensure that the training effort is put into those problem areas across the company where there will be the most cost-beneficial return. So attention must be given first to those areas having a critical impact on the firm's survival, and crucial to its future stability.

### STEP 6   Apply Budgetary Constraints
Although, with this approach, the training manager may not have his own budget, but be paid from the budgets held by line managers, he must have a clear idea of what the business overall, and particular departments within it, are likely to be able to afford for the training they are asking him to do. All training must therefore be costed very carefully, and when line managers hold budgetary control, close attention also needs to be given to 'hidden' costs like lost opportunity costs, the costs of having people away from their jobs for a period of time, eg by paying overtime, getting in part-time help, etc.

### STEP 7   Communicate Results
With the problem-centred approach, initial requests for training must be acted upon quickly, and information about training or development activities that will, in fact, be going ahead must be communicated to the managers concerned as soon as possible. In other words, there must be feedback on the final action that will be taken with regard to the plans generated in STEP 4. Yet where the problem-centred approach is used, certainty can rarely be built in to any stage of the cycle, so action plans may even at the last minute have to be cancelled or postponed because of some unexpected contingency. Communications at that point must work particularly well to ensure that everyone is informed about the reasons for the changes, and that (wherever possible) alternative ways of responding to the initial request (assuming it is still valid) can be agreed.

### STEP 8   Monitor and Evaluate Training
With the problem-centred approach, evaluation is essential in order to ensure that scarce money is being used effectively. If the problem and intended outcomes have been clearly specified then evaluation, however informal, should be done by the training manager and line manager without too much difficulty, using observable increases in knowledge, skills, attitudes, and overall performance as indicators.

Thus, to summarize the main learning points in this section, the four ways in which success in training is evident using either a total or a problem-centred approach, are that training is seen to be:

### A Means to an End
Training is seen as a means to an end which is identifiable and agreed between the training manager and all the interested parties.

### Cost-effective
Training is fully cost-effective, because the training manager is able to identify and justify all expenditure on resources.

### Essential
Training is seen to be an essential function, not an optional or peripheral activity.

### Collaborative
Training is a genuinely collaborative activity.

Furthermore, with both strategies the training manager and line managers know at all times:

- exactly what HAS been done

- exactly what NEEDS to be done

- exactly what CAN be done

- at what COST

if training is to make its full contribution to the business.

## Drawing Up a Training Plan
Training plans can be drawn up using many different formats. Essentially, however, they must include the following information:

### Purpose and policy for training
A statement of the purpose and policy for training in the organization. This will help to give a context to the training plan, so that everyone can understand its rationale and its desired outcomes.

### Details of training to be done
Details of what training will be done in the period of the plan, to what objectives, for what groups, sectors or individuals in the organization, at what cost, over what period/s of time, and who will be responsible for carrying out and administering that training.


## CONCLUSION

After reading this chapter and completing the various activities it contains, you should now:

1   Understand the difference between a purpose, policy and plan for training in an organization

2   Be able to choose an appropriate strategy for assessing an organization's training needs and developing a training plan

3   Know how to draw up an organization's training plan.

The main learning points related to these objectives are:

**1   Establishing a purpose, policy and plan for training**
When preparing to formulate a purpose, policy and plan for training in the organization, careful analysis must be made of the organization's:

* Environment

* Goal and Tasks

* Structure

* Technology

* Workforce

* Political system.

Planning training involves establishing a training:

* *Purpose*
  to express clearly the overall reason why the organization is investing in training

* *Policy*
  to give the guidelines to be followed in the organization's training activities

* *Plan*
  to explain in detail what will be done in order to realize the training purpose and policy in a practical way.

Training purpose and policy establish the framework within which the training plan can be drawn up.

Training purpose and policy should consider 4 categories of possible training need, related to:

- Staff newly appointed from outside the organization

- Newly promoted staff

- Existing staff

- Staff facing change.

## 2   Strategies for assessing an organization's training needs and developing a training plan

Strategy has been described as the art of directing and planning. When we refer to 'training strategy' we usually mean 2 things:

- The overall approach chosen to assess training needs

- The particular ways in which training will be carried out in the organization — eg on the job, off the job, buying in training, using outside courses or activities, etc.

There are 2 main strategies for assessing organizational training needs and developing a training plan:

- The total strategy

- The problem-centred strategy

The 8 steps involved in carrying out both approaches are:

- Agree the training needs

- Consider possible solutions

- Select training events

- Create the training plan

- Establish priorities

- Apply budgetary constraints

- Communicate results

- Monitor and evaluate training.

The 4 ways in which success in training is evident, using either of these strategies, are that training in the organization is seen to be:

- A means to an end

- Cost-effective

- An essential function

- Collaborative.

Furthermore, with both strategies the training manager and line managers know at all times:

- what HAS been done

- what NEEDS to be done

- what CAN be done

- at what COST

if training is to make its full contribution to the business.

## 3 Drawing up a training plan
Whatever its format, the organizational training plan should include:

- Purpose and policy for training

- Details of training to be done.

---

## REVIEW ACTIVITY

Finally, here are some questions which you can either tackle as essays (if you are a student); discuss with fellow-students or colleagues; or simply think about now that you have completed this chapter:

- 'All business plans contain a risk element'. What risks do training plans typically contain and how can a training officer reduce them?

- Explain with examples how you would decide whether or not training is the preferred approach to solving a problem.

- Find out if there is a training plan for your organization. If there is, check it to see whether it contains all the essential information, including a statement of the purpose and policy for training in the organization. If it does not, see if you can discover any of the missing information, and find out why it was omitted.

OR

- Contact THREE organizations with which you are familiar, or major local or national organizations likely to have a training function, and ask them if they could let you have copies of their organizational training plans together with information on how the plans were drawn up. (Explain why you are interested.) Compare the three plans, analysing them to discover which is the most informative and comprehensive, which the least, where there are omissions, and which show signs of the most systematic approach to assessment of needs.

## CHAPTER 7

# Organizing and managing the training function

## LEARNING OBJECTIVES

After reading this chapter and completing the various activities it contains, you should:

1 Understand the basic issues involved in carrying out the 'training manager' role, and in organizing a specialist training function

2 Understand the main activities involved in managing training resources

3 Be able to carry out a simple costing of training activities, and draw up and monitor a training budget

4 Understand the main factors involved in establishing a training record system.

### The Training Manager Role

As a starting point, we can expand the definition of the training manager role that was given in Chapter 3, so that it now encompasses the training function rather than just the specialist training section or department.

> **The training manager role is primarily concerned with the planning, organization, direction and control of the training function. The main activities it involves are to do with the management and development of training resources, and policy development and co-ordination.**

Having looked at training roles and responsibilities (Chapter 3), and at policy-making and planning (Chapter 6), in this chapter we will look at:

Organizing the training function

Managing training resources

Measuring the training investment

A strategy for the management of training resources

Establishing a training record system

## Organizing The Training Function

The training function must fit into the wider organization, both influencing and being itself influenced by the following aspects of the organization:

Environment

Goal/tasks

Structure

Technology

People

And, of course, it must interact effectively with the POLITICAL SYSTEM (see Chapters 2 and 3).

When a training function is being formally established, important decisions have to be made about its structural organization, relating to questions like:

- At what levels should there be responsibility for training in the organization, and what should be the roles of those with such responsibility?

- How centralized or decentralized should the function be?

- In particular, is training to be a responsibility solely of line managers, or will any specialist personnel be appointed?

- How should the function relate, structurally, to other functions, including to personnel?

- How far should training staff specialize or be flexible and wide-ranging in their skills?

- How far should training staff be a closely-integrated team or a loosely-knit group?

Whilst in practice many training managers, and probably many of the readers of this book, may have little direct influence over most of these decisions, they should have a part to play in at least the last two. It is in any case important for anyone in training to appreciate the issues raised by all of these questions, in order to be able to analyse the kinds of pressures and opportunities they present to the function. At this point we can return briefly to the case of Mansells, which was discussed in Chapter 6. It offers an excellent example of how the structure and organization of a training function responded positively to changes in the firm's situation.

---

### CASE STUDY: Mansells, Birmingham (Part 2)

The 'Mansells' case study shows how changes in environment, goal and training tasks, structure, technology, and workforce of a firm, and their interaction, determined the way in which the training function was organized over the years. The function's intelligent adaptation to the needs of the organization as a system ensured its centrality in the firm even when the future was at its most unpredictable. Although the culture of the firm was such that top management and the Personnel Director carried a direct and overall responsibility for training throughout the years, it took many changes before line managment reached their present position of fully supporting and collaborating in every stage of training; and that position has only been reached by increasing care being given to getting right the goal, tasks and organization of the function. Compare this with the many other training functions which are now closed down because of their failure to understand their position in changed times and respond creatively, and the need for the training manager to think analytically, and to organize and manage accordingly becomes self-evident.

---

Even if few of the readers of this book have responsibility for decisions about where and how the training function is to be placed in the organization's structure, most will now or in the future, in specialist or line management roles, be involved in managing training resources. Let us now, therefore, take a practical look at this area.

## Managing Training Resources

---

## ACTIVITY

### Training Resources
If you were asked to produce a list of your organization's training resources, what would you include in that list? Please write down as many as you can think of, categorizing them under three or four overall headings.

---

## FEEDBACK NOTES

You have probably produced a very long list. However, it will become more manageable once the items on it are grouped under three main headings, as follows:

### Internal and external resources
*Personnel*
Available within and outside the organization.

*Physical resources*
Accommodation, equipment, training materials, etc available within the organization.
Accommodation, equipment, training materials, etc available through external sources.

*Finance*
Finance available within the organization for the training and development of the workforce, whether allocated to a central training budget, or to departmental training budgets.
     Finance available from external sources for organizational training and development activities.

### Time
The time available to carry out any activities in training, including the management and development of training resources, will have a crucial effect on training policy and strategy, on managerial strategy and effectiveness, and on day to day training and managerial tactics.

### Natural learning resources
These are everyday learning opportunities available in the organization, in the normal course of work. We have already referred to these

in Chapters 4 and 5, and have seen how their good management can fully utilize the organization's potential as a learning system. Any training manager must identify natural learning resources, and decide how integration of work and learning can most effectively and efficiently be achieved. Guidelines for this kind of planning have been given in those chapters.

---

There are, of course specific techniques which can improve the management of staff, or develop skills in financial management. However, there are at least five fundamental steps involved in being an effective 'training manager':

OBSERVE AND REFLECT on the present situation. Look at the current training budget (or, if none is available, some equivalent figures that show the costs of running the training function and carrying out training activities) to establish what is done, and what it costs. Identify the other training resources available — materials, equipment, accommodation, personnel — and look at how they are currently being organized and used.

ANALYSE this information by reference to contextual factors such as the organization's external environment, corporate aims, structure, workforce; and at the kind of training technology that could be utilized. This analysis will help to establish whether the department's resources are being used rationally in pursuit of the organization's training objectives.

BE CREATIVE. Think of alternative ways of using resources, ie of deploying staff, choosing and using materials, equipment and accommodation, and investing money which would achieve the training objectives to the required standard, but more effectively or efficiently.

MAKE DECISIONS choosing the most feasible, cost-efficient and cost-effective action.

MONITOR AND EVALUATE choosing those methods that are both simple and effective enough for the purpose, and agreeing well in advance who is to carry out these processes, and when.

Thus good training management requires those same core skills to which so much reference has already been made in this book:

Observation and reflection

Analysis

Creativity

Decision-making/problem-solving

Evaluation

Here is a practical illustration (for Part 1, see p87).

---

## CASE STUDY: The New Training Manager (Part 2)

The Training Manager was told that the Personnel Manager would allow one of her ablest staff — an IPM-qualified young male Personnel Officer with three years post-college experience in personnel work, although none in training — to spend two days a week in the training section for at least one year, both as part of his career progression and in order to help in the task of developing an organizational training policy and of putting the various elements of the plan into operation.

### Observation and reflection

She gave some careful thought to how to make best use of this officer. She must, of course, decide on his tasks and targets, although she must avoid defining these too closely initially, in order that as the training section's work developed, his and her own aptitudes and interests could creatively influence the allocation of work and duties. Thus if she did eventually draw up a formal job description and personnel specification, especially to aid any future recruitment into the section, she would actively involve him in that process, and they would agree on what would go into those documents.

She would also have to ensure that as he made progress in the job she helped him relate this to his general career development plan. So some appraisal and counselling, no matter how informal, was going to be needed. She herself needed quite a high level of professional expertise in order to perform effectively across the spectrum of training tasks that would have to be performed, and she would have to find out from initial discussions where the Personnel Officer had strengths that could be used and developed. They could then agree on how best to organize his work and to involve him in learning opportunities which would develop his potential and improve his ability to take on further tasks as time progressed. The sort of tasks she had in mind are those inherent in a systematic approach to planned training events. and have already been listed in Chapter 6 (page 89):

Assessment of needs

Analysis of jobs/tasks

Appraisal of people

Specification of training objectives

Allocation of resources

Recruitment, selection and continuous assessment of learners

Design of learning events

Operation of learning events

Evaluation of learning, training and development

She was also going to have to help the young officer to develop the core skills of:

Observation and reflection

Analysis

Creativity

Decision-making/problem-solving

Evaluation

if she intended to use him as his qualifications, experience and proven ability merited, and give him as much autonomy as possible rather than simply delegating to him all the low level, routine tasks. As she read through the 1987 Manpower Services Commission paper 'Developing Trainers' which stressed the need for competency in the training profession, she realized the importance of managing and developing the Personnel Officer so that he could make a fully effective contribution to the operation of training in the organization.

### Analysis

As she reflected on these parameters and analysed their significance, it became obvious that what was really involved was almost the whole range of human resource development processes (already highlighted in Chapter 1 of this book (see pages 3 and 4)).

She herself must also consider how best to achieve effective leadership and teamwork:

### Leadership style

What should be her style of leadership — tight or loose, authoritarian or participative, task-centred or person-centred?

### Teamwork

How should the small training team (including the clerk) be organized? On a close-knit or semi-autonomous basis? With frequent checks and feedback of performance, or some other *modus operandi?*

She thought about the firm's and the function's environment. It was one calling for a creative and proactive role for training, and general agreement on and support for a training policy which would be followed by a simple plan based on meeting quickly the firm's key needs. Clearly, therefore, a 'task' culture and net structure would be the most appropriate one for the training function, both in itself and in relation to other functions and departments with which it must interact throughout the organization. Such a culture and structure also fitted the goal and tasks of training in the organization, the fairly simple technology available to the function, and the abilities and expectations of the people (mainly the young Personnel Officer) working for her. It seemed to make good political sense too for her to move out of the office from the start and go around the organization, using the small training team in a collaborative manner, helping the organization achieve its goals by offering advice and expertise to meet those problems which were amendable to a training response. Thus her analysis had been helped by using our now familiar model:

Environment

Goal/tasks

Structure

Technology

People

Political system

She would also need to ensure that the young officer had political sensitivity and interpersonal skills, especially since this was the first time that a training audit had been carried out in the organization.

### Creativity and decision-making
Having fully reflected on all this information, and analysed it carefully, she would now find it relatively easy to generate alternative ways of using the young officer, and to make shared decisions which would result in the small training section being organized effectively and efficiently.

### Evaluation
She would, of course, have to monitor progress and evaluate the results of their joint operations, in order to determine where changes were needed in the future.

---

## Measuring the Training Investment
The report *A Challenge to Complacency* (1985) singled out expertise in measuring the costs and benefits of the training investment as crucial to the task of changing organizational attitudes to training. The report called for the development of simple measures of training activity, and clear identification of its costs and benefits. In this section we will demonstrate how both these tasks can be carried out.

### Simple measures of training activities
The first place where one expects to find a categorization of training activities, and of their costs, is in the budget. Budgeting in training can take two main forms: there may be a budget for the training department, for which the training manager is responsible. This is the case at Northumbrian Water, and in Chapter 6 I have already explained how that budget is drawn up and managed. On the other hand, money for training and development may simply be held in departmental budgets for which managers are responsible. This is the case at Mansells, also examined in Chapter 6, and in many other organizations in private and public sectors.

Whoever is responsible for a training budget, it is essential that training resources and activities should be costed and managed in such a way that full value is obtained for available money, and that where at first sight priority needs cannot be met within current budgets, a sound case can be put forward for obtaining more money, or the needs can be met using alternative approaches.

There is no general format to be used in the presentation of financial information about training, since format must always depend on three factors:

### Why the information is needed
This will determine what information is to be collected, and what focus to give the costings.

### For whom the information is needed
This will determine the way the information is expressed, and the specific format to be used. If financial information is needed by the accounts department, this should follow the format and language used in their accounting system. If data on costs and benefits of one training solution compared to another is needed by a busy line manager to help them decide which solution to choose, then the data must be expressed clearly, using language that is meaningful to the manager, and that will make an immediate and unambiguous impact.

### When the information is needed, and what is available
If, as often happens, a request comes in today for information needed tomorrow, then it may prove impossible to obtain, in such a short time, all the data theoretically desirable. The format must then be tailored to match whatever data can be produced in time, so that the overall presentation is still meaningful even if not entirely comprehensive.

There are always, however, three pieces of information that are essential if training activities are to be identified and measured:

- The overall annual cost of running the training function

- How to recover that cost

- How to identify and compare costs involved in training alternatives

In relation to all three areas of information, two terms are fundamental:

### Trainer day costs
This refers to the daily costs involved in the basic running of a training function.

### Training day costs
This refers to the total costs involved in running a training function and in carrying out its specific training activities.

#### *Calculating the annual running costs of a training function*
First, we will look at how to calculate the basic annual running costs of a training fuction. On page 126 is an example of an approach that is relatively simple, and will suffice for most practical purposes. In this example it is used to establish the basic running costs of a training department. It can also be used to establish such training costs where there is no specialist department, as will be shown subsequently.

Thus we can see that a simple but acceptably accurate calculation of the basic annual costs involved in running a training department can be obtained by looking at personnel, overhead and administration costs.

Personnel and overhead costs are fixed (that is to say, the organization must pay them, whether or not training activities are carried out) but administration costs are variable, because they depend on what kind and extent of training activities are carried out.

It is important to stress that Figure 3 deals with basic costs, which do not include the costs of providing specific training activities (except in relation to administration costs, where in order to get any acceptable figure, we have to consider the sort of demands likely to be made). Those costs will be calculated separately, in our next examples.

If, however, there is no specialist training department, nor any training overheads, then the basic annual running costs of the training function can be calculated by reference to:

### Personnel costs
The number of days each manager spends in carrying out training and training-related activities for others, expressed as a proportion of their annual salary and employment costs.

### Administration costs
Identifiable administration cost caused by work on training and training-related activities, expressed in annual terms.

## EXAMPLE OF BASIC ANNUAL RUNNING COSTS OF A TRAINING DEPARTMENT

(employing 2 training officers and a secretary)

**Personnel**
Training staffs' salaries plus, say, 25% for
employment costs (pension, NI and other
payments)                                                    = £30,000

Support staff:
    Administrative staff
    Clerical/secretarial staff                              = £10,000

**Overheads**
Annual rent and rates (or some approximate
calculation of these) related to training
accommodation (1 training room; 2 offices)

Heating, lighting cleaning and other maintenance
costs of training accommodation                             = £  5,000

**Administration***
Estimated/actual:
    telephone and postal costs, printing,
    photocopying, etc costs, computer costs (if any
    — eg cost of computer time, software, etc)             = £  3,000

Total Basic Annual Running costs                            = £48,000

**Figure 3:   Basic annual running costs of a training department**
*(With acknowledgements to A. Rutter)*

*With regard to 'ADMINISTRATION' costs, if a forecasting exercise is being
carried out, then these figures can be estimated in one of two ways:

1   by taking an average of total administrative costs incurred during, say, the
    last two years' training activities, if those activities were similar to those
    planned for the forthcoming year. An inflation cost will have to be built in
    to this calculation.

2   If there is an organizational training plan like that produced by North-
    umbrian Water (see Chapter 6) then the training manager can look at the
    administration costs actually incurred by the activities involved in last
    year's plan. She can then estimate, looking at the sort of activities planned
    for the forthcoming year, how much more or less the related administra-
    tive costs are likely to be. Again, an inflation cost will have to be built in to
    the calculation.

**Recovering the cost of running the training function**
First, we need to find out what is the cost of a trainer day in an organization. Let us continue with the example we have just used, adding on some more information.

---

**EXAMPLE:** (continued)

## COST OF A TRAINER DAY

| | |
|---|---|
| Days actually worked by the 2 training staff (ie once holidays, etc have been taken) = 240 each | = 480 |
| Annual running cost of the training dept. (see Figure 3) | = £48,000 |
| So cost of each day the training staff are actually working | $\dfrac{£48,000}{480}$ |
| Cost of one trainer day | = £100 |

---

**Figure 4:  Cost of a trainer day**
*(With acknowledgements to A.Rutter)*

(This same approach can, of course, be used to calculate the 'trainer day' costs of anyone who carries out training or training-related activities, whether or not they are training staff.)

This very easy but absolutely crucial calculation of the trainer day cost tells us that, in order to recover the annual cost of running its training department (£48,000), this particular organization would need to provide training for 480 days a year (ie 240 days by each of the two training staff) and charge £100 per day for that training. So the basic running costs of a training department or function can be expressed as a trainer day cost, and this cost, as we have seen in Figure 4, can be calculated as follows:

$$\frac{\text{Annual running cost of the training function}}{\text{Number of days each staff involved in training work}} = \text{Trainer day cost}$$

But how can costs actually be recovered once identified? A case study should provide a helpful illustration at this point.

---

**CASE STUDY: Mintech Ltd (Part 1)**
(With acknowledgements to A. Rutter)

Mintech Ltd has a training department employing two training officers (Mike and John) and a clerk/secretary.

| | |
|---|---|
| The basic annual running cost of the department | = £30,000 |
| Number of days worked by the 2 Officers: | |
| Mike: 250 + John: 250 | = 500 |
| | |
| Trainer day cost | = $\frac{£30,000}{500}$ |
| | = £60 |

The Department is involved in two sorts of training activity:

---

| Training people | Assisting people to attend training done externally |
|---|---|
| The trainers keep a record of the number of days they spend on face to face training of people: | The trainers keep a record of the number of days they spend on work connected with external courses, ranging from analysis of needs through to evaluation of results: |
| Mike: 30 days | Mike: 220 days |
| John: 20 days | John: 230 days |
| Total: 50 trainer days | Total: 450 trainer days |
| Cost: 50 x £60 = £3,000 | Cost: 450 x £60 = £27,000 |

The trainers add up the number of days that staff spend participating in these events: Total training days = 300

The trainers add up the number of days that staff spend participating in these courses: Total training days = 3,000

Amount to be recovered for internal training activities £3,000 for 300 days' training

Amount to be recovered for external training activities £27,000 for 3,000 days' training

---

SO:  Total cost of internal training day = £10

Total cost of external training day = £9

BUT:  Additional costs (fees, travel, subsistence, accommodation, course materials, per person, per day) = £1

Additional costs (fees, travel, subsistence, accommodation, course materials, per person, per day) = £200

---

To recover its costs of £10 per person for everyone who undergoes internal training, and £9 per person for everyone who undergoes external training, plus covering the additional costs involved, Mintech's training department can do one of two things:

1  If it has its own budget, then it must include in the budget estimate enough to cover a cost of £10 per day for every member of the organization who will be attending internal training courses, and a cost of £9 per day for every member of the organization who will be attending external training courses, plus the additional costs of fees, travel, subsistence, accommodation, course materials involved in the training events concerned.

2  If there is no central training budget, but (eg Mansells, see Chapter 6) each department has its own budget from which training costs must be met, then it must charge departments £10 per day for every member of staff who will be attending internal training courses, and £9 per day for every member of staff who will be attending external training courses plus the additional costs of fees, travel, susbsistence, accommodation, course materials involved in the training events concerned.

The Mintech case study shows us that in order to calculate how to recover the costs involved in running a training department and in carrying out its training activities, the training day cost must be calculated, as follows:

$$\frac{\text{Trainer day cost}}{\text{Number of training days}} = \text{Training day cost}$$

Note that the number of training days is simply arrived at by adding up all the days it has taken to train people throughout the organization, in one case internally, in the other case externally. So if 100 people each went on 3 days external training in a year, then the total number of external training days would come to 300.

So we can conclude by saying that:

**The trainer day cost can be used to calculate the basic cost of running the training function, and the training day cost to calculate the charge to be made by the function for training in order that its running costs can be recovered.**

We have now seen how to provide two of the three crucial pieces of information that every training manager should possess: the overall costs of running a training function, and how to recover that cost.

### Identifying and Comparing Costs Involved in Training Alternatives

Using the same Mintech case study, we can look at a typical situation facing many personnel and training officers: staff requests to go on education or training courses. We will see how, by comparing the costs of internal and external supervisory training, a sound decision can be reached by someone who is concerned to achieve both relevant training and good management of resources.

---

**CASE STUDY: Mintech Ltd (Part 2)**
(With acknowledgements to A. Rutter)

Three supervisors from different departments have applied to the training department to go on a day-release supervisory training course at the local college. It lasts for a year, involves absence of half a day plus an evening (same day) over three terms, and ends with an examination in which, if they are successful, course members will obtain a national supervisory skills qualification.

In order to decide whether or not to recommend to the personnel manager that this request should be approved, Mike, one of the two training officers, first identifies the costs involved in sending the three supervisors away on the day release course. To help him do this calculation, he uses the 'training day cost' identified in Mintech Case Study, Part 1, page 128.

## OPTION A:

Sending supervisors on external training course leading to national supervisory qualification

| | |
|---|---|
| Fees (£500 per person per year) £500 x 3 | = £1,500 |
| Travel and subsistence (£1 per person per day at college): £1 x 3 x 30 days | = £90 |
| Materials (books and other items used by trainees on the course) £20 x 3 | = £60 |
| Administrative overhead cost External training day cost x number of days x number of trainees (£9 (already calculated) x 30 x 3) | = £810 |
| Total cost of sending 3 people on course | = £2,460 |

Theoretically, of course, Mike could have made out a more complicated list which would have included indirect as well as direct costs. The indirect costs would be the less tangible costs incurred by attending the external course: lost opportunity costs, reduction in output or quality of service of their staff due to less effective staff management during the periods of their absence, lost salary and related employment costs, due to the supervisors' reduction in hours worked 'on the job' during the period of the course, and so on. However, in practice such costs are rarely taken into account in situations like this, and only if there had been tangible payments occasioned by the supervisors' absence (for example, overtime payments due to their work having to be done by others) would costs other than shown in Mike's calculation normally be noted.

The next step is for Mike to think carefully about the external course, and about possible alternatives to it. In his own mind the benefits the course will bring to the supervisors, their departments and Mintech as a whole are not in dispute, but from the figures he has produced it is clear that to send three supervisors on the course will be an expensive undertaking, and it may not be possible to offer the same opportunity, in the current year, to any further supervisory applicants. What alternatives might there be? (At this point you may like to take over and do some creative thinking to generate a list of alternatives. For the purpose of this exercise, I am only developing one other option, but in fact several are possible.)

One such alternative is for the exact training needs of all Mintech's 16 supervisors to be identified through appraisal interviews and other methods (the company already operates an appraisal scheme related to current performance and development needs), and for the training department to organize internal courses to meet common needs, whilst individual needs could be met on some other appropriate basis. Mike now discusses this idea with his colleagues and they agree that three one-week courses run by the training department in its Conference Room would cover the necessary material well, and would be a real benefit to at least 12 instead of only three supervisors. But what will it cost?

## OPTION B:

Internal supervisory training course run by training staff

There would be three 1-week courses, to take a total membership of 12 supervisors, with four attending each course.

| | |
|---|---|
| Fees (Nil) | — |
| Subsistence Mid-morning and mid-afternoon refreshments for participants and trainer, @ 60p per head per day (60p x 5 people x 5 days x 3 courses) | = £45 |
| Materials (£20 per trainee) | = £240 |
| Administrative overhead cost Internal training day cost for training 12 supervisors for 5 days each (£10 (previously calculated) x 5 x 12) | = £600 |

Total cost of training 12 supervisors internally    = £885
(Cost of training 3 supervisors on these courses,

$$\frac{£885}{4} = £221.25)$$

Mike was interested to note the cost per trainee involved in each of the options:

| Option | Total cost £ | Number trained | Cost per trainee £ |
|---|---|---|---|
| A | 2,460 | 3 | 820 |
| B | 885 | 12 | 73,75 |

Thus Mike was able to show clearly, from his calculations, that the cost of the organization running their own supervisory courses, using their own staff, was very much less than sending three supervisors on an external course. He did this by identifying, in each case, the following costs:

Fees

Expenses

Materials

Administrative overhead costs

However, although through the various examples we have examined we have discovered how to identify the three crucial pieces of information noted at the start of this chapter:

The basic annual cost of running the training department

How to recover the running cost

How to identify and compare costs involved in training alternatives,

there is another activity that needs to be carried out in order to ensure that cost-effective decisions are made in relation to the use of training resources:

### Cost-benefit analysis

Cost-benefit analysis is concerned with establishing the costs of an activity, and comparing these with the benefits it is likely to confer. It should take into account efficiency as well as effectiveness in establishing the benefits.

---

## ACTIVITY

### CASE STUDY: Mintech Ltd (Part 3)

When Mike has finished his calculations, it is obvious that running an internal supervisory training programme using Mintech's own training staff would be by far the cheapest course of action. But is it the most cost-beneficial? On what main issues should Mike seek information, in order to make a final decision?

---

## FEEDBACK NOTES

There are important issues raised by the two alternatives, not least the potential clash between individuals' wishes to improve their career prospects by obtaining a recognized qualification, and the organization's wish to cut costs. The following list is not exhaustive, but shows at least six major issues which should always be considered when weighing up training alternatives, together with a sample of the kind of questions to be raised under each heading.

### Budgeting
Would either of the options be affordable in terms of Mintech's budget per department for training?

### Training purpose, policy and plan
Which of the options would be most consistent with Mintech's overall purpose, policy and plan for training, as well as with the training plans of the departments concerned?

### Training needs
Have supervisory training needs been carefully analysed? By whom, and using what criteria? Is there any conflict here between individual

and departmental or organizational needs? Which alternative would best meet a balance of needs, and why? Have adequate discussions been held with the supervisors and their managers on these points?

**Training benefits and evaluation**
Which of the options is most likely to help job performance, motivation, commitment, etc. of the supervisors; and/or which is most likely to carry other benefits for the organization, and for the individuals, both related to their everyday work and to their longer-term career development?

What information can be obtained about the value of each of the options, either from past initiatives at Mintech, or from organizations like Mintech who have been involved in such initiatives themselves?

**Transfer of learning**
What positive action will be taken to ensure transfer of learning for supervisors if they attend the external course? Would there be better transfer if they attended an internal course?

**Alternative courses of action**
Are there any other ways in which the same kind and level of results offered could be achieved? What about integration of work and learning through experiences like team briefings, quality circles, management by objectives? (Some firms offer financial incentives to their supervisors, either alone or coupled with those sorts of initiatives.)

What would be the costs of doing nothing? Would that lead to reduced motivation of the supervisors; to lack of development of their ability and potential; to longer learning time of new techniques; to poorer quality work, higher rates of absenteeism or sickness, and so on?

When Mike discussed the two options with his colleagues, and with the managers of not only the three supervisors who had come to him originally, but also of the other Mintech supervisors, it became increasingly clear to everyone that the company's supervisors needed two distinct kinds of training and development. It was agreed that the Personnel Manager would recommend to the Director of the company that there should be:

1  *A development programme for new supervisors, or those shortly to be promoted to that level, and for others whose inclusion would bring clear benefits to the company and to themselves.*
   This would include opportunities for up to four people each year to attend the external course, or for a greater number to do the

course by a distance learning package; and for such supervisors also to have planned work experience and guidance.

2 ***An internal training programme for all Mintech supervisors.*** This would not only meet areas of common need, but would also help the supervisors to develop a common language and team identity through the mechanism of a shared and work-related learning experience. There would be initial costs involved in designing the first course, which would need to be added to the costs shown in Mike's calculations relating to Option B. However, the design cost would not recur, and the more courses that were run, the quicker that cost would be recovered.

The costs involved were affordable within departments' training budgets, and the Personnel Manager was confident that the Director would see that the cost of an in-company programme would be more than offset by the benefits it would bring. Procedures for monitoring the programmes and for evaluation would have to be built in at the start, and responsibility for those processes clearly allocated.

---

## A Strategy for Managing Training Resources

What have we learnt about management of training resources by tackling the final part of the Mintech case study? We have seen how training (and indeed any learning) activities can be managed efficiently and effectively by ensuring:

### Accurate and meaningful costing

The cost of training activities must be estimated as accurately as possible, and expressed in a way that is meaningful to the managers of the organization concerned.

### Relevance to training policy and needs

Decisions about expenditure on training activities must be consistent with decisions about the training purpose, policy and plan of the organization as a whole, and must relate to real training needs and priorities.

### Consistency with other personnel policies and processes

Decisions about training activities must also be consistent with other personnel policies and processes, for example manpower planning and utilization, staff appraisal, promotion possibilities, career planning, financial reward systems, and so on.

**Considered alternatives**
Alternative ways of using resources and of achieving training and
development objectives must always be considered and costed
before final decisions are made. A 6-point checklist is useful here:

Budgeting

Training purpose, policy and plan

Training needs and strategy

Training benefits

Transfer of learning

Training alternatives.

**Cost-efficient and cost-effective decisions**
Compare costs and benefits of the alternatives that have been
produced, (including that of doing nothing). Make a decision which
strikes the best balance between being cost-beneficial, generally
feasible, and politically sensitive.

**Monitoring and evaluation**
All learning events must be carefully controlled, and their value as
well as their validity must be assessed. This point will be covered
fully in Chapter 15.

We have also seen how the very process of thinking through a range
of alternatives can act as a catalyst, producing further initiatives to
the benefit of the organization.

**Establishing a Record System**
There is, however, one more crucial activity involved in the
management of resources: establishing a training record system.
   In this section I do not propose to attempt the task of explaining in
any detail how to set up a record system or design training records.
There are excellent texts to give that practical help, some of which
are included in this chapter's reading list at the end of the book. My
concern is simply to outline the key factors to be taken into account
when establishing a record system.
   In training as in other personnel areas, what the record system
must ensure or show is that:

### Training activities can be identified and monitored
It should be possible at any time to check on how far, in what ways, at what cost, and with what results, the training purpose, policies and plans are being carried out in every part and sector of the organization. Therefore the more systematic and collaborative is the approach to training (see Chapter 6), the easier it will be to obtain and record that information. Training records must also be comprehensive, up to date, and accurate.

### Training and development of individuals is recorded
Personal records need to be kept showing numbers and kinds of people who have been trained and developed, and to enable monitoring to ensure non-discrimination. (See next heading.)

### The law relating to employment is being observed
It must be possible at any time to identify how far, and in what ways, the law relating to employment is being observed. Records must therefore pay particular attention to areas of training activity related to dismissal, redundancy, discrimination, health and safety, and data protection. In all of these areas, failure to ensure that employees have the right knowledge and skills can mean that employers as well as employees become liable for breaches of the relevant legislation. Discrimination issues are receiving increasing publicity at present, and the importance of records in that connection cannot be over-stressed. I have made the point elsewhere that:

> **Records and up to date information should always be available to show exactly what steps have been taken to prevent discrimination in the workplace, and to prove how people have been treated at work.**
>
> *(Harrison, 1986)*

### The record system itself adheres to the law
The record system must adhere to legal requirements. The Data Protection Act must therefore be carefully observed.

### The record system is cost-beneficial
The record system must be cost efficient and cost effective. It should be as simple as possible, using sophisticated systems and processes only where the ensuing benefits can be shown to fully justify the human, physical and financial resources and costs. Particular attention must be paid to questions like how detailed particular records should be; for how long records should be kept; who should keep records, and how often records should be updated.

**Training records are consistent with other personnel records**

Training records should have a positive relationship with records maintained in any other areas of personnel management in the organization. They should therefore whenever possible be drawn up using a format and technology that complements rather than confuses other personnel record-keeping and data analysis. As far as is possible their content should also avoid overlap with the content of other personnel records.

**Confidentiality is observed**

Particular attention must be paid to confidentiality, and therefore to what information goes on record; to who should have access to various records; and to how access can be protected.

These, then, are the main factors to be taken into account when establishing a record system. For detailed discussion of the many ways in which they can be tackled constructively, the reader is referred to texts noted in the reading list for this chapter, at the end of the book. The main point to remember about a record system is that, together with the budget, it is an invaluable aid to the control of resources. However, like the budget, the criteria for determining what goes into records depends, in the end, on three factors:

Why the information is needed

For whom it is needed

When it is needed, and what information is available.

## CONCLUSION

Having read this chapter and completed the various activities it contains, you should now:

1   Understand the basic issues involved in carrying out the 'training manager' role, and in organizing a specialist training function

2   Understand the main activities involved in managing training resources

3   Be able to carry out a simple costing of training activities, and draw up and monitor a training budget

4   Understand the main factors involved in establishing a training record system.

The main learning points related to these objectives are:

1  **The training manager role**
   The 'training manager' role is primarily concerned with the planning, organization, direction and control of the training function and of training resources.

2  **Organizing the training function**
   The training function must fit into the wider organization, both influencing and being itself influenced by the organization's

- Environment

- Goal/tasks

- Structure

- Technology

- People

- Political system

3  **Managing training resources**
   Training resources can be classified under three headings:

   TRAINING RESOURCES, internal and external:

     Personnel

     Physical resources

     Finance

   TIME

   NATURAL LEARNING RESOURCES

   Good management of training resources requires the exercise of the core managerial skills of:

- Observation and reflection

- Analysis

- Creativity

- Decision-making/problem solving

- Evaluation

## 4 Measuring the training investment
The format to be used in the presentation of financial information about training depends on 3 factors:

- Why the information is needed

- For whom it is needed

- When it is needed, and what information is available

### *Simple measures of training activities*
There are always three pieces of information needed as a measure of training activities:

- The overall annual cost of running the training function

- How to recover that cost

- How to identify and compare costs involved in training alternatives

The annual costs involved in the basic running of a training department can be obtained by looking at 3 items:

- Personnel costs

- Overhead costs

- Administration costs

  When obtaining the costs of running a training function where there is no training department or overheads, only 2 items need to be identified:

- Personnel costs

- Administration costs

Basic running costs can be expressed as a trainer day cost, calculated as follows:

$$\frac{\text{Annual running cost of the training function}}{\text{Number of days each training staff works}} = \text{Trainer day cost}$$

To decide how to recover the costs involved in running a training function and in carrying out its training activities, the training day cost must be calculated, as follows:

$$\frac{\text{Trainer day costs}}{\text{Number of training days}} = \text{Training day cost}$$

To compare the costs of various training alternatives, 4 items should be identified in relation to each alternative:

- Fees

- Expenses

- Materials

- Administrative overhead costs

### Cost-benefit analysis
Cost-benefit analysis is concerned with establishing the costs of an activity, and comparing these with the benefits its is likely to confer. It should take into account efficiency as well as effectiveness.

The very process of thinking through a range of alternative training and development possibilities can act as a catalyst, producing further initiatives to the benefit of the organization.

### 5  A strategy for managing training resources
Training activities can be managed efficiently and effectively by ensuring:

- Accurate and meaninful costing

- Relevance to training policy and needs

- Consistency with other personnel policies and processes

- Considered alternatives: a 6-point checklist is useful here:

Budgeting

Training purpose, policy and plan

Training needs and strategy

Training benefits

Transfer of learning

Training alternatives

- Cost-efficient and cost-effective decisions

- Monitoring and evaluation

## 6  Establishing a record system

What the training record system must ensure or show is that:

- Training activities can be identified and monitored

- Training and development of individuals is recorded

- The law relating to employment is being observed

- The record system itself adheres to the law

- The record system is cost-beneficial

- Training records are consistent with other personnel records

- Confidentiality is observed

Three factors should determine what goes into training records

- Why the information is needed

- For whom it is to be provided

- When the information is needed, and what information is available

## REVIEW ACTIVITY

Finally, here are some questions which you can either tackle as essays (if you are a student); discuss with fellow-students or colleagues; or simply think about now that you have completed this chapter:

- Outline the steps you would take and the factors you would take into consideration in preparing a cost-benefit analysis of the desirability of setting up a company management training centre.

- What is meant when trainers are described as resource managers? How useful and how feasible is this view of the training practitioner's role?

- Outline the factors to be taken into account and the problems you would expect to encounter in developing an effective system of training records.

- With reference to the organization of your choice, explain (a) the stages in the development of the approved training budget, and (b) how expenditure of the budget is controlled.

## CHAPTER 8

# Assessing needs at operational level: job training analysis

## LEARNING OBJECTIVES

After reading this chapter and completing the various activities it contains, you should:

1  Understand what kind of overall strategy to use when analysing jobs for training purposes

2  Know the main approaches and techniques used in job training analysis

3  Be able to choose the relevant approach and techniques to use in analysing a particular job.

Job training analysis requires much practice before anyone can claim to be able to do it well, and therefore the learning objectives for this chapter stress understanding and knowledge rather than skill.

### Job Training Analysis

When designing training in relation to particular jobs or tasks, information must be produced which shows clearly and in detail the type and level of skills, knowledge and (as relevant) attitudes which must be learnt in order to perform adequately in those jobs or tasks. This process is called 'job training analysis'.

> **Job training analysis is the process of identifying the purpose of the job and its component parts, and specifying what must be learnt in order for there to be effective work performance.**

A crucial part of the analysis is to identify the performance standards required in a job in order that objectives for a training programme can be set, and evaluation of the training can subsequently be carried out. It should also emphasize those aspects of a job which make it difficult to learn, so that special attention can be given to them during the training programme.

The job training analysis process aims to produce a job training specification. This is a document produced to aid the design of a training programme.

**The job training specification describes in overall terms the job for which training is to be given, or the problem which training will enable learners to tackle. It then specifies in detail the kinds and levels of knowledge, skill and, where relevant, attitudes needed for effective performance, together with the standards that will operate in the job, and the ways in which performance will be assessed.**

How does one start the process of job training analysis? First, all jobs can be seen to consist of three broad components:

**Skills**
Skills may be, for example, manual, diagnostic, interpersonal or decision-making; they include any component of the job that involves 'doing' something.

**Knowledge**
Knowledge may be, for example, technical, procedural, or concerned with company organization, but always relates to what must be 'known about' or 'understood' in a job.

**Attitudes**
It may be important in a job that staff clearly show certain attitudes at all times, eg courtesy and sensitivity in dealing with customers or clients; flexibility and co-operation when working in a close-knit team; or calmness and patience in coping with various critical pressures in a job. Although attitude training will not be needed for every job, certain attitudes are so crucial to particular jobs that keeping that component in mind when analysing is always to be recommended. If in the specific case there are no attitudes that need to be emphasized, then it is quite simple to make a note to that effect on the job training specification.

It is important to collect information about these three components when analysing any job, because each have different implications for training design and methods: the ways of developing 'skills' are usually different to the ways of imparting 'knowledge' and of producing or changing 'attitudes', and indeed the whole structure and time period of training will be affected by the relative importance of those three categories in a particular job or task.

It may be necessary to analyse a wide variety of skills, knowledge and attitudes. Furthermore jobs differ greatly in their range, autonomy, and environment, as well as in the level (as distinct from simply the type) of skills, knowledge and attitudes that they involve, and therefore different analytical approaches and techniques are necessary.

Since there are so many books easily available on job training analysis, and Kenney and Reid (1986) in particular have an excellent and detailed section dealing with the topic, on which I draw at many points in this chapter, I am only going to deal in outline with 3 interrelated areas:

- A strategy for carrying out job training analysis

- Four main job training analysis approaches

- Eight main job training analysis techniques

## A Strategy for Carrying Out Job Training Analysis

(In this section I am particularly indebted to Kenney and Reid's (1986) excellent chapter on job training analysis)

A strategy for carrying out job training analysis can be divided into six steps:

### STEP 1   Initial investigation

As was noted in Chapters 6 and 7, any request for training should always be met first by investigatory questions such as:

#### *Is training really the answer?*

For example, poor performance may be due to ineffective supervision, lack of financial or other incentives, or innate lack of skill. If any of these is the primary cause, then training is not going to improve performance, and so job training analysis is pointless.

#### *Is training the most cost-beneficial answer?*

There may be other ways in which knowledge, skills or attitudes can be developed without involving the expense of formal training: for example, careful integration of work and learning may be more cost-beneficial; or buying in the training skills or some other non-training solution.

#### *Is analysis really necessary?*

Perhaps reliable and up to date information already exists about the job? Perhaps there is already a job training specification, either produced by someone within the organization or outside it?

### Is the job likely to change?

This would require new analysis to take place whenever change took place. If change is likely, why, how often, and over what period of time? Or is it a routine and stable job, which will not be changing significantly through time, and therefore will repay detailed analysis now? Is it a job that many people are performing, or will be performing, or is it unique?

### Should the person be adapted to the job, or the job to the person?

With certain jobs, especially those at the top level of the organization, or which are very specialized, or involve a high degree of innovative talent, it is much more a question of the job-holder 'making' the job within quite loosely defined parameters to produce unique kinds and levels of performance, than a question of job-holders being trained to carry out specific tasks with given types and levels of knowledge and skill. In such a situation a job training specification is not likely to be needed, and certainly a query should be raised at this stage to that effect.

### STEP 2   Select the analyst

In most organizations except small firms (where a line manager or a consultant may have to do the task) it is specialist staff who carry out job training analysis. However, it is the line manager and the person who actually does the job who know most about the job's components, and the knowledge, skill and attitudes needed to perform well in it, so whoever carries out the analysis must be both technically competent and acceptable to those with whom he or she works. Much of a sensitive nature can be uncovered during the process of job training analysis: motivation, discipline and supervision problems; misunderstandings caused by ill-defined responsibilities; conflict and inefficiency arising from inappropriate organization structures or cultures. Even though the analyst is concentrating on training matters, he or she will have to contribute to resolving or at the least making known such difficulties if not to do so means that the training effort will be wasted.

### STEP 3   Gain co-operation

Because of its sensitive nature, before this analytical activity begins, everyone involved in and likely to be affected by it must be approached with a full and clear explanation of its purpose, how it will be carried out, by whom, over what period of time, and with what probable outcomes. Only when the full co-operation of all the key parties is ensured should the process begin. Ignoring the 'political' aspect of job training analysis can lead to a barrier of problems developing which can end in the abandonment of the whole project.

## STEP 4    Approach and techniques
Information obtained in the previous stages will enable the analyst to decide which approach and techniques to choose (these will be explained in the next section). However, it is essential that choice is governed not just by consideration of what is technically best, but also of what will be acceptable to those from whom she will have to obtain information during the analysis. This takes us back to the importance of ensuring the co-operation of all the interested parties.

## STEP 5    Carry out the analysis
Here, the analyst needs to know the sources of information to use and the depth of analysis needed.

### Sources of information
*Written sources* are liable to be produced on differing bases, and may be out of date or not comprehensive. Care must therefore be taken when referring to technical manuals, or to records of various kinds. Accurate records should give important information like, for example, whether the job is one where there are many problems in performance, or one where good standards of performance are the norm and are relatively easily achieved; also whether there are trends in labour turnover, absenteeism, sickness or lateness that could indicate problems that are being experienced in the job.

*Oral sources* of information, eg the job holder, the job holder's manager, co-workers, are all liable to be biased, and to contradict one another in their perception of both the contents and characteristics of the job and — very important − in the priorities to be achieved within it: they can be deliberately or unintentionally misleading.

Deciding which sources of information to use, and how to collate and interpret the data that is then produced, is thus a difficult stage, calling for considerable interpersonal and analytical skills.

### Depth of analysis
In job training analysis the general principle to observe is to see a total job in terms of its constituent tasks, or elements. So, regardless of which analytical approach is chosen, how much detail is needed about a task and the skills, knowledge and attitudes required to do

it? Annett *et al* (1979) suggest that every task in a job should continue to be broken down and described until the point is reached where the remainder of the task can be readily learnt without training, and where even if inadequate performance were to result, it would not be a serious matter.

The analyst must also look for any problems, either social or work-related, in the workplace that could make it difficult for the trainee to apply learning form the training programme. The training programme must not only develop skills, knowledge and attitudes in the learners, but must also relate adequately to the kind of job environment which they will enter, or re-enter, after training.

### STEP 6   Produce the job training specification
When the process of analysing the job has been completed, and the information checked in order to be sure that it is valid, the analyst can write a job training specification, ensuring that it is agreed as being accurate by the key parties: the managers and, if relevant, unions involved.

Now let us think in more detail about step 4: choosing a job training analysis approach.

### Job Training Analysis Approaches
Currently, again as Kenney and Reid (1986) explain, there are four major job training analysis approaches:

Comprehensive analysis

Key task analysis

Problem-centred analysis

Core analysis

### Comprehensive analysis
Here, as the words imply, a very detailed examination takes place of every aspect of the job, until each task has been fully described in terms of its knowledge, skills and (if relevant) attitudes. It must also be described by reference to the objective of each task, the frequency of each task, the required standard of performance in each task, and how that performance is to be measured. Clearly it is an extemely time-consuming analytical approach, and requires much skill. The first question to ask is, therefore, in which circumstances would you recommend this approach, and in which

would you not?

The following reasons form a set of general criteria where the use of comprehensive job training analysis would be recommended (with acknowledgements to Kenney and Reid, 1986, page 159):

*Tasks are unfamiliar, hard, and must be learnt quickly and to standard*
Most of the tasks the trainees must do are unfamiliar to them, are quite hard to learn, and must be done quickly and accurately, with experienced worker standard needing to be reached as soon as possible after recruitment.

*Change is unlikely*
The job is unlikely to change in the foreseeable future, and a training programme drawn up now will for that reason, and because of the regularity of intakes of new recruits, be used frequently.

*Job is closely prescribed*
Little or nothing in the job is left to the initiative of the job holder.

*Resources are adequate*
There are enough resources (eg time, skill, numbers of staff) to carry out this detailed, complex and time-consuming approach to job training analysis.

So how does one apply the comprehensive approach? Basically it is a matter of two things:

### Produce a job description
A broad statement of the purpose, scope, responsibilities and tasks which constitute a particular job (Department of Employment, 1971). The job description should contain:

- the title of the job

- the overall purpose of the job, preferably expressed in a sentence, which sums up why the job is there at all as far as the organization is concerned

- the name of the department in which the job holder works

- the title of the person/s to whom the job holder is responsible:

a) directly

b) ultimately (if (b) is different from (a)

- brief details of any other key relationships, for example with staff in another department or unit; with people or institutions outside the organization, etc

- brief description of any major resources for which the job-holder is accountable: finance, physical resources, personnel

- an indication as to whether the job holder works mainly on their own, or as part of a fixed team, or is expected to move through various teams according to task needs

- a list of major tasks only, simply to give a picture of the main elements of the job

- the job description should also give brief details of any particular difficulties commonly experienced in the job: obviously these must receive attention in any training programme.

### Produce a job training specification

This should show, for every task of the job, split as necessary into sub-tasks or elements, the skill, knowledge and (if relevant) attitudes required; the standards of performance to be reached; and how performance will be measured in order to ensure achievement of standards. The way the specification is laid out and the kind of information it contains related to those three basic categories will depend on the analytical techniques used (see page 159), but it must be remembered that as it is a guide to action (i.e. drawing up a training programme) it should have a simple, easily-understood format, and be expressed in clear, meaningful language.

### Key task analysis

This approach takes only the crucial tasks within a job — ie those tasks in which performance of a certain kind is absolutely essential to effectiveness in the job overall. Whilst comprehensive analysis is used most commonly for jobs consisting of simple, usually manual, repetitive and unchanging tasks, jobs involving more complex skills such as those referred to already in this book — observation and reflection, analysis, creativity, decision-making and problem-solving, evaluation — would in their essence be obscured rather than revealed by the plethora of information that an attempt at comprehensive analysis would produce. What is wanted in those instances is a clear overview of the job, followed by a focus on only what is most essential for successful performance: the key tasks.

Once again, therefore, there will be a brief job description, exactly as in comprehensive analysis, but the job training specification will be selective, covering only those tasks crucial to effective job performance. So key task analysis is appropriate for any type of job where the following conditions apply:

*Tasks are varied, and not all are critical*
**The job consists of a large number of different tasks, not all of which are critical for effective performance, and it is assumed that the job holder does not normally require training in minor or non-key tasks;**

*Changes are likely*
**The job is changing in emphasis or in content, resulting in a continuing need to establish priority tasks, standards of performance and the skills and knowledge required**
*(Kenney and Reid, 1986, page 160)*

Appendix 2 shows an extract from a 'key task' job training analysis produced by a student on our Institute of Personnel Management Stage 2 Year 1 part-time course in 1985, as one of his Employee Development assignments. It shows what key task analysis involves, and the kind of information it produces for the training designer. It is not intended to be a 'model example', but simply a lay person's attempt to apply the approach to a particular job.

## Problem-centred analysis
With this approach the focus is on defining problem/s which have been agreed to have a training solution. Thus the analysis is concerned with describing the nature and causes of each problem, and the skills, knowledge, and attitudes (if relevant) needed to cope successfully with it. The analytical process also actively involves job-holders in considering what kind of training they would find most effective. Warr and Bird (1968) have done major work on this approach, with their 'training by exception' technique, developed when they felt that their attempts to use both comprehensive and key task analysis approaches in connection with supervisory training needs were inadequate, because of the enormous diversity of tasks in each supervisor's job, and the amount of time taken to analyse them compared to the ultimate usefulness of the information obtained by using those approaches.

The problem-centred approach is best used when:

### Training is urgent, but analytical resources limited
There is an immediate need for training but limited resources to do the analysis.

### Performance is generally satisfactory
The job holder's work is satisfactory except in one or two 'problem' areas.

### Involvement of learners in analysis is important
It is particularly important to use a method of analysis that will actively involve the potential learners, both in diagnosis of their needs for training and in suggestion about preferred and effective training media and methods.

With the problem-centred approach there is no one way of gathering and collating the information, although whatever methods are used must, of course, ensure that the perspectives of both job holder/s and their supervisors, managers and any other key parties (eg unions) on the problems are obtained. Nor is there a job description or job training specification, but simply a description of the problems and how they can be tackled in training. What comes out of problem-centred analysis, typically, is:

### Common training needs
Knowledge, skills and attitudes, the need for which is evident in the responses of large numbers of those being questioned. These can form the basis of a common training programme.

### Individual training needs
Needs which are so specific to individuals that they require to be met at an individual, not at a group, level.

### Suggested training media and methods
Those training media and methods which the key parties, and particularly the job-holders, feel would be best and most feasible to meet the needs which analysis of the problem/s has revealed.

### Commitment of the learners
Because of the nature of the analytical approach, it is one which is highly successful in obtaining the commitment of those who will be the learner group in the subsequent training programme. Since they have taken a leading part in the diagnosis and analysis of their problems and needs, and in suggesting training solutions, the objectives and relevance of the training programme are obvious to them.

Again, a practical example will be useful, and I am showing in Appendix 3 a peice of work done by another student on our 1985 Institute of Personnel Management Stage 2 Year 1 course who attempted the problem-centred approach in his assignment. Often the problem-centred approach is used to analyse the needs of large numbers of personnel, but in this instance it was used to examine problems relating to only a few; his introductory notes comment on this. He has made use of Warr and Bird's (1968) recommended analytical techniques, and these too receive comment in his introduction.

### Core analysis

An area of training analysis which is now of major importance is youth training, where analysts are confronted not with needs specific to a particular organization, but with needs ranging across many different jobs in many different kinds of organization and context. In such a situation the three approaches already examined clearly have their limitations. Instead, an approach called 'core analysis' has been developed, focusing on the analysis of core skills.

Core skills are those which are transferable through a range of jobs or tasks which have them at their core. Throughout this book we have referred regularly to a particular set of core transferable skills. Do you recall them now?

---

## ACTIVITY

### Core Transferable Skills

There is a group of skills which are relevant to all learning tasks or managerial jobs. Please list these skills, and explain from which body of theory they derive.

---

## FEEDBACK NOTES

The core skills are:

Observation/reflection

Analysis

Creativity

Decision-making/problem-solving

Evaluation

They derive from Kolb's (1974) explanation of learning as a circular process involving experience, reflection, abstract conceptualization, and experimentation. (Chapter 4 contains the full explanation.)

---

The possession of core skills can therefore lead to competency in an occupation rather than just in specific jobs in particular organizations. The Manpower Services Commission (MSC, 1984) lists 103 core skills in four major areas: Number, Communication, Problem-solving and Practical.

Let us look at an Activity related to core analysis, but carried out in the context of a particular organization. This will show how core analysis has a local as well as a more universal value.

---

## ACTIVITY

## CASE STUDY: The Core Skills Analysis Task

Here is the MSC's list of core skills involved in 'MONITORING':

11.    MONITORING: KEEPING TRACK OF PROGRESS AND CHECKING

11.1   Check that he/she is performing a task to standard

11.2   Monitor a process or activity

11.3   Monitor the availability of stocks or materials

11.4   Check the quality and condition of equipment, materials or products

11.5   Check written information

11.6   Monitor the safety of the workplace

11.7   Notice that things have gone wrong, and that action is required

An analyst is collecting information which will be used to design an in-house programme for a trainee Training Officer in her organization. She is told by the Training Manager that one crucial task in the job of a training officer is:

> ...the task of making sure that training activities go as planned, and don't actually cost more than estimated in our training budget. So every training activity has to be checked to see that it's done what it was meant to do, and hasn't cost more than it should. There will be various written records to examine, amongst other kinds of information. We do a host of long training courses, so those have to be monitored at different stages as they go along, to make sure costs are not adrift. If anything goes wrong, cost-wise, then quick action has to be taken, because otherwise we're really in trouble!

Use the MSC list shown opposite to define what are the skills related to MONITORING that will achieve competent performance in this training task.

---

**FEEDBACK NOTES**

If we look at the list of core skills under 'MONITORING', we can see that the analyst should record the following skills:

- Check that activities are being performed to standard

- Monitor activities

- Check written information

- Notice that things have gone wrong, and that action is required.

Of course, other skills will be involved, for example related to finding out and providing information, and planning and decision-making, but for our purposes we have just looked at one set of core skills. Note how in every case skill is explained very simply but clearly by using an active key word, such as 'Check', 'Monitor', or 'Notice'.

In our example, the analyst would next have to take all the other key tasks of a Training Officer and discover which core transferable skills were involved in the job, using the MSC list to describe them. This will eventually aid not only training design but also the selection of applicants for the job: applicants who can show that they have competence in the core transferable skills involved in the trainee Training Officer job should be assessed as strong contenders for it.

---

However, at this point Mansfield (1985) makes the important observation that two people performing the same job in two different contexts have to master more than the *occupational* skills involved in the job. They also have to know how to manage all the tasks in the job, and carry out the job successfully in its specific *environment*. A training manager going from private to public sector organization will not only need expertise in occupational skills common to all training jobs; she will also have to be able to manage all the tasks that make up her new job in the particular situation in which she finds herself, and must be able to understand and operate effectively in the particular system that she has now joined. Thus there are three components involved in effective job performance:

**Task related skills**
**Those used in carrying out tasks.**

**Task management skills**
**Those used to manage a number of tasks including planning, problem-solving and decision-making.**

**Job/role environment skills**
**Include working directly with people outside the workplace, working in a hazardous environment or one which can be critical in terms of cost, such as dealing with highly confidential work.**

*(Kenney and Reid, 1986, page 162)*

Core analysis enables these three kinds of skills to be precisely defined.

From what has been said so far it is clear that there are many tasks in organizations which have at their core a shared body of skills. And since core analysis can also identify the organization-specific 'task management' and 'job/role environment' skills which are essential to the competent performance of a job, its use will enable a clear and flexible document to be drawn up which will be an aid to many personnel processes, as well as being expressed (if using the MSC's list of core skills) in a 'universal' language.

As an approach, core analysis differs from key task analysis (which at first sight it resembles closely, since both are concerned to identify those tasks crucial to effective performance in a job, and break them down into elements in which training can then be given) mainly in the focus it requires on core transferable skills, and in its use of a 'universal' rather than 'local' language to describe those skills. It also, of course, offers advantages that relate to a wide range of personnel processes rather than just to the formulation of a job description and a job training specification.

The use of core analysis is relevant in any of the following situations:

### Skills must be transferable
Skills acquired in a particular training programme must be transferable to a variety of tasks and jobs in many different sorts of situations and organizations.

### Core transferable skills must be identified
It is important to discover which are the core transferable skills common to groups of tasks in a workplace, the possession of which will ensure competence in those tasks.

### Analysis should promote discussion of learner progress and needs
It will be particularly helpful to use an analytical approach which will promote the shared recording, discussion and assessment of the learner's achievements; informed and task-centred appraisal of their strengths and weaknesses; and the highlighting of their training needs.

In this section we have looked at 4 job training analysis approaches:

Comprehensive analysis

Key task analysis

Problem-centred analysis

Core analysis.

## Job Training Analysis Techniques
Once the overall job training analysis approach has been determined, there are many techniques that can be used to obtain information about the skills, knowledge and attitudes that make up a task or job, and about the standards and methods that are applied to performance. Widely-known ones that are too well described elsewhere to need repetition here include:

ACTIVITY ANALYSIS (Miller, 1962)

MANUAL SKILLS ANALYSIS (Seymour (1954; 1966) and Gentles (1969), and see also King's (1968) warning about the danger of drawing up training programmes based on such a detailed technique when one change to an operating method is enough to require the whole analytical process to be carried out again from scratch.)

CRITICAL INCIDENTS ANALYSIS (Flanagan, 1954)

FAULTS ANALYSIS (Kenney and Reid, 1986)

STAGES AND KEY POINTS ANALYSIS (Ibid)

However, there are two further sorts of techniques which are perhaps less well-known, but are so important, especially in relation to more complex jobs, that some comment may be helpful:

Role analysis

Interpersonal and interactive skills analysis

**Role analysis**
In supervisory and managerial jobs especially, it is vital to be clear about the role, or roles, that the job holder must carry. Certainly training for anyone who had to move into a training manager's job would greatly benefit from being based on role analysis along with the more immediately obvious analytical techniques, because of the frequency of role problems in training jobs. It is a technique derived from the behavioural sciences, notably from the work of the industrial psychologist McGregor (1960), who emphasized how important it was, if a manager was to be effective, to build up a shared perception of his/her role between different members of the manager's role set (i.e. the people with whom the role holder regularly interacts). French and Bell (1978) summarize the various procedures involved, which basically require job holder, superior and (usually) one or more other members of the job holder's role set to each produce a list of the duties and behaviour that they perceive necessary if the job holder is to be effective. A role description is then produced from joint discussion of the different lists, showing most of the important features of the job.

Durham Business School use role analysis in their 'Expectations' approach. Machin (1981) shows how the technique highlights any disagreements amongst job holder and members of the role set about the role in question, and generates open discussion to the point where, hopefully, full understanding of the role has been achieved, most of the disagreements have been resolved, and a job description can be drawn up. If, however, there should be conflicting perceptions and expectations, then the analyst should bring this to the attention of management, since clearly such conflict will impede successful job performance, create organizational problems, and produce situations for which training is not a remedy.

**Interpersonal and interactive skills analysis**

A wide range of jobs, especially those that are supervisory, managerial, professional and technical, make heavy demands on the job holder in terms of their requirement for a high degree of skill in dealing with face-to-face situations, and in achieving the effective interaction of people and tasks in a work cycle. Such skills are difficult to analyse, but there are now a number of useful techniques available. These include Rackham, Honey and Colbert's (1971) techniques for analysing interactive skills; transactional analysis, described very fully by Carby and Thakur (1977); and the diagnostic techniques and instruments related to teamwork skills that have been developed by writers like Woodcock (1979). Readers who need further information are referred initially to the work of the authors already mentioned, together with the articles by Cuthbert (1984) and by Simpson (1984), and the books by Argyle (1970) and by Sills (1973).

Finally, it is important to emphasize that the analysis of a job holder's performance will show any problems being experienced or likely to be experienced in reaching required performance standards; typical faults encountered in the work and how to deal with them; and much other valuable information. Performance analysis is therefore yet another technique (if it can be so called), and it should virtually always be included, no matter which job training analysis approach is used. More is said about how to treat information arising out of performance analysis in Chapters 9,10 and 11.

In this section I have referred to eight analytical techniques that can be used singly or in various combinations, given the particular job training analysis approach that is chosen and the situation to which it is applied:

Activity analysis

Manual skills analysis

Critical incidents analysis

Faults analysis

Role analysis

Interpersonal and interactive skills analysis

Performance analysis

## CONCLUSION

Having read this chapter and completed the various activities it contains, you should now:

1 Understand what kind of overall strategy to use when analysing jobs for training purposes

2 Know the main approaches and techniques used in job training analysis

3 Be able to choose the relevant approach and techniques to use in analysing a particular job.

The main learning points related to these objectives are:

**1  Job training analysis**
Job training analysis is the process of identifying the purpose of the job and its component parts and specifying what must be learnt in order for there to be effective work performance.

The job training specification describes in overall terms the job for which training is to be given (or the problem/s which training will enable learners to tackle), and then specifies in detail the kinds and levels of knowledge, skill, and, where relevant, attitudes needed for effective job performance, together with the standards that will operate in the job, and the ways in which performance will be assessed.

All jobs consist of 3 broad components:

• Skills

• Knowledge

- Attitudes

## 2 A strategy for carrying out job training analysis
The 6 steps involved in job training analysis are:

- Initial investigation

- Select the analyst

- Gain co-operation

- Select approach and techniques

- Carry out the analysis

- Produce the job training specification

## 3 Job training analysis approaches
There are 4 main job training analysis approaches:

- Comprehensive analysis

- Key task analysis

- Problem-centred analysis

- Core analysis.

The use of comprehensive job training analysis is recommended when:

- Tasks are unfamiliar, hard, and must be learnt quickly and to standard

- Change is unlikely

- Job is closely prescribed

- Resources are adequate

The use of key task analysis is recommended when:

- Tasks are varied, and not all are critical

- Changes are likely

The use of problem-centred analysis is recommended when:

- Training is urgent, but analytical resources limited

- Performance is generally satisfactory

- Involvement of learners in analysis is important

What comes out of problem-centred analysis, typically, is:

- Common training needs

- Individual training needs

- Suggested training media and methods

- Commitment of the learners

Core analysis can identify 3 types of skills often involved in effective job performance:

- Task related skills

- Task management skills

- Job/role environment skills

The use of core analysis is recommended in any of the following situations:

- Skills must be transferable

- Core transferable skills must be identified

- Analysis should promote discussion of learner progress and needs

**4   Job training analysis techniques**
There are 8 techniques widely used in job training analysis, either singly or in various combinations:

- Activity analysis

- Manual skills analysis

- Critical incidents analysis

- Faults analysis

- Stages and key points analysis

- Role analysis

- Interpersonal and interactive skills analysis

- Performance analysis

---

## REVIEW ACTIVITY

Finally, here is a short case study and a question which you can either tackle as coursework (if you are a student): discuss with fellow-students or colleagues: or simply think about now that you have completed this chapter:

- You have been asked, in an organizational context of your choice, to set up a training programme to ensure that the flow of information between shop floor and management improves. The aim is to improve industrial relations. Identify what seem to you to be the critical issues and outline the steps you will take to deal with this request. Please include in your recommendations the job training analysis approach, or approaches, and analytical techniques which would be useful in this situation.

- Critically examine the various ways in which jobs may be analysed for training purposes. Which are used in your organization and what would you recommend to improve your organization's job training analysis activity?

## CHAPTER 9

# Assessing needs at individual level
# 1 Personnel specifications and records of performance

## LEARNING OBJECTIVES

After reading this chapter and completing the various activities it contains, you should:

1  Know the main ways of analysing training needs at the individual level

2  Be able to draw up a personnel specification which can help the training designer

3  Understand the main factors that explain the performance of a job holder

4  Know the main considerations relating to the use of performance records of various kinds in the analysis of an individual's training needs.

As we saw in Chapter 8, the end product of job training analysis is a job training specification which clearly sets out the nature of the job in question, and the types and levels of skill, knowledge and attitudes necessary for effective performance in that job. However, this information in itself is not enough for the training designer. It is also necessary to know something about the needs and characteristics of the individuals who will be receiving training. Once the demands of the job and the needs of the person are put together, training objectives relevant to both can be formulated, and a training programme designed which will aim to close the gaps between the existing and the desired performance of the learners.

### Individual Training Needs
As we saw in Chapter 6, (page 93) four categories of training need should always be considered, relating to:

Staff newly appointed from outside the organization

Newly promoted staff

Existing staff

Staff facing change

Whoever is responsible for training in the organization or a part of it should find out what type of training is needed for each of the categories shown above. Ideally, of course, everyone should have the opportunity to undergo all four types as their working life progresses:

Induction training

Basic skills training

Continuous development

Training for change

There are many sources of information about potential learners, and in this and Chapters 10 and 11 we can only look at some of them. The task of the training manager (or whoever is responsible for planning training and development programmes) is to collect as much relevant information on the learners as is feasible, and use it to help with the design of training.

This Chapter examines the following sources of information:

Personnel specifications

Performance records

In Chapter 10 we will continue by looking at:

Trainability tests

Assessment and development centres

Self assessment

In Chapter 11 we will conclude by looking at:

Appraisal of performance

## The Personnel Specification

The personnel specification, which of course has far wider uses than for training design alone, is a document which specifies, under relevant headings, the kind of person who will perform well in the job in question.

If, as ideally should be the case, specialist and line management staff work closely together in the recruitment, selection and training processes, then once the job training specification has been drawn up, a discussion should take place between the parties, out of which should come agreement on the personnel specification which will be used as an aid to recruitment and selection. This is a far more logical process than drawing up a job training specification and a personnel specification separately.

Thus the personnel specification should clarify the kind and level of human characteristics, experience and potential that a new job holder should possess, as distinct from those that induction, initial training and subsequent continuous development will help them to achieve.

The format of a personnel specification is not predetermined. Well-known formats include Rodger's 7-Point Plan (1952), and Fraser's 5-Point Plan (1971), but it is equally valid to use any categorization system, providing that the categories are comprehensive, and have minimum overlap.

The specification should begin with the kind of job description to which we referred in Chapter 8 (page 151) so that the relationship between the nature of the job and the kind of person needed to do it can be clearly seen. Then come the assessment categories within which are noted the type and level of human characteristics required. It is useful to draw up two columns in specifying these characteristics, one to show those essential for effective performance, and the other for those additional desirable requirements which would lift performance to above, or well above, average.

At this point, let us try a practical activity, but before attempting it, the following revision points from this and the previous chapter will be useful:

- All jobs can be viewed as consisting of three broad components:

    Skills

    Knowledge

    Attitudes

- There are three levels of competency involved in effective job performance:

  Task related skills

  Task management skills

  Job/role environment skills

- There are four major categories of potential learners:

  Staff newly appointed from outside the organization

  Newly promoted staff

  Existing staff

  Staff facing change

- There are four major types of training and development:

  Induction training

  Basic skills training

  Continuous development

  Training for change

Now let us try the Activity.

---

## ACTIVITY

### The Personnel Specification Task

First, please turn to Appendix 2 which shows an extract from the Job Training Specification document for a Principal Assistant (PA) (Personnel and Training) at the North Eastern Electricity Board. Then examine carefully the Personnel Specification for the job, shown in Appendix 4. This shows the kind of person who will actually be recruited into the job, and who will be going through the training programme.

You are the Training Manager who has been asked to design a

programme for the new recruit to the PA job. The appointment is due to be made in two months' time.

1 What information do the two documents already give you?

2 What further information should you seek, before being able to design that programme?

---

## FEEDBACK NOTES

1 The Training Manager has three important pieces of information:

- The Job Description at the start of the Job Training Specification shows the overall purpose and key parameters of the job

- The rest of the Job Training Specification shows the knowledge, skills and attitudes required for effective performance in the job

- The Personnel Specification indicates the kind of person who will be recruited into the job

2 Before designing a training programme, information is needed on many points, and the list below is therefore not exhaustive: you may well have included other areas where data is required.

- *Previous programmes*
  Have we run a programme for this job before? If so, are there any evaluations of it, formal or informal?

- *Job changes*
  Have there been any changes in the job — its purpose, key tasks, etc — since the Job Training Specification and Personnel Specification were drawn up? If so, do those changes have training or development implications?

- *Training standards*
  Is the training programme expected to take the new recruit up to the 'desirable' level indicated in the personnel specification, or to ensure that tasks are performed to the 'essential' level only? If this is an internal appointment, then is it known how far the new recruit is likely not only to have core task related skills, but also to be familiar with the task management, and job/role environment skills involved in the job?

- *Level of requirements sought*
  Is it known at this stage whether the new recruit will be expected
  to have already only the 'essential' or also the 'desirable'
  requirements indicated in the Personnel Specification, in each of
  the five categories shown? (If the new recruit is expected to have
  already all the 'desirable' requirements, then the programme
  could concentrate on induction, appraisal and continuous
  development, whereas if he or she is expected to have gaps in
  areas of the 'essential' requirements, then that is a strong
  indicator that basic skills training will also need to be included in
  the programme.)

- *Sources of recruitment*
  Is it known whether the new recruit will be coming from within
  or outside the organization? (This will affect the extent to which
  the programme must develop job/role environment skills in
  addition to the task related and task management skills indicated
  in the Job Training Specification. We discussed these three
  categories of skill in Chapter 8, under 'Core Analysis'.)

- *Timing of the training programme*
  How long will there be between the appointment being made,
  and training having to be provided? (As is clear from the above
  list of points, much of the information needed to enable a
  completely relevant and effective training programme to be
  drawn up cannot be provided until the identity of the new recruit
  is known. If the job holder is to go straight into training, then
  certain assumptions will have to be made now in order to design
  the programme; and to the extent that these assumptions are
  proved later to be invalid, the programme itself will lack validity.)

- *The type of programme required*
  Analysing all the above information, what learning strategy
  should be pursued? Induction and basic skill training only?
  Some other form of organized learning? Continuous development of the job holder? A combination?

---

You may have noticed that in doing this Activity certain difficulties
were encountered because the training designer was not given
information about how far the recruiters were going to look for
someone who met only the 'essential' or also the 'desirable'
requirements shown in the personnel specification. The personnel
specification itself, however, was a clear aid to training, because:

- It showed those areas where 'potential' rather than existing skills were important (implications here for training and development activities)

- It also showed the type of training, experience and development needed to take someone from merely adequate to very good performance in certain areas (see under 'Qualifications' and 'Occupational Experience')

- It expressed requirements in terms which clearly indicated whether what was needed was knowledge, skills or attitudes (see especially under 'Motivation')

- Without specifically using these terms, it made clear which were task mastery, task management, and job/role environment areas of skill. (See, for example, in the 'Desirable' column under 'Occupational Experience' where job/role environment skills are indicated and under 'Motivation', where many task management skills are clearly outlined.)

As can be seen from the Activity you have just carried out, in using the personnel specification as an aid to training, five major issues are involved:

### Planned interrelationship between job description, job training specification, and personnel specification

There should be a planned interrelationship between the job description, the job training specification, and the personnel specification, and their use in the recruitment, selection and training processes.

### Accurate information

The information they contain must be up to date and comprehensive, and gaps in information must be filled in before the training programme is designed.

### Identification of training-related elements

The personnel specification used for training purposes must clearly identify training-related elements, either within the body of the specification or in a separate section at the end of the document.

### Categorization of learners

There must be clarity about the type of learners involved.

## Categorization of training
There must be clarity about the type of training or development involved.

## Understanding Performance
Information about how a person is performing, or might perform, in a job for which training is to be provided is crucial, but before examining such information, it is important that the analyst should have a clear understanding of two major factors:

Factors underlying performance

The relationship between job holder and manager.

## Factors underlying performance
Performance can be explained as the final outcome of the interaction between a person's needs, their perception of the results wanted from them and the rewards being offered to them, and the amount of effort, energy and ability they have available or wish to apply to the task at hand. Handy (1985, page 34) calls this the 'motivation calculus', and what it means is that in trying to understand a person's work performance, we should find out:

### Needs
How far, in their mind, does the job or task relate in any positive way to needs that the individual brings to work? What we should try to discover is not all a person's needs, but only those by which they are influenced at work. If a particular task or job only relates to those needs in a minor way, then clearly we cannot expect more than minimal performance from the individual.

### Results
How far does the person really understand what is wanted from them? Do they fully understand what the job is, what results they are supposed to achieve, and within what context of opportunities, constraints, etc? Have they had any opportunity to set work targets jointly with their manager, rather than simply having these imposed on them? There is much evidence to show that the joint formulation of work plans and targets is a vital aid to a shared perception of the job between manager and job holder, and to increased motivation and commitment in the job holder.

### Rewards
Does the task or job offer rewards to the individual that they value, in

relation to their needs? Rewards can take many different forms: not just money and position, (quite often those sort of 'rewards' have less impact than is commonly supposed, as well as not usually being readily available to distribute to staff) but status, praise, recognition. Talking and listening to staff about what is seen as a reward, instead of simply acting on assumptions about this crucial factor, can be a very instructive activity.

### 'E' Factors

How far does the job holder see it as worthwhile to expend effort, energy, excitement and ability in the task, given the results that are required and the rewards it appears to offer them? And what level of those 'E' factors does the job holder actually possess? Are assessments about this accurate, or are incorrect assumptions being made, so that either less or more is expected of the job holder than they can in fact offer?

So to summarize, performance has to be examined by reference to four parameters:

Needs of the individual

Results the individual is expected to achieve

Rewards offered for their achievement

'E' Factors: the individual's effort, excitement, energy, ability available in relation to the task.

Let us take a case study and try applying our analytical model to the information it contains.

---

## ACTIVITY

### CASE STUDY:   The Reluctant Worker

A member of staff is invited by his manager to work on a new project that has come into their department. The manager knows that she cannot force him to take it on, as he already has a heavy workload, and there are other staff who could cope with it satisfactorily. However, having observed him working over the two years he has been a member of his group, the manager believes he is motivated strongly by ambition, and since the task is a crucial one, and (she also believes) he is likely to be highly effective in carrying it out, she tries to enlist his commitment by telling him that if he does it, and does it well, it will significantly advance his prospects of promotion. To her surprise, he turns the opportunity down. Using the concepts involved in analysing performance:

Needs

Results

Rewards

'E' Factors

produce a list of possible reasons for his decision.

---

## FEEDBACK NOTES

There are a great number of reasons why the member of staff may not be motivated to apply much effort to the task in question. Using our analytical model, the following come immediately to mind:

### Needs
Even though he may be ambitious, promotion may not be a reward that means anything significant in relation to this need. He may be driven by the need not for the increased responsibilities or high level of skill that promotion would involve, but for some form of status in his profession. That need may be satisfied by doing well in his present work, and in making sure that his wider professional body knows about his successes. Another possibility is that he may want status in the eyes of his colleagues at work, again by being regarded as highly effective in his present job. Taking on another task when he is already expending maximum effort on his existing workload could mean a reduction in his overall effectiveness, and the loss of such status. Or he may have a need for power which is already being satisfied by the influence he can exercise over members of his existing workgroup. In other words, a generalized term like 'ambition' does not adequately explain the complex motivation that could be involved in his behaviour. Such generalizations are very commonly used by managers to explain the performance of their group, and lead to what is often serious mismanagement, causing reduced morale, commitment and motivation of that group.

### Results

He may have misunderstood the results he is being asked to achieve, and feel that the task involves too much effort. Unless tasks and targets are clearly explained, and preferably jointly agreed, motivation of the job holder may, again, be reduced.

### Rewards

As already explained under 'Needs', the reward being offered — an increased chance of promotion — may simply not be relevant to the needs he brings to the work situation. On the other hand, his ambition may well be satisfied by promotion, but he may not believe that such a reward would actually occur, either because his manager is known to make promises that she does not fulfil in order to get people to take on extra work, or because events have proved that she does not have the power to carry out her promises.

### 'E' Factors

He may feel unable to expend any more effort or energy on new tasks, given his heavy existing workload. Or he may not know his manager's opinion of him, and may feel, or know, that he does not have the necessary ability. Again therefore, he will not be motivated to perform the new task.

---

What is interesting in the above case is to note the complexity of the interrelationship between needs, results, rewards, and 'E' factors in explaining motivation and performance. Over time, the performance records of such a member of staff may show increased levels of absenteeism, sickness, and of refusal to take on new tasks, and such records may result in very unfavourable assessments. Finally, therefore, such information may lead the manager and training staff to see the individual as one to whom training and development may make little difference; in other words, the individual may be 'written off' as an uncommitted and difficult member of staff. Yet with more insights into the factors that lie behind performance, and a more searching analysis of the information, together with discussion with the member of staff, a quite different understanding of the person may emerge. This would lead to important conclusions about the recruitment of staff, the allocation of work, the leadership style, and the appraisal methods that prevail in that department.

Thus we can summarize by saying that:

**Performance is the outcome of a complex interaction between perceived and actual needs, results, rewards and 'E' factors.**

This definition emphasises the importance of understanding not only the actual needs, results, rewards and 'E' factors, but how these are perceived by job holders and their superiors. It is *our* perception of life that primarily governs our behaviour, rather than any other person's perception of it: so in understanding performance at work we must find ways of analysing issues related to behaviour and performance. Accurate analysis is most likely, in the case of the training manager, to come from building up such close and regular informal as well as formal interactions with managers and other personnel in the organization that he/she develops valid insights, rather than being governed by the view of one party or the other.

**Relationship between job holder and manager**
The other important dimension related to performance is, of course, the relationship between the job holder and their manager. As we have already seen in the Activity just completed, there are so many ways in which that relationship crucially affects the performance of the job holder, to the extent that, given a different manager, the individual could give quite a different kind of performance, either much better or much worse. Performance records alone will reveal nothing of that relationship, so we can sum up this section by the following statements:

> **The relationship between the job-holder and their manager is a crucial influence on the job-holder's performance, and will not be revealed by performance records.**

> **The training analyst needs to know the different managers well enough to be able to assess for him/herself the effects their style, methods and general 'culture' are having on individuals.**

This assessment will be particularly important when examining records of appraisal interviews (which form the subject of Chapter 11).

**Performance Records**
When examining records relating to an individual's present or potential performance, then the analyst must first carefully consider the two parameters we have just been discussing:

Factors underlying performance

The relationship between job holder and manager

As to analytical techniques, we have already, in Chapter 8, referred to several that can, in fact, also be applied to the analysis of the person in the job, with the aim of obtaining insights into the existing methods and levels of skill and knowledge of the job holder, and any difficulties they encounter in performing their job. Other indicators relating to the job performance of the individual may be found in records of output, quality, lateness, absenteeism, sickness, and evaluations of performance including those recorded in appraisal interviews.

## CONCLUSION

Having read this chapter and completed the various activities it contains, you should:

1  Know the main ways of analysing training needs at the individual level

2  Be able to draw up a personnel specification which can help the training designer

3  Understand the main factors that explain the performance of a job holder

4  Know the main considerations relating to the use of performance records of various kinds in the analysis of an individual's training needs.

The main learning points related to these objectives are:

**1  Individual training needs**
The training manager should consider 4 types of individual training need, relating to:

• Staff newly appointed from outside the organization

• Newly promoted staff

• Existing staff

• Staff facing change.

The training manager should therefore consider 4 types of training and development:

- Induction training

- Basic skills training

- Continuous development

- Training for change.

There are 6 major sources of information about individual training needs:

- Personnel specifications

- Performance records

- Trainability tests

- Assessment and development centres

- Self assessment

- Appraisal of performance.

## 2 The personnel specification
In using the personnel specification as an aid to training, 5 things are essential:

- Planned interrelationship between the job description, the job training specification, and the personnel specification

- Accurate information

- Identification of training-related elements

- Categorization of learners

- Categorization of training.


## 3 Understanding performance
When considering the actual or potential performance of an individual, 2 major factors must be examined:

- Factors underlying performance

- The job holder/manager relationship.

Specifically, there are 3 points for the analyst to remember:

- Performance is the outcome of a complex interaction between perceived and actual needs, results, rewards and 'E' Factors

- The relationship between the job-holder and manager is a crucial influence on the job-holder's performance, and will not be revealed by performance records

- The training analyst needs to know the different managers well enough to be able to assess for him/herself the effects their style, methods and general 'culture' are having on individuals.

## 4 Performance records

When examining records relating to an individual's present or potential performance, the analyst must first carefully consider:

- Factors underlying performance

- The job holder/manager relationship.

Records of performance which may be useful to the training analyst include those relating to output, quality, lateness, absenteeism, sickness, and evaluations of performance including those recorded in appraisal interviews.

## REVIEW ACTIVITY

Finally, here are some questions which you can either tackle as essays (if you are a student); discuss with fellow-students or colleagues; or simply think about now that you have completed this chapter:

- What can the personnel specification contribute to the analysis of training and development needs?

- 'Performance records are one of the best sources of information for the diagnosis of training needs of individuals'. Critically discuss this statement, using practical illustrations wherever possible.

## CHAPTER 10

# Assessing needs at individual level
## 2 Trainability tests, assessment centres and self-assessment

**LEARNING OBJECTIVES**

After reading this chapter and completing the various activities it contains, you should:

1 Know in which situations and for which types of staff trainability tests and assessment centre methodology are likely to be relevant

2 Be able to show someone how to carry out self-assessment in order to diagnose learning needs

3 Know how self-assessment can be incorporated in the overall process of analysing an individual's learning needs and of encouraging their self-development.

**Trainability Tests**

First, let us look at a major source of information about the extent to which potential learners are in fact 'trainable', and how their potential not only for training but for development thereafter can be assessed: trainability tests.

Trainability tests for manual workers have been pioneered by Sylvia Downs at the Industrial Training Research Unit at Cambridge.

> **The trainability test comprises the detailed instruction of a job applicant in a piece of work which is part of the job being applied for. The applicant then has to perform the task without any further assistance while under scrutiny from the instructor. He or she is rated according to the number and type of errors made while performing the operation.**
>
> *(Kilcourse,* Personnel Management, *May 1978)*

Trainability tests have the following special features:

- They are designed to include parts of the training which trainees find difficult, as well as elements of the job itself

- They involve a structured learning period

- They include the use of detailed error checklists written in behavioural terms.
  *(Downs,* Personnel Management, *October 1984)*

Thus the focus is very much on how the individual learns the task, so that:

**The principal advantage of trainability tests is their ability to weed out those applicants who are untrainable or who will take too long to train to acceptable standards,**
*(Kilcourse, 1978)*

There are a number of factors that need to be considered, however, before a decision is made to use trainability tests:

### Cost
A trainability test is a specialized instrument. Each job has to have its own test, so that this is quite an expensive way of obtaining information about an individual's learning potential.

### Design and validation
Tests need to be very carefully designed and validated, and those who administer them must be fully trained to do so.

### Time
Trainability testing is also time-consuming and therefore expensive.

### Insurance
Finally, of course, there must be special attention to the matter of insurance against accidents for non-employees who take the tests. In spite of these provisos, there is no doubt that trainability tests have proved to be a major aid to selection and training in a wide range of manual jobs, especially in the clothing industry, and a very interesting evaluation exercise involving tests in the mining industry has been carried out by Cowling and Gripton (1986).

As to applicability to non-manual jobs, work is being done in developing trainability tests for supervisory and managerial positions, and in this connection 'Task Observation', whilst not amounting to full trainability testing, can provide useful information about existing level of ability in certain key tasks. The individual is asked to perform a typical activity which is an important part of the total job (for example, an applicant for a managerial position may be put through an in-tray exercise, or asked to present a brief report on a particular topic to a Board of Directors) and their existing level of competence is then assessed. Work sampling of this kind, taken to its logical conclusions, leads to the comprehensive and structured methodology of assessment and development centres, which will be briefly described next with a view to seeing how far they can offer useful information to the designer of training and development programmes.

## Assessment and Development Centre Methodology

In an informative article Stevens writes:

> **An assessment centre is a systematic approach to identifying precisely what is required for success in a particular job and then labelling these requirements in terms of a short list of tightly defined criteria. Leadership, integrity, tenacity and team-building skill are typical criteria which might be included for a management position.**
>
> **The 'assessment centre' combines a series of job-related exercises which are designed to enable the applicant to demonstrate whether he or she has the skills required. The exercises are observed by a (trained) team of company managers who later pool their information and reach an agreed objective assessment of the candidate. *The approach not only ensures that sound decisions are made on which candidate has the closest 'fit'; it also provides a list of each candidate's training and development needs which can be used as the basis for that individual's development plans.* (Italics mine)**
>
> *(Stevens, Personnel Management, June 1985)*

Stevens then describes how Deloitte Haskins, Woolworth and Pedigree Petfoods all use assessment centres as the basis for their appraisal process, out of which training, career development and promotion planning decisions are made. In another article Shepherd (1980) describes the success enjoyed by Ford in their use of assessment centres to aid the selection and training of first line supervisors. All these accounts, whilst demonstrating some of the difficulties and dangers involved in the introduction of assessment centres or assessment centre technology give striking evidence of their advantages, particularly the following:

### Improved decision-making

Decisions relating to the selection, transfer, promotion, and to training needs of staff are based on substantially more 'facts' than in the past.

### Improved feedback

Assessment centre methodology offers an increased opportunity for meaningful feedback related to performance and potential, and this is especially valuable in relation to career and other counselling services.

You may have noticed that, although our heading for this section included reference to development centre methodology, we have so far only discussed the use of assessment centres. What, if any, is the difference between the two approaches? Well, to many writers there is no difference, and Stevens (1985) makes it clear that he, for instance, sees assessment centres as not only a way of assessing potential, but also a way of helping to diagnose people's training and development needs related to current performance. However, increasing use of the term 'Development Centres' makes it worthwhile briefly defining it here.

In a recent article describing the use of development centres at British Telecom, the difference between 'Assessment' and 'Development' Centres was explained as follows:

> **In both cases groups of participants gather to take part in a variety of job simulations, tests and exercises with assessor observers, who assess against a number of predetermined, job-related dimensions. If the collected data is used to diagnose individual training needs, facilitate self-development or provide part of an audit for OD (Organizational Development), then a 'development centre' would seem the more appropriate, less ambiguous term (ie than 'assessment centre').**
>
> *(Rodger and Mabey,* Personnel Management, *July 1987)*

They emphasize that development centres are entirely about assessing individual strengths and weaknesses in order to diagnose individual and organizational development needs and therefore that this objective should be fully understood and agreed from the outset by those assessing and being assessed.

The following points emerge as vital to the success of any assessment programme aimed at highlighting learning needs:

### Assessment must be in context
The need to place the use of assessment/development centres in a firm context of major training and development programmes, so that they are seen to be a positive aid to all who go through them, rather than a threat.

### Involvement of management
The need to involve line management from the start in the development and operation of assessment/development centre methodology.

### Confidentiality
The need to be clear about who will have access to the information produced by the assessment processes: without this, the trust and commitment of those being assessed cannot be achieved.

### Action
The need for assessment to lead to action, although, as Rodger and Mabey (1987) observe, 'for a whole host of reasons development activities may not happen immediately'.

### Evaluation
The need for full evaluation of the results achieved by the use of such methodology, including analysis of the effects its introduction has had on personnel at various levels in the organization.

## Self-Assessment and Self-Development
Assessment of learning needs at the individual level can also be done by the individual, in order to determine their strengths and weaknesses, formulate appropriate ways of meeting the needs that are thereby revealed, and plan for on-going monitoring and evaluation of their performance.

Pedler, Burgoyne and Boydell (1978) have done much to popularize self-assessment for managers, and I have run workshops incorporating diagnostic exercises in their book for my own management and personnel management students, to considerable effect. There are four stages involved in self-assessment:

Self-assessment

Diagnosis

Action planning

Monitoring and review

The three authors have drawn up a very detailed questionnaire to help a manager to carry out those four processes. Such questionnaires can be completed in three ways:

**By the individual alone**
He or she goes through the questionnaire, considering each area of skill in turn and rating themselves as best they can. From this kind of information can emerge a diagnosis of areas of strength and learning need, which will help the individual to formulate a self-development 'Action Plan'. This kind of exercise can go further, and form the basis of a major programme involving 'sets' of learners from one or more organizations — for example, the Middle Management Development project-based certificate programme run by Durham University Business School for British Gas.*

**By the individual working with someone else**
Each can then interview the other, in an attempt to make the partner think through their levels of competence in each skill area as fully and objectively as possible. Particularly interesting discussions always take place in the area of interpersonal skills where, left to themselves, individuals often arrive at facile self-assessments (usually favourable!), but where, probed by someone else, a much deeper and more critical self-assessment almost invariably emerges.

This way of tackling self-assessment also has the advantage of developing diagnostic and even counselling skills in the partner who, in the process of questioning, also has to practice and learn more about those skills of observation, listening, discussion and appraisal that Singer (1979) highlights as vital to the good coach. The more productive the skills are found to be, the more mutual learning emerges from the whole exercise.

The individual can also, of course, carry out self-assessment with the aid of a colleague, perhaps someone who is also involved in a self-development programme, or just someone interested in the process and willing to help. A friend or husband/wife can often be just as effective in the role as someone at work.

**By the individual as part of a wider organizational scheme**
To anyone concerned with development of people in organizations, it is essential to see the individual not as the 'servant' of the organization but as someone with the power to either expend or

*Durham University Business School Centre for Management Development, Mill Hill Lane, Durham DH1 3LB

withdraw effort, energy and ability, and therefore someone whose willing commitment must be obtained if lasting development and change is to occur. This leads to the concept of individual and organization as bound together not only by a legal contract that specifies duties, terms and conditions, and material rewards, but also by a 'psychological' contract consisting of felt and perceived expectations, needs, and rights that form the framework of an ongoing relationship.

Acting on this concept, Burgoyne and Germain (1984) have worked on a project at Esso Chemicals whereby career development is 'negotiated' between the organization and the individual, and centres on three processes:

### Organizational planning
This involves the organization in producing short- and long-term business plans from which decisions are made about the work that is to be done, the structure required for the organization, the roles needed within the structure and, ultimately, the work and targets of the individual.

### Individual planning
This involves the individual in thinking through their overall life goals, what part their work will play in relation to those goals, and therefore the kind of career plans that will be appropriate and feasible to follow. This process is helped by a 'Workbook' with a diagnostic self-assessment questionnaire.

### Joint career planning
This involves individual' and manager (or some other person or body responsible for the organization's career development schemes) in exchanging information from the previous two processes, and then in negotiating career decisions.

The concept of using self-assessment as a way of helping the individual to analyse learning needs, both short and longer-term, and then to articulate those needs clearly and fully in a development discussion with their manager, is a potentially very productive one, and can be seen to relate to a discussion about self-appraisal in Chapter 11. However, whereas self-appraisal simply involves the individual in thinking about their work performance in order to arrive at an overall judgement about it, self-assessment involves the individual in rating themselves in each area of skill in their job along a continuum (however expressed) from highly satisfactory to not yet competent

The Institute of Personnel Management (IPM) is carrying out a lot of work on self-assessment and continuous development as part of its 'A Boost for Continuous Development' campaign. Let us now try an Activity which is included in the invaluable 'Teaching Pack for IPM Course Tutors', compiled by Pike *et al* (1985), and available from the IPM. It demonstrates what is involved in the kind of exercise which I have already described, and can be used as part of a wider and on-going analytical and self-development process. All my second year IPM Stage 2 students completed the exercise as an Assignment after the 2-day Continuous Development Workshop to which I have referred in Chapter 5, and I, in the role of 'training manager', felt that I learnt more about their individual learning needs and about the interactions between their life and career goals through this one diagnostic exercise than through a year's joint learning activities.

## ACTIVITY

### Self-Assessment Exercise

In Appendix 5 you will find an IPM Self-Assessment exercise to complete. Before attempting it, the following points will be useful. They elaborate on instructions given in the IPM Pack which contains this exercise.

The exercise is divided into three parts:

### 1   Assessment

The 3-page Questionnaire. This can be completed either on your own, or after discussion with someone else — anyone who is interested in your career development and willing to give up about an hour to help you think through your answers to the various questions.

### 2   Diagnosis

The 'Assessment of Learning Needs' sheet. This is filled in after the self-assessment exercise has been completed, using the insights generated by that exercise.

### 3   Action planning

One sheet, which should be copied and used for each component of the overall Plan. The Plan should tackle whichever learning needs (listed on your 'Assessment of Learning Needs' sheet) you feel need the most immediate attention. Thus, should you decide to tackle three areas of need in the forthcoming period, three separate sheets should be drawn up.

Please note, when completing your Action Plans, that there is an extra page in the Appendix that shows a range of possible developmental methods. This reminds us that development can take place not only at work, but away from work, and not only through formalized activities, but in a wide range of informal ways. For example, belonging to clubs, committees or other activity or interest groups outside work can offer opportunities to develop skills, knowledge and attitudes highly relevant to your longer-term career aspirations.

Before completing the Assessment, please write a brief introduction, in which you explain who you are: your job, role and level in the organization; your overall life goals and your career aspirations in the light of those goals; any barriers and/or aids to learning and development that currently exist in your work situation, and in your non-work situation; and how you carried out the self-asssessment exercise (by yourself, or with the help of someone else). When considering barriers and aids to learning, think of the learning process in the way it was described in Chapter 4, as consisting of four stages (Kolb, 1974):

*Experiencing* something — a problem, a need, a situation.

*Observing and reflecting* — suspending judgement whilst gathering information, making comparisons, looking for patterns, similarities and differences to previous experiences.

*Conceptualizing* — analysing the information; forming a set of concepts about it, and/or trying to fit it into some existing body of theory in order to 'learn' from the experience; diagnosing the crucial issues.

*Experimenting* — trying out a different or amended approach to this sort of experience, suggested by the processes of reflecting and theorizing.

Pike *et al* (1985) explain that the sort of barriers to learning and development that you might experience at work include structural and cultural barriers, as follows.

## Barriers to Learning and Problem Solving

### Barriers to EXPERIENCING
*Structural barriers:* Activities are closely defined and specialized. They are routine, predictable, undemanding, low in variability, uninvolving, not stimulating.
*Cultural barriers:* General preference for distance and detachment.

People tend to be reserved, non-expressive, impersonal. Code of behaviour that stresses 'Don't get your hands dirty or muck in: don't get involved,' etc.

### Barriers to OBSERVING AND REFLECTING
*Structural barriers:* Poor communications and information flow. Inadequate feedback. Geographical or structural isolation. Fast pace of work and other pressures.
*Cultural barriers:* The organization/department is preoccupied with the present. Tendency to be secretive and distrustful. Norms of behaviour include 'Let's get cracking. What's next? That's just history — live for today. Keep your opinions to yourself. Don't wash your dirty linen in public. Keep your cards close to your chest', etc.

### Barriers to CONCEPTUALIZING
*Structural barriers:* Emphasis on results at work. Interruptions and short time-scales. Lack of reviews. Lack of procedures for 'post-mortems', policy-making, planning, and 'think-tanks'.
*Cultural barriers:* Action oriented. Pragmatic. Over-responsive. Typical views are 'Thinking is for academics. Ignorance is bliss. No use sitting around on your backside', etc.

### Barriers to EXPERIMENTING
*Structural barriers:* Over-prescribed duties, methods, rules and procedures. Red tape. High costs of failure. Lack of encouragement to experiment or innovate.
*Cultural barriers:* Cautious. Conservative, traditional, conforming. 'Tread carefully. Don't rock the boat. We don't do it that way here', etc.

When you have finished the exercise, please write a brief note on how each Action Plan will be monitored and reviewed, when, and by whom.

---

## FEEDBACK NOTES

Feedback for this kind of exercise is difficult, because everyone will tackle it in different ways. However, the exercise should lead to an increased understanding of the four stages involved in self-assessment:

**Self assessment**
preceded by careful analysis by the individual of their work and life situation

**Diagnosis**
of the individual's learning needs

**Action planning**
identifying objectives, aids and hindrances to action; resources (including people) needed to carry out the action plan; and a timescale

**Monitoring and review**
procedures must be determined, and a timescale determined for those processes to take place.

---

# CONCLUSION

Having read this chapter and completed the various activities it contains, you should now:

1  Know in which situations and for which types of staff trainability tests and assessment centre methodology are likely to be relevant

2  Be able to show someone how to carry out self-assessment in order to diagnose learning needs

3  Know how self-assessment can be incorporated in the overall process of analysing an individual's learning needs and of encouraging their self-development.

The main learning points related to these objectives are:

**1  Trainability tests**
Trainability tests can identify individuals who are untrainable or who will take too long to train to acceptable standards.
    There are 4 major factors that need to be considered before a decision is made to use trainability tests:

• Cost

- Design and validation

- Time

- Insurance.

## 2  Assessment and development centres
Advantages claimed for assessment centre methodology include:

- Improved decision-making

- Improved feedback.

If the collected data is used to diagnose individual training needs, facilitate self-development or provide part of an audit for OD then the term 'Development Centre' rather than 'Assessment Centre' is increasingly being used.

Five points are vital to the success of any assessment programme:

- Assessment must be in context

- Involvement of management

- Confidentiality

- Action

- Evaluation.

## 3  Self-assessment and self-development
Self-assessment can be done in 3 ways:

- Alone

- With a partner

- As part of an organizational scheme.

Four activities are involved in self-assessment:

- Self-assessment

- Diagnosis

- Action planning

- Monitoring and review.

When carrying out self-assessment as part of a wider organizational scheme aimed at diagnosing an individual's development needs and relating them to career plans, 3 processes are involved:

- Organizational planning

- Individual planning

- Joint career planning.

---

## REVIEW ACTIVITY

Finally, here are some questions which you can either tackle as essays (if you are a student); discuss with fellow-students or colleagues; or simply think about now that you have completed this chapter:

- 'It is possible to look on trainability tests as practical and structured interviews or as condensed probationary periods. They have a number of advantages over conventional selection tests'. Discuss, with reference to a workplace of your choice.

- What sort of information does assessment centre methodology offer to the training analyst? Would you recommend the use of an assessment centre (or methodology) in your organization? Please give detailed reasons for your reply.

- How can self-assessment aid the process of analysing the training and development needs of an individual? Please relate your answer to a practical example.

## CHAPTER 11

# Assessing needs at individual level

## 3: Appraisal of performance

### LEARNING OBJECTIVES

After reading this chapter and completing the various activities it contains, you should:

1 Be able to evaluate your organization's appraisal system and identify areas where improvements are needed

2 Be able to advise on how to plan a motivating and developmental appraisal interview that should lead to the understanding of work performance and the accurate diagnosis of learning needs

3 Know a range of activities that could form part of an individual's development plan, arising out of the appraisal discussion.

Appraisal is at the heart of training and development, as it is of so many other personnel processes. It decides who will or will not be developed, and why, and if appraisal is ineffective then ineffective development is almost inevitable.

Our focus in this section is on how to carry out appraisal in such a way that it will make a positive contribution to the training and continuous development of people in an organization. Here, the crucial questions are:

- What produces successful appraisal of performance?

- What are the main factors influencing the appraisal discussion?

- How to plan an effective appraisal discussion that should lead to the accurate diagnosis of learning needs?

### Successful Appraisal

As we shall see throughout this chapter, if appraisal related to training and development is to succeed, there must be:

### Shared perception of purpose
Appraiser and appraisee must have a shared understanding of the purpose and value of the discussion, and a shared commitment to its objectives.

### Mutual learning
In the course of the appraisal discussion both parties, not just the appraisee, should learn more about themselves and about each other, so that not only performance but all constraints and opportunities related to it are understood and evaluated.

### Objectivity
The discussion should be supportive and centred on work objectives, not with a subjective emphasis on blaming or judging.

### Integration of appraisal into the overall development process
Appraisal, as has already been observed, is part of a much wider process related to the development of people in an organization. Any scheme of performance appraisal must, therefore, be consistent with other developmental activities. More on this point follows in the next section.

The outcomes of the appraisal discussion should always include:

### Motivation
Sustained or improved motivation of the appraisee.

### Understanding
An increased understanding on both sides about issues related to the appraisee's performance.

### Diagnosis
Accurate diagnosis of learning needs, and a related action plan.

### Development
A development step for the appraisee within the discussion itself.

## Factors Influencing the Appraisal Discussion
However, the appraisal discussion cannot be viewed in isolation. It always takes place within a context, and that context has a very significant effect on its conduct and outcomes. Major contextual factors are:

The organizational culture and structure

The overall development process

The organization's appraisal scheme

The appraiser/appraisee relationship

**The organizational culture and structure**
We have already seen in Chapters 2 and 3 how pervasive is the influence of the whole system of the organization on whatever happens in the training function. Of the major elements we examined there it is the structure and culture of the organization (or of that part of it within which the appraiser and appraisee work) that have some of the most significant effects on appraisal schemes and discussions. It is no accident, surely, that so many rigid and paper-bound appraisal schemes are to be found in bureaucratic role cultures (although role cultures, and appraisal within them, can be effective, if there is the willingness to make them so): or that it is so often in task cultures that one hears about innovative and developmental appraisal schemes.

Here is a practical example, showing how interaction between culture and structure, appraisal, and people in an organization produced an appraisal scheme with the characteristics to which we have already referred as necessary if the appraisal discussion is to be effective.

---

**CASE STUDY:   Appraisal at Newlands Preparatory School**
(by permission of Newlands Preparatory School, Gosforth, Tyne and Wear)

Newlands, a day preparatory school for boys on the outskirts of Newcastle upon Tyne, introduced formal appraisal into the school in 1987, with the objectives of aiding work planning and performance, and diagnosing staff training and development needs.

**The culture and structure**
Since 1977 the school (capacity, 235 boys, 4—13½ years old) under Nicholas Barton's leadship has gone from the threat of closure to being one of the most highly regarded and successful in the North East.

He has developed a genuine task culture and matrix structure. He interacts closely with the Governors, who are mostly local business people and are all passionately committed to the school's welfare. They work with him at several levels. Teamwork takes place to an equal degree between Headmaster and teaching staff, and is clearly evident in the dedication shown by the staff to the school, to their educational task, and to the all-round development of the boys.

The boys too are actively involved, especially the senior groups (aged 11 upwards), with the prefects and Head Boy having responsibilities that keep them in everyday contact with the staff and the Headmaster. Finally, parents, the all-important customers, are fully involved, not in any proceduralized way but through a range of initiatives which contribute much to the life of the school and to the enormous enjoyment generated by belonging there, whether as staff, pupils, or parents.

## The product
The constant expenditure of effort and ability involved in keeping going this small but thriving and profitable organization is very great: and yet it is successful even on lower fees than are charged in most other local prep schools. There is a waiting list for entry, and although there is no policy of taking in only boys above a certain level of academic ability, since the aim is to have boys of all levels and from a wide variety of backgrounds, Newlands maintains a consistently excellent record of examination and sporting success.

## The appraisal scheme
In such an organization, whose mission is clear to all, and shared by all, it is not surprising that the tricky issue of appraisal (this is, after all, the educational sector, where so much suspicion and acrimony surrounds that topic) has been grasped, and not at the demand of Governors or Head but at the request of the staff themselves. It is equally unsurprising that in the simple but developmental appraisal scheme that operates, the emphasis should be on a genuinely two-way, open and supportive process.

The Headmaster appraises his staff, but he does it using a self-appraisal scheme which gives the initiative in the discussion to the member of staff. In the course of it staff also give their views of his performance, as it relates to his management of them and to his teaching as a member of the whole teaching team. His own performance is also appraised by the Governors by means of the Report that he presents termly to the full Governors' Board.

The average appraisal interview lasts for about two and a half hours, and one of the first comments made by the Headmaster was 'I never realized how much I could learn from this!'. One of the most important characteristics of successful appraisal, mutual learning, has been readily achieved and welcomed. In the first year of operation, appraisals have led to significant timetabling and wider organizational changes. Staff's views are already proving valuable spurs to action, so that the overall team culture which helped to produce such a scheme in the first place is being reinforced by its operation. (See also Harrison, 1988)

---

At Newlands School there is an absolute consistency between the culture and structure of the school and the appraisal scheme that operates there. To have established a complex, paper-bound, hierarchical scheme would have been quite at odds with the culture that has been so successfully developed, and this represents a general principle:

**In inception, design and operation, the appraisal scheme should be consistent with the organizational culture and structure of which it is planned to form a part.**

### The overall development process

The point has been made at the start of this chapter that appraisal is part of a wider process: that which relates to the general development of the people of an organization. At Northumbrian Water (whose approach to training has already been described in detail in Chapter 6), there is an extensive management development programme, which has led to many interesting changes in career direction amongst employees. The programme is directed by a Management Development Committee comprising Northumbrian Water's top directors, and chaired by the Chief Executive with the Training Manager as Secretary. The scheme for appraisal of individual performance of managers is seen as a crucial element in the programme, linking in to many other developmental activities. Their interrelationship is shown in Figure 5, and illustrates our point:

**Appraisal should always be planned and perceived to be not an end in itself, but a part of the wider process of development of people in an organization.**

### The organization's appraisal scheme

One part of that wider development process has such an important effect on the appraisal discussion that it merits a separate heading: the appraisal scheme. It is not necessary, of course, to have a formal appraisal scheme in order for appraisal discussions to take place, because such discussions can be informal, or at the level only of individual initiatives (and there should be regular informal discussions of performance in any well-managed workplace). However, where the organization does have a formal appraisal scheme it will, of course, have a profound effect on whatever appraisal discussions and decisions take place within it. For the effective appraisal of performance, regarding work review, work planning, and the diagnosis of training and development needs, research has shown repeatedly that the characteristics and outcomes necessary can best be achieved by an appraisal scheme, no matter how informal, that takes the following form:

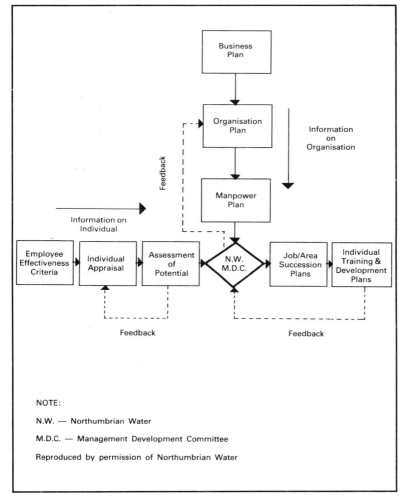

**Figure 5: Overview of the Northumbrian Water Management Development Process**

### The objectives of the scheme are clear and shared

They must be objectives to which line managers, not just specialist personnel and training staff, are committed.

### Objectives are limited in scope and number and are not mutually conflicting

A scheme whose focus is appraisal of current work performance, work planning for the forthcoming period, and diagnosis of learning needs (three objectives which do not conflict with one another) must not also have objectives related to pay, promotion etc. Such objectives are threatening to the appraisee, and can only lead to a tendency to hide weaknesses and overemphasize achievements, rather than to discuss actual performance and the reasons for it. Of course, judgements relating to pay, promotion, discipline etc must be made, but not all in a single scheme! Long (1986) in her recent survey of appraisal in a large sample of British organizations in both the public and private sector notes an increasing tendency for British firms to restrict the number of objectives served by a single appraisal scheme.

### Line managers are involved in the design of the scheme and the planning of its implementation

The principle here is an obvious one: the more managers are able to share in the creation of a scheme the more committed to it will they become. Often a consultant is used where there is either no personnel or training professional, or no-one who is acceptable to the managers, and the managers use that expert as a catalyst and learning resource. They not only find out how to evaluate their existing scheme, and have immediate access to information about other types of scheme that could be devised; they also develop task-related and teamwork skills that are absolutely essential to the successful operation of the final scheme. In this way, the task of evaluating appraisal in the organization and designing, running and monitoring a revised or new scheme becomes in itself a vehicle for the continuous development of managers and specialist as a team, and this in turn helps the organization to develop: an excellent example of integrating work and learning to achieve operational goals and individual, team and organizational development.

### Top management are an intrinsic part of the scheme, appraising and being appraised

We saw in our case study about Newlands School that the 'top manager' is appraised not only by the Board (a familiar model in industry) but also by his staff. The process for doing this may be informal and unstructured, but the fact that it is done is what matters. It is evidence of that commitment from the top which is essential.

### The mechanics of the scheme accurately reflect its objectives

If the scheme's objectives are to aid work planning and perform-ance, and diagnose training and development needs, then there is no necessity for complex forms to be filled in, or ranking systems to operate. Only the most basic information needs to be recorded, sufficient to ensure that work targets and ways of measuring performance are agreed, and that plans for training and develop-ment are passed to those who will need to approve and take action on them, together with equally simple monitoring systems where necessary. Support for this kind of approach is given by Long (1986), who found that in some organizations the problems in rating and ranking schemes (bias, skewedness and unequal standards) had led to the complete abandonment of such schemes. Anderson, Hulme and Young (1987) go further and suggest that appraisal could actually be carried out without forms at all, but feedback on such a system did indicate that to rely entirely on memory could result in the demise of the system.

### Training in appraisal skills is given

It is almost always necessary to give training in appraisal skills, not only at the inception of a new scheme, but as the scheme continues, in order to check on and refresh people's skills. The training must not only be concerned with helping appraisers and appraisees understand how to operate the organization's scheme — such training is fairly common. It is absolutely essential that it helps both parties develop the skills needed to carry out an effective appraisal interview. Such training, alas, is by no means the norm, yet without it a scheme can easily degenerate into a paper exercise, promising much but achieving very little.

### The appraisal scheme is regularly monitored and changed as necessary

Without this, even the best scheme will decline in effectiveness and relevancy, as personnel and situations change, and new demands are placed on the organization and its members.

To summarize, there are seven characteristics of an effective appraisal scheme:

- Clear and shared objectives

- Limited scope

- Line management involvement

- Top management commitment

- Appropriate procedures

- Training

- Review

**The appraiser-appraisee relationship**
The relationship between the manager and the appraisee, to which we have already drawn attention in previous chapters, is of course of central importance, and unless it is operating in an open, supportive and developmental manner, it is most unlikely that appraisal will bear fruit. It is one of the dilemmas of whoever is trying to use appraisal information as an indicator of training and developmental needs, that the relationship that produced that information may clearly be so poor that not only will the validity of the information be suspect, but any development may be frustrated once the appraisee is back in the work situation, being stifled by an unchanging relationship with their manager.

In this section, we have been discussing four major contextual factors influencing the appraisal discussion:

The organizational culture and structure

The overall development process

The organization's appraisal scheme

The appraiser/appraisee relationship

Now let us examine the appraisal discussion itself.

## Planning the Appraisal Discussion
In order to carry out the kind of discussion that will lead to valid diagnosis of learning needs, and a related plan of action for the appraisee, the appraiser should plan the discussion carefully. This is not the place for a detailed explanation of how to carry out an appraisal of performance: our interest in appraisal is the part it can play in clarifying an individual's training and development needs. However, that part of the discussion cannot be successful if elsewhere in the appraisal there are tensions. So it is worth using, or

encouraging appraisers to use, a simple checklist with headings like the following:

Preparing for the discussion

Getting started

Work review and planning

Training and development

Action planning

Conclusion

Follow up and monitoring

Let us look briefly at each of these now:

**Preparing for the discussion**
Five points should be covered:

*Information*
The appraiser should decide what should be the overall purpose for the discussion and should then collect, check and study carefully as much information as possible relating to the forthcoming discussion. Where there is to be examination of the individual's development needs, information will need to be obtained about:

- the individual's performance, and potential for development;

- future departmental and organizational goals and new work coming into the department;

- methods of measuring peformance used or to be introduced in the department, and how these relate to the work of the individual who is to be appraised;

- the individual's career objectives;

- different sorts of developmental experiences that could be provided for the individual.

*Objectives*
Next, the appraiser must decide on the specific outcomes to be

achieved through the discussion. Appraisal, incidentally, should never be rushed, in both the manager's and the appraisee's interests. The average time is two hours (Long, 1986), but if everything cannot be covered in one interview, then a second discussion should be arranged.

### Structure

The appraiser must decide how much structure to build into the discussion, remembering that when the discussion is actually under way there must be enough flexibility to cope with any unexpected information or incident that may arise.

The situation itself will help to decide how much or little structure there should be. For example, if there is a management by objectives scheme in operation, there will be a document drawn up at the time of the last appraisal interview which contains a detailed work plan for the coming period, showing the job holder's key targets. This document can form the basis of the discussion, which would therefore tend to be fairly structured.

If there is not such a document, or if this kind of management by objectives approach would be too rigid, then the skilful manager should still guide the appraisee through the key areas of the job, managing in the discussion to link areas and point up the interrelationship that should exist between them, and where the main priorities lie.

Training and development needs should be related to the different areas that are discussed, to the work plans that arise out of that discussion, and to the individual's longer-term developmental plan.

### Discussion strategy

In any discussion the appraiser must always have a strategy — a way of dealing with the appraisee in order to achieve the objectives of that discussion. The most effective strategy is likely to be an objective-centred one based as far as possible on self-appraisal and mutual learning.

A self-appraisal strategy for the interview is as follows:

- Appraiser and appraisee decide together at least a week or two in advance when and where the interview will be held, and are clear as to its purpose and expected type of outcomes

- Each then prepares for it, helped if possible by a simple form on which each notes, in relation to the appraisee, factual information like that shown in Appendix 6

- At the start of the interview, the appraiser clarifies with the appraisee the purpose and objectives of the discussion

- In the ensuing discussion the appraisee is asked for his or her view of the purpose and specific objectives of their job, and of their performance in it, together with their beliefs about priorities in the job. The appraiser probes and responds to these views until enough mutual learning and understanding has been achieved for performance to be appraised and for shared agreement on this, hopefully, to be achieved

- The appraiser and the appraisee always talk things through so that both learn about the reasons for performance rather than just about outcomes

- The appraiser emphasizes successes and strengths, rather than failures and weaknesses. The appraiser should aim at getting the appraisee to identify any shortcomings, rather than the appraiser doing so

- The appraiser encourages the appraisee to see any failures or weaknesses as learning points. Never make an appraisal discussion into a disciplinary interview. Take especial care therefore with any interviews that begin to look as though they may have to lead to corrective or disciplinary action.

Of course, self-appraisal has its drawbacks; people can give an over-optimistic appraisal of their own performance. But if the discussion is carried out in the way just described, and in the context of the overall strategy advocated here, there is a great deal of evidence to show that it can be highly motivating, developmental and positive on both sides.

**Setting**
The appraiser must plan carefully when and where to hold the discussion, paying particular attention to trying to choose a time for the interview when relationships are at a friendly point, and avoiding a time when the appraisee has had a glaring failure.

**Getting started**
Here, the appraiser needs to think about how best to introduce the discussion, in order to ensure that both parties have a shared understanding of the reasons for the discussion, and of its intended outcomes. Often, for a variety of reasons, the appraiser and the appraisee actually hold different perceptions and expectations

related to the discussion, and unless these are sorted out at the start, frustration and confusion will build up on both sides.

Once the interview has been introduced, the appraiser must build up rapport with the appraisee. A supportive start, a self-appraisal strategy, and a determination on the appraiser's part to listen and to learn are all key points in building up good rapport.

### Work review and planning

How should the appraiser discuss the person's work performance? Four general points should be born in mind, regardless of the specific approach that may be adopted. They should lead naturally to an open discussion of training needs.

#### Objective-centred discussion

Ensure that the discussion centres on agreed key tasks and targets of performance, not on generalized, non-job-related issues. When discussing future objectives:

- Explain the future plans of the organization, department and section, and how the individual's job and ongoing work fits in

- Agree on the objectives that the individual will aim to achieve, and what resources are needed in order to achieve them

- Agree on standards to be achieved, related to those objectives; and on how performance will be measured.

#### Examine task priorities and interrelationships

Ensure that the discussion looks at the priorities and interrelationships between tasks, and not just at the outcomes of specific tasks. For instance, in a lecturer's job it is essential to find out from the lecturer what other key areas than lecturing they consider to form part of their job, and what should be the 'trade-off' between the various tasks. Is it more important to devote maximum time and energy to classroom sessions, and to achieve outstanding results as a teacher, or to reduce the very high degree of effort expended in teaching tasks in order to be able to give more time and energy to administration, or to research, or to consultancy work?

#### Understand performance

The appraiser must strive to understand not just what performance there has been, but why the job holder has performed to that level and in that way. This means looking carefully at those factors that underly and explain performance, as well as at the performance itself. (See Chapter 9.)

### Substantiate judgements

The appraiser must never make judgements that do not rest on agreed facts; to do otherwise may lead to reduced commitment and motivation from the appraisee, and even the possibility of a formal appeal against the results of the apraisal interview.

### Training and development

The appraiser should always diagnose needs for training and development related to current work performance and the work plan for the forthcoming period, as well as to the longer-term, continuous development of the individual. Plans should be agreed by both to be realistic and appropriate, given the needs of the individual and of the organization.

Training and development should be considered for everyone, no matter whether the appraisee is 'upwardly mobile' or can only expect to stay in their present job, or at their present level, for the rest of their employment with the organization. Everyone has a right to development, and it is in the organization's interest to ensure that such rights are honoured.

The manager should help individuals to learn how to take control over their own careers, and think through what exactly are the goals that they seek to achieve. Three processes are helpful here, and have been referred to at various points in this book so far:

Self-assessment

Self-learning

Self-development

It is in this part of the discussion that counselling, guidance and coaching can and should take place, no matter how informal.

Reaching agreement on learning needs is rarely easy. There are three common problems:

1  Getting the appraiser and appraisee to discuss current perform-ance openly and supportively enough to enable an accurate diagnosis to be made of learning needs.

   Some appraisees may not admit to failings, and become hostile and defensive at any attempt to discuss them.

   Some may have too low an opinion of their performance and potential, and may lack self-confidence.

Some may have too high an opinion of their performance and potential, and be over-confident.

Some may feel that criticism is unjust, and will not accept it.

Some appraisers may not be skilled enough to deal with these forms of behaviour.

Some may not feel able to discuss poor performance on a face to face basis.

Some may not know enough about the detail of what the individual actually does in their job, or about technical aspects of it, to feel able to give an appraisal, or to diagnose learning needs.

2   Reaching agreement on priorities. The manager, for example, may think that the appraisee has a major need for interpersonal skills development, whereas the job-holder may think that this relates to only a very minor problem, and see other training or development as much more important.

3   Being 'fair'. The appraisee may not be able to appreciate why they are being denied opportunities for development or training that another colleague enjoys, and will require very convincing reasons if motivation is not to be seriously affected. If the appraiser cannot supply such reasons, then clearly the job holder has a justifiable grievance.

What can be done about these problems? Four major aids for the appraisers, where the personnel or training specialist should be able to act as a resource, are:

- Skills training which forewarns them about likely problems and equips them with a basis of techniques and self-development to deal with them

- Ongoing guidance and counselling to help them try out and improve their new skills

- Their use, in appraisal interviews, of an objective-centred, self-appraisal strategy resting on talking things through, and on mutual learning

- The existence, within the appraisal scheme, of a procedure which gives the appraisee the right of appeal should there be genuinely irreconcilable differences.

**Action planning**
In deciding how to meet the individual's needs, a range of alternative courses of action should be explored. There are three reasons for this:

*A learning process*
The very process of jointly considering which of a range of alternatives may be appropriate is a learning experience for both parties. They discuss the possibilities together and so generate a range of ideas.

*Improved working relationship*
Generating and discussing ideas together is an activity which in itself should strengthen an already good working relationship, or improve one which is unsatisfactory.

*Contingency planning*
It is necessary to agree upon some alternative courses of action, in case the one that is first proposed later proves for some reason not to be possible.

The final Action Plan should note:

- Individual's training and development needs

- Recommended action

- Period of time over which action is to be taken: dates and duration as relevant

- Resources needed to support the action (personnel, physical, financial)

- Distinction between immediate job-related training and development, and activities to promote the longer-term and continuous development of the individual.

ie   Needs

  Action

Timescale

Resources

Immediate and longer-term development

**Conclusion**
Appraiser and appraisee must leave the discussion with a clear and shared understanding of the outcomes of the discussion, and when, by whom and how action plans are to be progressed thereafter.

**Follow-up and monitoring**
All action agreed on, both to do with work planning and to do with training and development, must be monitored regularly.

Where there is an effective work relationship between manager and individual, such monitoring and fairly informal review will take place naturally. Where such a relationship does not exist, however, there may be problems — and so procedures of some kind to ensure that checks are made may well have to be devised.

In relation to training and development, it will be necessary to proceed in 2 stages:

- The manager will need to pass on the action plan proposals to any others whose agreement and/or co-operation will be needed in carrying out the plan.

- The manager must ensure that the appraisee is informed by an agreed date about the action that it has finally been possible to arrange, and to discuss any proposals which have had to be postponed or cannot be carried out. Alternatives may be possible where the latter occurs.

Final formal review should take place at the next appraisal discussion.

Now, let us perform a short exercise. It can be tackled either as shown in the instructions below, or as a role-play activity. Try to use what you have just learnt, remembering especially our 7-point checklist related to appraisal discussion planning (page 203).

The appraisal scheme itself must also be monitored and reviewed regularly. Long (1986) found that, after three years, most appraisal systems need overhauling, if not replacing. The appraisal discussion offers an opportunity to find out from appraisees how they feel the scheme is progressing.

## ACTIVITY

## CASE STUDY/ROLE-PLAY:    The Training and Development Problem

*Stage 1*
In Appendices 7 and 8 you will find a brief for a manager who is about to carry out an appraisal interview. Having read the brief carefully, imagine that you are the manager, and decide how you are going to run the interview. Give a short explanation, with special reference to what you think will be the objectives, expectations and attitude of the appraisee. Do not look at Appendix 9 until you have completed this exercise.

*Stage 2*
When you have completed Stage 1 of the exercise, turn to Appendix 9 where you will find the appraisee's brief. It will tell you his expectations and attitudes related to the interview that you have just planned. Please read it carefully, and then look again at your plan.

---

## FEEDBACK NOTES

Since I cannot guess at the detail of your plan for the interview, I will instead pose a few questions which may help you to judge how far the plan would have been likely to produce an effective and productive interview, using our 7-point check list for planning appraisal discussions.

**Preparing for the discussion**
Reading the appraisee's brief, how far was your assessment of his likely objectives, expectations and attitude correct? Why do you think your assessment was correct, or incorrect?

Would your plan have ensured that you would both have had a shared and clear understanding of the objectives of the interview from the start? Note that this is not a straightforward appraisal interview. The basic issues involved are:

- Mutual antagonism between appraiser and appraisee

- A manager who needs to convince his appraisee of the need for more development of the appraisee's staff

- A manager who does not initally understand the appraisee's reasons for tackling the appraisal and development of his staff in the way that he does.

The appraiser's main objective should be to help the Quality Assurance Manager to see another point of view related to appraisal and development, and accept the need to change his (the QA Manager's) approach in order to get more fully-developed people with opportunities to realize their potential. However, in order to do this the antagonism on both sides must be overcome by a strategy of focusing on objective, job-related issues. The manager must also uncover the appraisee's reasons for tackling the appraisal and development of his staff as he does, and must be prepared to discuss those reasons constructively, not in a judgemental way. The manager must be willing to see that the appraisee's point of view has some validity too.

How far do you think that your plan would have enabled you to elicit the crucial information from the appraisee that is contained in his brief? Would your structure, setting, and discussion strategy have enabled you to build up the kind of atmosphere in which antagonism could have been reduced, and some kind of joint problem-solving approach have been developed? Tactics that would ensure mutual learning are absolutely crucial in this case, where the perceptions of the two men about one another, and about the central issues, are so opposed.

Did you have a contingency plan if you found out during the interview that your initial assumptions about the QA Manager's attitudes and managment of his staff were incorrect or incomplete?

### Getting started
How were you going to deal with the tensions bound to be involved in this particular discussion? Again, did you remember the importance of listening tactics?

### Work review and planning
Even though this interview does not focus on work review and work planning, reference to these areas will be inevitable, and direct discussion will have to take place on key issues to do with the appraisee's development and general management of his staff. How did you plan to discuss his work performance? Did you intend to use a self-appraisal, objective-centred approach, focusing especially on the individual's own perception of his performance, and his explanation of it? Did you remember that a major aim throughout should be for the appraiser to learn, rather than to judge? How did you reconcile that aim with the need to try to change the QA Manager's views on development of his people? Were you able to

think of any strengths and achievement that could be brought out in the discussion?

### Training and development
Your discussion and any plan you agreed should relate both to meeting immediate needs, and to the continuous development of the appraisee, in line with longer-term career planning. Did you allow for a thorough discussion of his and your perception of where his career might go from here; of a number of developmental actions that might be possible in the forthcoming period; and of final agreement on a developmental plan for him?

### Action planning
Did your plan for this relate to the five parameters?

Needs

Action

Timing

Resources

Immediate and longer-term development

### Conclusion
Did your plan emphasize the need for summary of points and agreed action at the end of the interview?

### Follow-up and monitoring
Did you remember about the need to follow up and monitor any training and development plans?

Thus, using our 7-point checklist, a plan for the appraisal discussion can be drawn up which should enable the major problems inherent in such discussions to be tackled effectively, and for positive outcomes to be achieved.

---

## CONCLUSION

Having read this chapter and completed the various activities it contains, you should now:

1  Be able to evaluate your organization's appraisal system and identify areas where improvements are needed

2  Be able to advise on how to plan a motivating and developmental appraisal interview that should lead to the understanding of work performance, and the accurate diagnosis of learning needs

3  Know a range of activities that could form part of an individual's development plan, arising out of the appraisal discussion.

The main learning points connected with these objectives are:

**1  Successful appraisal of performance**
It is necessary to ensure 4 things in appraisal related to training and development:

- Shared perception of purpose

- Mutual learning

- Objectivity

- Integration of appraisal into the overall development process

There should always be at least 4 outcomes of appraisal of performance related to training and development:

- Motivation

- Understanding

- Diagnosis

- Development.

**2  Factors influencing the appraisal discussion**
The appraisal of performance is always influenced by the context in which it takes place. 4 major contextual factors are:

- The organizational culture and structure

- The overall development process

- The organization's appraisal scheme

- The appraiser/appraisee relationship

In inception, design and operation, the appraisal scheme should be consistent with the organizational culture and structure of which it is planned to form a part.

Appraisal should always be planned and perceived to be, not an end in itself, but a part of the wider process of development of people in an organization.

Successful appraisal schemes have 7 characteristics:

- Clear and shared objectives

- Limited scope

- Line management involvement

- Top management commitment

- Appropriate procedures

- Training

- Review

The ongoing relationship between the manager and the appraisee is of central importance, and unless it is operating satisfactorily, appraisal itself cannot be effective.

**3  Planning the appraisal discussion**
A 7-point check list for planning an appraisal discussion is:

- Preparing for the discussion

- Getting started

- Work review and planning

- Training and development

- Action planning

- Conclusion

- Follow-up and monitoring

***Preparing for the discussion***
Here we are concerned with 5 aspects:

- Information

- Objectives

- Structure

- Discussion strategy

- Setting

***Getting started***
Here, the appraiser needs to think about 2 points:

- Introduction

- Rapport

***Work review and planning***
Four points are useful to remember in connection with work review and planning:

- Objective-centred discussion

- Examine task priorities and interrelationships

- Understand performance

- Substantiate judgements

***Training and development***
Discussion of training and development needs should relate to two things:

- Current job-related needs

- Continuous development needs

Three key processes are interrelated, and should be discussed at appraisal:

- Self-assessment

- Self-learning

- Self-development.

**Action planning**
When the individual's needs for training and development have been identified and analysed, a range of alternative courses of action should be explored. There are 3 reasons for this:

- A learning process

- Improved working relationship

- Contingency planning.

The final Action Plan should note:

- Needs

- Action

- Timescale

- Resources

- Immediate and longer-term development

**Conclusion**
Must summarize:

- Main points of the discussion

- Agreed action.

**Follow-up and monitoring**
All action promised must be followed up, monitored, and reviewed at the next appraisal discussion.

---

## REVIEW ACTIVITY

Finally, here are some questions which you can either tackle as essays (if you are a student); discuss with fellow-students or colleagues; or simply think about now that you have completed this chapter:

- How would you establish the training needs of a group of supervisors, most of whom have been in their posts for many years?*

- How would you identify the training needs of a graduate taking up his or her first post in a personnel department?*

- What would you suggest to make appraisal activities in your organization (a) more collaborative, and (b) more closely linked to operational needs?

*In answering these questions, you will also need to use information related to Chapters 8 and 9

CHAPTER 12

# Designing the learning event
# 1: The learning task

## LEARNING OBJECTIVES

After reading this chapter and completing the various activities it contains, you should:

1 Know the major factors to be considered when designing a learning event

2 Understand what is meant by 'the learning task', in order to be able to use the concept in a practical way when designing a learning event

3 Be able to draw up an overall purpose, and final and intermediate behavioural objectives for a learning event

4 Know how to analyse the characteristics of a learning group, and relate these to the design of a learning event.

### The Learning Task in Context

In Chapters 4 and 5, in our discussion of the organization as a natural learning system, we saw that it is not necessary to have a detailed training plan, or designated 'events', for valuable learning to be achieved. Using ongoing work as a vehicle for continuous learning can also develop individuals, groups and the organization as a whole, both immediately and in the longer term. In those chapters we saw how the organization can be managed in order to promote such work-based learning, and how to generate attitudes and practice conducive to continuous development in the workplace.

However, in most organizations there will always be a need also for a range of structured learning events, and it is with the design of these that the next three chapters are concerned. Guidelines are offered here to whoever is responsible for the design of learning events, be they courses, workshops, coaching sessions, or a programme of varied activities and processes. Since designing learning events involves considerable skill and practice, the chapter's learning objectives focus on a general knowledge and understanding more then on a particular skill.

In the design of a specific learning event, there are five sets of factors to consider:

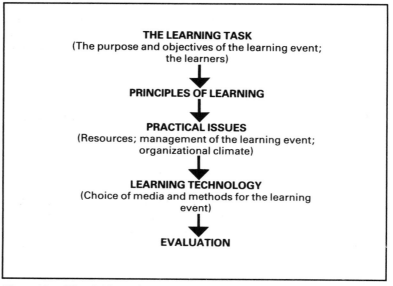

**Figure 6:    The design of a learning event**

In this chapter we will consider the learning task. The other factors will be examined in Chapters 13 to 15.

The learning task consists of the following main elements:

The overall purpose of the learning event

The learning objectives

The learners.

### The Overall Purpose of the Learning Event
The first activity in the design of a learning event is to review why it has been thought necessary in the first place, and, once clear

answers have been established, to formulate an overall purpose which will clearly relate to that need. Through this activity, the context, or framework, of the learning event is established.

Here, we are going back to what we discussed in earlier chapters: it is essential to be clear what the designer is being asked to do, what need the learning is to serve, and whether there is, in fact, a need for learning to take place, and to take place in this way. If there have been errors in that initial diagnostic process, then expensive resources are going to be wasted in carrying out an unnecessary activity. It is therefore essential to define the overall purpose of any learning event, as well as its learning objectives, since this reminds everyone — the learners, the providers and eventually the evaluators — what the entire learning event is intended to achieve.

Thus we can say that:

> **The overall purpose of a learning event answers the question 'why', whereas its learning objectives define 'what'.**

## The Learning Objectives
Now let us look at learning objectives.

> **The objectives of a learning event define what outcomes are to be achieved by that event in order to realize its overall purpose. They explain the kinds of behaviour of which the learner should be capable at key stages of the learning process.**

Ideally, the designer of the learning event should have been centrally involved in formulating its objectives, in line with an overall purpose which has already been agreed with a 'client' in the organization. However, in reality the designer may have to work to objectives that have already been established by someone else. This can pose many problems, such as when it seems clear that objectives should be changed or modified in some way, but such change seems impossible. Here is a case study based on fact. It represents a situation which will be familiar to many lecturing staff in universities, colleges and polytechnics.

---

## CASE STUDY: 'X' College and the Course Review

'X' college was concerned at its consistently poor level of examination success in a three-year part-time professional course. An internal review produced the following information:

1   The professional body in question had become preoccupied in the last four or five years with producing 'competent practitioners' rather than, as in the past, knowledgeable and informed graduates who would develop skills once they moved out into their first professional apprentice posts.

2   With this changed overall purpose in mind, the learning objectives for the national professional examinations had become almost entirely skills-orientated. However, the final method of assessment remained what it had always been: a series of formal examinations. The questions in these examinations required students to show not only what they knew, but also to explain what they would do, in relation to specific situations, but the format of each examination remained a three-hour paper, closed book, with a choice of four out of ten or twelve questions.

3   Students who passed the examinations, and those who scored highest in them, tended repeatedly to be those with trained academic abilities, rather than those who had been found to be competent in a variety of practical activities and assignments on the course. Clearly the task of mastering a complex body of professional knowledge in order to answer 'what would you do if . . . ?' questions posed very considerable difficulties for those who had not been through a similarly taxing academic course before, or had not reached quite a high level of intellectual development before embarking on this course.

4   The skills-orientated objectives called for classroom, material and staffing resources which the course tutor could rarely obtain: his team had to struggle with large classes of 30 to 40 students, (necessary to recruit because of the financial situation of the college) in classrooms without adjacent (and often without any) syndicate rooms, with no possibility of team teaching. Practical work, especially that done in groups, was therefore extremely difficult to organize satisfactorily.

5   Access to film, closed circuit television, video or computer equipment was difficult, because of the scarcity of those resources compared to the demands made on them; technical support was also patchy and unreliable.

6   When they started the course the students were very heterogenous in their existing skills and knowledge related to the course content, as was to be expected in such a large part-time course. They also had quite different levels of learning ability, and different types of learning skills and styles. Many had no ongoing experience at all of one or more of the key subject areas, so that activities during class time (case studies, role play exercises, discussions with other students) provided the only medium through which they could be helped to 'acquire' such experience. Visits to organizations were usually out of the question, because of the large numbers of students, and timetabling problems. Outside speakers were used, to very good effect, but since financial stringency made it impossible to pay more than one per term, the staff had to rely largely on voluntary speakers.

The review concluded that the examination failure rate was understandable in the circumstances, and was likely to continue until such time as the professional body concerned could be persuaded to reconsider either the overall purpose of its examinations, or the learning objectives, or the type of final assessment which was used. Many other colleges had come to a similar conclusion, and the professional body did in fact begin to look at those three factors, with a view to producing a purpose, objectives and method of assessment which were less mutually contradictory. The professional body did, however, point out to the colleges that when it came to recruitment and selection of learners, and resources made available for the course, this was the responsibility of the colleges themselves: it was unreasonable and inappropriate to expect a professional body to consider such localized and temporary factors when setting permanent standards of entry to a profession.

---

In this case study, what is important to note at this point is the influence exercised by the overall purpose and the learning objectives of the course in question. Discrepancies there started off a chain of difficulties which led, in the end, to unsatisfactory outcomes of the whole complex learning event. If the tutor and staff themselves had looked more critically at purpose and objectives before designing their course, at the least they could have alerted the college to the likely problem. There might then, given sufficiently powerful arguments, have been the provision of better resources, or the beginning of a dialogue with the professional body that might have led more quickly to the eventual review of the purpose, objectives and method of assessment in the final examinations.

We can conclude our examination of this case study by stating that:

**The designer of the learning event should always challenge or rethink its learning purpose or objectives if they seem inappropriate in some important way.**

Except in very simple learning situations, it is helpful to formulate learning objectives at two levels, final and intermediate:

### Final behavioural objectives
Sometimes known as 'Ultimate' or 'Criterion' or 'Overall' objectives, these explain the kind of outcomes which the learner should have achieved once the learning event is completed.

### Intermediate behavioural objectives
Sometimes known as 'Interim' or 'Specific' objectives, these explain the kind of outcomes which the learner should have achieved at key stages of the learning process.

You may have noted the use of the phrase 'behavioural objectives' in the above definitions, and the reference to 'outcomes'. This is because the clearest guide to design can be obtained, not so much by stating what the learning event aims to do in general terms, but by closely specifying what the learner should be capable of at certain stages and by the end of the event. To illustrate this point, consider the difference between two ways of defining the objective of the same learning event, in relation to this chapter.

---

## ACTIVITY

### Behavioural Objectives
Please read the following examples carefully, and then answer the question on them.

#### Example 1
One of the aims of this chapter is to explain the term 'the learning task'.

#### Example 2
After reading this chapter and completing the various activities it contains, you should be able to understand what is meant by 'the learning task' in order to be able to make practical use of the concept when designing a learning event.

In what ways does Example 2 give better guidance to the reader, and help the author to better understand the kind of structure and content relevant for this chapter?

---

## FEEDBACK NOTES

From the reader's point of view, Example 1 tells what the chapter aims to do, but not why; and so he/she probably does not understand its purpose, or what use it might be. Example 2 gives concise information on both those points. It therefore should act as a stimulus (providing that the outcome is desired).

From the author's viewpoint, if the only brief given was Example 1, it would be hard to decide what to put into the chapter. But with Example 2 it is clear that a simple explanation of 'the learning task' will not be enough. The reader must achieve an understanding of the meaning of the term 'learning task', and be able to make practical use of the concept in designing a learning event. So the author will have to ensure that the type of readers likely to be going through this chapter are given whatever aids are possible and feasible to help them achieve both understanding and the ability to relate that to designing a learning event. This logically leads to including practical illustrations, exercises (like this one), and review activity.

---

This example helps us to understand how expressing objectives in behavioural terms results in there being as clear an explanation as possible, not only of what the learning event aims to do, but of what sort of skills, knowledge or attitudes the learner has acquired.

**Behavioural objectives give a clear focus to the learning event by explaining the outcomes it will help learners to achieve.**

Ideally, objectives should include an explanation of the conditions under which the learners will ultimately carry out the learning, and the standard they will need to achieve. We can therefore conclude this section on the purpose and objectives of the learning event by stating that:

**The most helpful behavioural objectives are those which describe not only the kinds of behaviour to be achieved at the end of the learning event, but also the conditions under which**

that behaviour is expected to occur, and the standard to be reached in that behaviour.

## The Learners

A major feature of the learning task facing designer and trainer is the kind of learner or group who will be involved. Here, it is essential to analyse three sets of characteristics:

Their learning styles and skills

Their motivation

Their existing skills, knowledge and attitudes

### Learning styles and skills

In Chapter 5 we looked in detail at learning styles. We noted Honey and Mumford's (1986) ideas about many learners tending to be primarily either activitists, reflectors, theorists or pragmatists. It was also noted that people can usually develop learning styles in more than one mode, and that a number of people can move easily between the four modes, able to learn equally well in any of them.

In terms of the skills of learning, Mumford, in an article about learning from everyday work experiences, lists the following as the key skills:

**Ability to establish effectiveness criteria for oneself**

**Ability to measure one's own effectiveness**

**Ability to identify one's own learning needs**

**Ability to plan one's learning**

**Ability to take advantage of all learning opportunities**

**Ability to review one's learning processes**

**Ability to listen to others**

**Capacity to accept help**

**Ability to face unwelcome information**

**Ability to take risks and tolerate anxieties**

Ability to analyse what other successful performers do

Ability to know oneself

Ability to share information with others

Ability to review what has been learned

(*Mumford,* Personnel Management, *August 1981*)

Learning styles and skills have a primary influence on how well the learners can organize and control themselves in relation to the learning event: how effectively and efficiently they are able to bring their attention to bear on the learning process, keep it there, and make progress in learning. Learning styles and skills are usually formed at quite an early age, and this leaves little possibility that they can quickly be altered or improved for a particular learning event. Initially, therefore, it is a matter of designing or choosing an event which will take them adequately into account. For example, many people may find distance learning unexpectedly hard to cope with (Mann 1988) but can learn quite effectively in a face-to-face learning medium; those who do not learn well when lectures predominate may respond much better to more active or pragmatic forms of learning like group and practical work; those who cannot review their own learning processes can be helped to do so by using a learning styles inventory, and by regular discussion with a trainer or 'mentor' about how they are coping and which learning processes they most or least enjoy.

However, in designing the learning event it is important to consider not only how the event can adapt to the learners' primary learning styles and skills, but also to what extent the event should itself seek to change or develop those styles and skills. Honey and Mumford (1986) suspect, for example, that trainers as a profession may tend to be activists rather than reflectors or theorists. If this suspicion is valid (and getting the learning group in question to fill in their questionnaire on one or two separate occasions before the course should give some helpful indicators), then any course for trainers should surely aim to redress that imbalance by offering ways of learning that will develop styles and skills in all four modes, rather than simply encourage a dependance on and preference for only the activist approach to learning.

When a learning event calls for learning styles and skills of quite a high order, and the type of learner who will be involved is unlikely to have reached the required level, then a 'Study Skills' input can serve a very useful purpose before the main course begins; or a full

'Foundation' course which introduces the main topics but at a lower level, thus developing the skills over a longer period of time and in a different way.

## Motivation
Little useful learning can occur without the drive to learn, and so it is important to assess the probable needs and expectations learners will bring to the learning event, and to consciously respond to these at the design stage and thereafter. Motivation can be considered under two headings (Gagne, 1965): social motivation, and motivation related to task mastery.

*Social motivation* concerns the social situation in which the learners are placed: their social needs, characteristics, problems and types of relationship with each other and with the training staff. All these factors will have positive or negative motivational effects and so the learning system should aim to build on the former and reduce the latter. For example, designing a course in a new and difficult area of skills for a group of employees, whether from the same or from different organizational departments or levels, calls for skilful use of social factors. If the learners are brought together into a cohesive group from the start, sharing expectations and concerns, this will help build up an atmosphere of social supportiveness which will stand them in good stead as they tackle the various learning tasks. To this end, my own polytechnic has introduced an 'Outward Bound' weekend at the start of some of our part-time management courses, when the new students will begin to develop into a strong social group, motivated and able to approach their 2-year learning experience as a team rather than as a heterogenous collection of individuals.

*Motivation related to task mastery* raises the issue of what drives different learners to succeed. Some may be spurred on by a need to 'win', achieving most in a competitive learning situation; others may be stimulated by any opportunity to learn something new — a 'curiosity' motive. But whilst classifying learners in such ways may prove to have considerable practical value in some design situations,* generalized assumptions must be avoided. As was explained in Chapter 11, performance is the final outcome of a complex interaction between a person's needs in a particular situation, their perception of the results wanted from them and the rewards they

---

*See C. P. Otto and R. O. Glasser *The Management of Training*, London, Addison-Wesley, 1972, for a detailed classification system.

perceive they will obtain by achieving those results, and their effort, energy and ability in that situation. Design of any learning event must therefore pay careful attention to those four factors.

In Chapter 13 there is. a practical checklist (page 243) offering guidelines for achieving and sustaining learners' motivation, and for stimulating them to master learning tasks.

To summarize: motivation presents many learning design problems:

### Unpredictability
It is to a major extent unpredictable, even with types of learning events that have often been run before.

### Individual differences
There can be significant individual differences in motivation and expectations in a group of learners.

### Dynamism
Motivation is dynamic, and can change during the learning event.

Thus there must be a preparedness and an ability to monitor and respond to these problems, and to spend time at crucial points at the start of, during, and at the end of the learning event in diagnosing the needs and expectations of the learners, and in responding to them. This requires close collaboration between designer and trainer (if the two processes are carried out by different people) from the outset so that any problems that have arisen can be carefully analysed, and relevant changes can be made in the design of the learning event.

### Existing skills, knowledge and attitudes of the learners
These may, by their standard and relevance to the learning tasks, be very helpful to the learner; or they may be counterproductive in the new learning situation, requiring early attention if they are not seriously to impede the learning process. Information on skills, knowledge and attitudes of the learners should be obtained from whatever relevant sources are available (Chapters 9, 10 and 11 deal with several sources in detail), because they will also have a major influence on deciding what the content of the learning programme is to be; the more the learners already know and can do, the shorter the learning event needs to be. Conversely, the less they know and can do, the more has to be achieved in the learning event.

At this point it is important to stress the significance of the age factor in any discussion not only of the skills, knowledge and attitudes of learners, but of learning styles and skills and (as already indicated) of motivation. Very useful practical guidance about training young people is given in the publication *Helping young people to learn* (Institute of Personnel Management and Manpower Services Commission, 1983), and for those dealing with older learners, the work of the Belbins (1972) is invaluable.

Let us end this section on 'The Learning Task' by tackling a real-life consultancy assignment (although minor details have been changed to ensure anonymity of the client organization). The main purpose of this Activity is to reinforce what we have learnt in this section. However, because the assignment itself is about appraisal schemes and skills, you might like to refer before starting it to that part of Chapter 11 which deals with 'Factors influencing the appraisal discussion' (page 195), and especially the section on 'The appraisal scheme', (page 197) since the material there is highly relevant to the technical side of this Activity. A summary of relevant points raised in Chapter 11 is as follows:

The appraisal of performance is always influenced by the context in which it takes place. Four major contextual factors are:

- Organizational culture and structure

- Overall development process

- Organization's appraisal scheme

- Appraiser/appraisee relationship

Successful appraisal schemes have 7 characteristics:

- Clear and shared objectives

- Limited scope

- Line management involvement

- Top management commitment

- Appropriate procedures

- Training

- Review

In your overall analysis of the Activity, try to use the headings established in this chapter:

Overall purpose of the learning event

Behavioural objectives of the learning event

The learners

---

## ACTIVITY

## CASE STUDY: The Retail Store's Appraisal Project (Part 1)

You are a management consultant, and, following a telephone call three days ago, you have been invited to visit the big local branch of a national retail store in order to discuss the possibility of carrying out training in appraisal skills for about 15 managers and supervisors. The work is to be done in the next two months.

You arrive at 9.00 a.m., and are met by the Personnel Officer, a woman of about 55, who has been accepted as a member of the IPM by the 'age and experience' rather than examination route. You already know her slightly, and she has a reputation for being well-informed in the practice of personnel management, and well-liked by employees generally. She is a loyal and long-serving member of the store, having worked there for 25 years, moving up gradually from secretarial positions to her present job. She tells you that the Managing Director (MD), with whom you are both going to spend the morning, is new to the job, having being appointed six months ago from a senior management position in another chain of stores. He is 38, with an impressive record of success in his previous posts. He is already establishing himself as a man of action, absolutely committed to increasing the store's turnover, and full of ideas about how that can be done. Whatever he decides to do he quickly carries out, and his time-scale for results to start coming through seems to be about 18 months. Throughout the subsequent discussion, the Personnel Officer says very little, since the aim of that discussion is for the MD and yourself to talk about the proposed assignment, and arrive at some conclusions about it.

You start off by asking the MD to explain what the assignment is about. He replies that he wants you to 'train all the managers and supervisors (about 15) in appraisal so that I can find out what their performance really is, get a few standardized disciplinary procedures sorted out, diagnose training and development needs, assess potential, and get the managers working together as a team'. He wants the training done within the next two months.

He goes on to explain that the store, a long-established one, is profitable but that its turnover has declined in the last five years, and competition is increasingly strong. The store has had a paternalistic role culture for some years, and this has stifled the drive and initiative of its managers and supervisors, most of them in their 40s and 50s and long-serving. A few have become complacent, because profits (due to cost increases and customer loyalty) are still good: they see no need to change their ways. At the time the new MD arrived there were some redundancies amongst catering and domestic staff, approved although not initiated by him, and a makeshift appraisal scheme was used to determine who should go. This caused quite a lot of trouble and has led to a belief in some quarters that the MD himself is a hatchet man, with a 'list' of those he intends to get rid of in the next year of so. This is, in fact, a quite mistaken belief: the MD is genuinely determined to build up a high calibre, enthusiastic team of people who will regain the store's former position in the market. He has already broken down the structure immediately below him with two directors in their early 30s who work closely with him, and are fully committed to his way of doing things. His style is open and positive. He sets high standards, and rewards those who achieve, whilst seeking to understand reasons for poor performance before passing any judgements. His views on appraisal can be summed up in the phrase:

**I may not know much about the detail of appraisal, but I know what I want it to achieve for me.**

Expanding on the consultancy assignment, he says that he will probably start with closed assessments, because he thinks anything else at this stage would be 'too threatening'. By closed assessments he means that each appraiser should produce a written report on their staff; that may or may not be followed up by an appraisal discussion with the staff concerned, but in any event, staff will not be able to see the reports on them. The reports will then 'be pushed through the system', to enable him to see what sort of skills and potential exist in his workforce, and what kind of performance is being achieved, together with needs for training and development. The MD adds that he does not want a complicated ranking system on the reports, just something simple and understandable. He would be involved in the training, being himself appraised by the Chief Executive of the group of stores, and appraising his two Directors. The appraisal 'chain' would stop at supervisory level, with supervisors being appraised but not, at this stage, doing any appraisal themselves.

What issues will you raise with the MD, and what will you try to achieve during your discussion with him, in order to reach agreement on the learning task that you will help the organization to carry out?

---

## FEEDBACK NOTES

The initial discussion between the consultant, the MD and later on the Personnel Officer in reality took almost a day. However, at the end of that time the crucial issues had been straightened out, leaving the way clear for agreed action to take place. Obviously you will have all sorts of ideas about how to tackle the discussion, and all I can usefully do, therefore, is to tell you the major issues that any similar discussion needs to confront, and how they were actually dealt with in this case.

### The Learning Task

#### 1  The overall purpose of the learning
The first issue to clarify is the true reasons for the consultancy assignment. At present there is no clear overall purpose, and there is also an inconsistency in objectives, so that many questions relating to the initial need for training must be asked. There is also a confusion in terms; the MD refers at one point to 'appraisal' and at another to 'assessment', as if they are the same activity, whereas to the consultant they are quite different activities, the former related to examining current work performance, the latter to diagnosis of potential. Terms must be defined at the outset, and a common language developed. This is always essential to achieve at an early stage in consultancy discussions, if any reliable final agreement is to be reached between the parties.

What really is the need that has brought appraisal to the forefront of the MD's mind? He mentions the need to find out about people's abilities and performance, but also a need to develop fair disciplinary procedures. He refers to a need to discover about people's potential, but also a need to find out their training and development requirements. He talks about a major need for teamwork, but then refers to closed appraisals. These are mutually contradictory needs; no single activity, training or otherwise, can deal satisfactorily with all of them, and meeting one set of needs could only be at the expense of several others. Too many of the results he wants from appraisal will appear as threatening to his managers and supervisors and would result almost certainly in their opposition to appraisal, and lack of any motivation to enter actively into any training related to it.

Discussion of this issue did, in fact, lead to agreement that what was more important to him than anything else was to introduce appraisal as an aid to reviewing work performance, helping work planning, and diagnosing training and developing needs. If this could be achieved as a first step, then developing disciplinary activities, sorting out how to carry out assessments of potential, and so on, could be done as separate activities at a later date, when confidence in the least threatening process, that of appraisal related to current work and to training and development, had built up and when an appraisal scheme was working well. This part of the discussion also looked at what MD and consultant meant by the terms 'appraisal' and 'assessment'. The MD admitted to using the terms indiscriminately, as many people do, and once the distinction between them had been clarified and agreed, many other things became clearer, and a shared frame of reference and language began to develop between him and the consultant.

## 2 The learning objectives

The next issue is the behavioural learning objectives. The MD has referred to 'appraisal skills training', but what, specifically, are to be the outcomes of any training that takes place? Initially, his one answer, that his managers should be able to operate a closed system of appraisal, presupposes three things; that there is an appraisal scheme already in existence, to which training can be related; that it has the support of his managers and supervisors, so that they will welcome training; and that closed appraisal is consistent with his overall purpose of using appraisal as an aid to reviewing work performance, helping work planning, and diagnosing training and development needs.

Discussion of this issue took a long time, but in the end significant progress was made. It emerged that:

> **there was no appraisal scheme worthy of note; the one used for selection for redundancies was agreed to be unsuitable from every point of view. Therefore before skills training could take place, an appraisal scheme would have to be designed;**

> **closed appraisal, especially coming at this particular time, would be viewed with great suspicion; it would be seen as imposed, threatening, and with many ulterior motives. It would be far better to involve the managers and supervisors in the design of an appraisal scheme, opening up the entire**

design as well as operational process from the start. Such an approach would also be consistent with the MD's other major need, to bind his managers and supervisors together into a close-knit managerial working team: the design task could start to build up that relationship;

if the objectives of the appraisal scheme were simply to do with work review and planning, and the diagnosis of training and development needs, then no rating or ranking system related to performance was needed; and to dispense with it would, again, reduce fears of the managers and supervisors that there was some ulterior motive behind the exercise, to do with selection for redundancy or for promotion.

## 3   The learners

The third issue is the learners. What are their characteristics and situations? It is vital to get as much information about them at this early stage as possible, in order that the whole of the learning task facing the consultant is clearly understood.

Discussions on this issue confirmed that the managers and supervisors were mainly in the 40—50 age range; most had been with the store since youth. In terms of learning styles and skills, they had no management training or education, although they had whatever technical and professional qualifications were needed; they would tend to be activists in the learning situation, distrustful of theories and simulated situations unless these were very clearly relevant to their work situation.

As to motivation, over the last ten years with a rather old-fashioned, complacent and authoritarian leadership right at the top of the store, some managers had become disillusioned and pessimistic about their futures. Others felt that they had received little support from the top in their attempts to perform efficiently and effectively, and this bred lack of confidence as well as confusion and some stagnation. Overall, energy and excitement were at quite a low ebb, and although the MD had a high opinion of their real levels of ability and potential, it was essential to restore their original enthusiasm and excitement. Also, one or two seemed to see no need to work harder or differently from the way in which they worked at present. What, asked the consultant, was therefore going to be the incentive for them either to design an appraisal scheme, or to undergo skills training for it — or indeed to do any of the things desired by the MD? The MD believed that the motivation would come as they began to realize all the possibilities that lay before them; a market which they could start to win back and develop; the opportunity to become a small, cohesive, high-calibre and high-achieving professional team, with rewards for those who proved their worth in meeting challenging standards. It was also evident as he spoke that he was quite determined that appraisal would be introduced; there was absolute commitment from him to both the concept and the reality of appraisal. Furthermore, his two Directors would be positive in their support for the initiative, and this would do much to convert any apathy or suspicion into willingness to experiment, and to a commitment to try to make appraisal work, once there was a belief that this was not just one more 'flavour of the month' technique but a strategy offering benefits rather than danger or disadvantage.

In terms of relevant skills and knowledge, few of the managers (including, said the MD, himself) really knew anything about appraisal.

### The Agreement on the Learning Task
The final issue was to establish, after all this discussion, what the learning task should actually be. The following agreement was reached:

1  The consultancy assignment would proceed in stages, with both consultant and client able to withdraw at the end of any stage if that seemed necessary or desirable.

2  Stage 1 would consist of initial information-gathering by the consultant, to determine whether the kind of diagnoses made in this initial discussion were valid, or whether other needs and problems existed which called for a review of the tentative conclusions reached at this stage by him and the MD.

   If the diagnoses did prove to be valid, then the consultant would run a workshop for all 15 managers and supervisors, with the aim of working with them to design a simple appraisal scheme for the store. Initially it would be a pilot scheme, covering only managers and supervisors. If subsequent evaluation proved positive, it would then be extended to the rest of the store. Recommendations for a scheme would be presented to, and discussed and agreed with, the MD at the conclusion of the workshop, in order that he could present a report on them to the Board of Directors.

3  Stage 2 would consist of appraisal skills training, to develop those skills needed to introduce and operate the pilot scheme. The details of that stage (which again would fall into the two components of initial information-gathering and a workshop) would be determined once a decision had been made on

whether or not the consultant was to go ahead and carry out that stage.

4   Stage 3 would come at a later date, once a pilot scheme had been introduced and was under way. It would consist of a review day in which consultant, management team (which included those titled 'supervisors'), MD and Personnel Officer would come together to review the scheme and the way it was operating, and agree on any further action that might be relevant.

Thus agreement between consultant and client was reached by a process of jointly talking through the whole learning task, and the specific learning events within it, and of looking in some detail at the number and characteristics of the learning group who would be involved in those events. This resulted in establishing the learning task in its three parameters:

Overall purpose

Behavioural objectives of the learning events

The learners

Note how important were the consequences of the consultant doing what was advised early on in this chapter:

**The designer of the learning event should always challenge or rethink learning objectives if they seem inappropriate in some important way.**

---

## CONCLUSION

After reading this chapter and completing the various activities it contains, you should now:

1   Know the major factors to be considered when designing a learning event

2   Understand what is meant by 'the learning task', in order to be able to use the concept in a practical way when designing a learning event

3   Be able to draw up an overall purpose, and final and intermediate behavioural objectives for a learning event

4   Know how to analyse the characteristics of a learning group, and relate these to the design of a learning event.

The main learning points connected with these objectives are:

## 1   The learning task in context
In the design of a learning event, there are 5 sets of factors to consider:

- The learning task

- Principles of learning

- Practical issues

- Learning technology

- Evaluation

The learning task related to a particular learning event consists of 3 main elements:                                                        --

- The overall purpose of the learning event

- The learning objectives

- The learners

## 2   The overall purpose of the learning event
The overall purpose of a learning event answers the question 'WHY', whereas its learning objectives define 'WHAT'.

## 3   The learning objectives
The objectives of a learning event define what outcomes are to be achieved by that event in order to realize its overall purpose. They explain the kinds of behaviour of which the learner should be capable at key stages of the learning process.

The designer of the learning event should always challenge or rethink its learning purpose or objectives if they seem inappropriate in some important way.

It is usually helpful to formulate learning objectives at 2 levels:

- Final behavioural objectives
- Intermediate behavioural objectives

Behavioural objectives give a clear focus to the learning event by explaining the outcomes it will help learners to achieve.

The most helpful behavioural objectives are those which describe not only the kinds of behaviour to be achieved at the end of the learning event, but also the conditions under which that behaviour is expected to occur, and the standard to be reached in that behaviour.

## 4   The learners

With any group of learners, we need to examine 3 sets of characteristics:

- Their learning styles and skills

- Their motivation

- Their existing skills, knowledge and attitudes

In designing the learning event it is important to consider not only how the event can adapt to the learners' primary learning styles and skills, but also to what extent the event should itself seek to change or develop those styles and skills.

Designers and trainers should consider motivation under 2 headings (Gagne, 1965):

- Social motivation

- Motivation related to task mastery

Motivation presents the designer with many problems, including the following:

- Unpredictability

- Individual differences

- Dynamism

Motivation must therefore be monitored and responded to during the learning event, and evaluation must establish whether future design needs to be changed in view of any problems encountered in the learning event.

## REVIEW ACTIVITY

Finally, here is a design task which you can either tackle as coursework (if you are a student); discuss with fellow-students or colleagues; or carry out on your own now that you have completed this chapter.

- Take any training design task .you like, in the context of your own organization or one with which you are familiar. Describe its overall purpose, its learning objectives, and the characteristics of the learners who will be involved, and explain the implications of these for the general design and content of the learning event.

## CHAPTER 13

# Designing the learning event
## 2: Applying 'principles of learning' to design tasks; practical issues affecting design

---

## LEARNING OBJECTIVES

After reading this chapter and completing the various activities it contains, you should:

1   Be able to apply to the design of a learning event eight practical guidelines related to principles of learning

2   Understand what sort of practical issues need to be considered in designing learning events and be able to analyse such issues in order to identify the constraints and opportunities they present to the designer.

### Applying Principles of Learning to Design Tasks

In Chapter 4, we noted when discussing the Stimulus-Response model of the learning process, that 'principles of learning' can be summarized under four main headings:

Drive

Stimulus

Response

Reinforcement

In this chapter we are going to develop a set of guidelines from those basic principles to help in the practical task of designing a learning event.

First, let us recall what was said in Chapter 4 (page 64)

**Throughout the learning process there must be stimulation and reinforcement of learning.**

Now here is an Acitivity to try to identify some helpful practical guidelines for incorporating the major principles of learning into the design of a learning event.

## ACTIVITY

### Preparing a Talk

There are a number of practical points to be observed when designing a learning event so that it incorporates the four main principles of learning. Thinking back on your own EXPERIENCES of giving and listening to talks, please REFLECT on those experiences, ANALYSE what it was that produced good and bad talks, and then PROBLEM-SOLVE. Your 'problem' is that you have to give a talk to colleagues on any subject of your choice. What general guidelines should you follow in order to ensure that your talk really helps them to learn? I have written down one. Try to think of six or seven others.

### Stimulate the learners

Make the talk *stimulating* enough to gain and keep the attention of the audience throughout.

## FEEDBACK NOTES

There are many possible answers to this question, but eight of the most important points would be the following (and in making them I have drawn significantly from Gagne's (1965) ideas: his book not only offers a scholarly and clear discussion of the psychology of learning, but also excellent practical guidelines about the design of learning events). They constitute an 8-point checklist for incorporating the main principles of learning into the design of a learning event:

Design an appropriate structure and culture

Stimulate the learners

Help understanding

Include appropriate learning activities

Build on existing learning

Guide the learners

Ensure that learning is retained

Ensure that learning is transferred.

Explanation of each of these points follow:

**1  *Design an appropriate structure and culture*** for the learning event. By *structure* is meant the framework of the learning event: the way it is 'shaped' and the type of interactions planned to occur within it.

'Structure' also refers to how tightly or loosely controlled by the trainer the whole learning event should be; in other words, how much structure should actually be built into it. For example, where active participation is particularly desirable in a training programme, how structured or unstructured should that programme be? Should the whole programme be so unstructured that the learners actually decide for themselves (given certain learning objectives, resources, and a timescale) what the design, content, learning media and methods should be, virtually running the event themselves, and using the trainer/tutor as a resource and final reference point? Some programmes, particularly in management education, do operate in that way. Or should there be very tight structuring of the participation, so that where, for example, group work is used, it is set up with detailed instructions, and with group leaders selected by the tutor; it then has to function to strict time-limits; and feedback is engineered by the tutor to lead in all cases to the conclusions that the tutor wants to achieve?

*Culture* means the norms and values that pervade the learning event, expressed by statements like 'this is the way we like to do things in this programme/course/activity'. 'Culture', in other words, is about the ways in which tutors or mangers of the learning situation and the learners themselves are expected to behave in relation to one another, and to the learning event; it is also about the values they share in relation to the learning event.

Decisions about the kind of structure and culture for any learning event should be taken in the light of:

The learning task .        .

Principles of learning

Practical issues

**2** *Stimulate the learners.* For learning to succeed it must be presented in ways that arouse the attention of the learners, making enough impact so that learning is achieved. To stimulate the learners initially, help them to relate to the overall purpose and the learning objectives of the event; if they cannot identify with those, then the basic drive to learn will be missing, and stimulation then becomes difficult if not impossible. To ensure continued motivation throughout the learning event, consider a variety of methods like films, slides, computer-assisted learning, and participative methods like discussions, group work, and practical activities of various kinds. Think also about how to emphasize the most important parts of the event — the ones that it is essential should be learnt accurately. This is what is called giving 'perceptual distinctiveness' to key parts of the learning event.

Remember that we observed in Chapter 12 three particular problems related to motivation:

Unpredictability

Individual differences

Dynamism

Thus even in planning a talk we should allow sufficient flexibility to change our way of interacting with the learners if we find we need to improve or actively sustain motivation.

**3** *Help understanding.* Choose content that is relevant to the overall purpose, the learning objectives, and the learners' characteristics (see Chapter 12). If learners can see the relevance of learning, both to some overall need that they have, and to their ongoing practical situation, this will help them to understand the learning and to have confidence in it.

There should be a clear explanation at the outset of the talk of its purpose and the outcomes that will follow from it for them. Then there can be a brief outline of the content before going into it in detail. Thereafter, try to illustrate main points in ways that will help the learners to relate them to their own needs and experiences.

**4** *Include appropriate learning activities.* Even in a talk, small activities can be built in: a point in the talk when questions are asked for from the audience; an overhead slide containing points about which they make notes before the next slide is shown; you might distribute some information before the talk, and ask for it to be read and questions on it prepared, in order to provide a focus. But always choose interesting and relevant activities, given the objectives, the content, the key points and the major difficulties contained in the learning event, and the type of learners with whom you will be interacting.

**5   *Build on existing learning*.** Try wherever possible to develop rather than destroy or minimize the existing skills, knowledge and attitudes of the learners. In this way learning becomes both easier for them and a positive, incremental activity. There is almost always some area of ability or experience which they can apply in the learning situation, or some attitude that will help them in dealing with it. A simple question like 'does anyone know anything at all about this, just to give us a lead in to the discussion?' can elicit quite a variety of responses, providing that it is phrased in such a way as to reduce fears of being singled out for any kind of stringent questioning!

**6   *Guide the learners*.** It is essential that the learners should have feedback and guidance available as they move through any type of learning event, from a talk to continuous development in the workplace. This is for four main reasons:

to  REINFORCE key learning points or stages;

to  help learners OVERCOME DIFFICULTIES;

to  give learners regular CHECKS on their progress;

to  maintain learners' MOTIVATION.

The longer the event, the greater the need for processes like appraisal, coaching and counselling. Learners will tend to need attention at different stages, and the trainer will not only have to be technically competent in instructional functions, but also skilled at the interpersonal level in order to build up and maintain a supportive relationship with the learners. Once this has been achieved, the whole learning task becomes a joint effort rather than a didactic experience.

**7   *Ensure that learning is retained*.** There are two major, and quite complex, points to consider here:

### Practice

Practice reinforces learning until the point is reached when the new behaviour patterns become habitual. But how much practice? The concept of 'learning curves' is useful here, even in the context of a short talk. A learning curve means the average amount of time it takes a particular type of learner to fully 'learn' something. Learning curves vary greatly from task to task and from person to person, being related to three major considerations.

#### Difficulty of task
the innate level of difficulty of the task

#### Learner characteristics
the characteristics of the particular learner/s concerned

#### Practice periods
the duration and frequency of practice periods.

'Learner characteristics' does not just mean the skills and knowledge of the learners, but also their attitudes, their learning styles and skills, and their motivation. All these will have considerable effects on the rates at which they are likely to master particular kinds of learning, and therefore on the amount and frequency of practice or repetition of information they will need.

We can rarely give the ideal amount and frequency of practice in relation to every piece of learning that must be acquired; we must choose the learning which is most important and/or most difficult (not always the same thing) and give priority to that. Thus, for example, in this chapter I have built in activities and examples of various kinds around not every learning point, but those which are either the most important, or those which can be expected to be the most difficult to understand for the average reader. The activities and examples are also spaced out in order to give variety and interest to what would otherwise be a mass of material that most readers would find less and less interesting and easy to absorb as the chapter went on.

With these considerations in mind, the designer or trainer should build up a store of information about learning curves in relation to the sort of learning events in which he or she will be involved. Past performance should give acceptably valid indicators of the sort of practice periods to build into the learning event, and the way in which those periods should be spaced. Where such information does not yet exist, then careful examination of the three key factors:

Difficulty of task

Learner characteristics

Practice periods

should prove helpful. However, careful monitoring of the learning process will always be necessary, with enough flexibility to allow for changes to the duration or sequencing of practice periods if necessary. One audience may absorb most of your talk in minutes, where another has problems which require you to expand, illustrate and interact for very much longer.

### Reward or punishment?

A response can be reinforced positively by a reward or an attempt may be made to 'punish' an incorrect response. Quite simple rewards for the learners, such as a smile, a word of praise, a pat on the back may be enough. However, it is also important to explain why they have been successful, in case they have only achieved the correct response by chance.

Punishment of incorrect responses, on the other hand, is less predictable in its consequences. A critical comment, a harsh word, or more obvious types of punitive reactions to someone's failure to learn may frighten or shame the learner into renewed efforts to succeed, but equally they may cause negative reactions which inhibit further learning. Indeed, in the extreme case the learner may simply refuse to go on trying. Usually, failure is in itself punishment enough. To correct it, slow demonstration by the trainer, followed by repeated practice by the learner, may be effective: or a repetition of the initial instruction session, using slightly different methods; or a joint discussion of precisely what the learner has found to be an obstacle, and how they may be helped to overcome that obstacle. There are a great many ways in which initial failures can be overcome, and confidence and motivation sustained, providing always that the basic ability is there.

Where the ability is lacking, or there is no drive to learn, these represent fundamental problems that have usually been caused by errors in the initial selection process, and may prove impossible to deal with in any way except by the removal of the learner from the programme. There should, therefore, always be provision for counselling and guidance of the learners in any except very short learning events, and exit points and procedures must always be designed into the programme. In your short talk, you should encourage audience participation in order to deal with any problems or complete misunderstanding and sort them out at the time rather than let them gather momentum throughout the whole period.

**8** *Ensure that learning is transferred* positively both from and to the learner's 'real life' situation. Transfer of learning from a previous job or experience into the new learning situation will be positive if that previous job or experience provides skill, knowledge and attitudes that can be used in the new situation. It will, however, be negative if previous knowledge, skills and attitudes cannot be used, or are actually counter-productive. Thus a manager who has previously managed people successfully in a unit or small-batch production firm may find it difficult to see why he needs to learn how to manage people in a mass production system. Yet Woodward (1980) makes it clear that the difference between those two types of technology are so significant that they present many learning needs to such a manager. However, his attitudes and previous experience may put such barriers in the way of learning new attitudes, knowledge and skills that there is only negative transfer of learning.

At the end of the learning event (where learning has not been continuously integrated with work, but has been separately organized) learning must be transferred to the learner's real life situation, and this too can be difficult. To a significant extent, successful transfer will depend on ensuring:

**Appropriateness of the purpose and objectives of the learning event**
If the event is one of questionable relevance to the learner's needs, or beyond their capabilities to master, or has not been agreed with their manager, then transfer is unlikely to occur.

**Relevance of learning throughout the learning event**
By reference to the guidelines explained above.

**Learning outcomes are achieved**
Learning cannot be effectively transferred if it has not been fully mastered; checks, tests and discussion are some of the many ways to measure achievement.

**Learning will be used after the learning event**
Some of the best aids to effective transfer of learning into and out of the learning event are briefing discussions before and after the learning event, between the learner and someone responsible for them and/or for the learning event; their manager, or the training or personnel manager, for example. Pre-event briefings can establish with the learner exactly what the purpose and objectives of the event are, and how they relate to the learner's needs; also how the learning will be used in the work situation once the learner has finished. Post-event de-briefings can encourage the learner to discuss what has been learnt; to give their views on the learning

event; and to agree on how the new learning can best be used in the work situation. Where learners are not in employment, or are pursuing learning on their own initiative (eg in a distance learning course), careful thought needs to be given by the learning designers as to how transfer can best be achieved.

## Practical Issues

The final section of this chapter is to do with practical issues relating to the learning event. The designer must consider any issues relating to practicality and feasibility of a planned learning event. As a guideline, however, the following are the major issues needing analysis:

Resources, opportunities and constraints

Management of the learning event

The organizational climate

## 1   Resource management

We have covered the management of training resources in Chapter 7, and so most of what is to be said under this heading takes the form of a review of learning points made in that chapter. The most relevant points are the following:

### *Training resources*

These comprise:

INTERNAL AND EXTERNAL RESOURCES

Personnel

Physical

Financial

TIME

NATURAL LEARNING RESOURCES
Those experiences through which learning can occur regularly in the course of the organization's ongoing work.

As far as the training designer is concerned, she must analyse what resources are available, and the opportunities and constraints that these present; and also what considerations are important regarding attitudes in the organization towards the proposed learning event. Careful analysis is essential, because it is at this stage that even the overall purpose, let alone the specific objectives, of a learning event may need to be abandoned or modified, or changes in the numbers or kinds of learners may have to be made.

## 2 Management of the learning event

Learning events all need management — planning, organizing, directing, controlling and evaluating. Some, especially those that are longer-term and/or complex, may require responsibilities to be allocated to a number of different people; others to personnel or training specialists or to designated line managers.

Many of the most effective learning events, as we have seen throughout this book, can be of a continuous and relatively unstructured kind, based on the integration of learning and work. Many others will need to be systematically planned and carefully designed. Although this chapter is primarily concerned with the latter kind of learning event, it is important to recall at this point the discussion in Chapters 4 and 5 of the organization as a learning system: it was stressed then that management of that system requires there to be clear policies, responsibilities and skills to guide people at every level in the organization in the process of continuously developing themselves, their teams, and/or individuals.

## 3 Organizational climate

It is important for the designer to establish what is the general climate in the organization, in relation to the proposed learning event. Is is supportive, antagonistic, neutral? Does a particular climate of opinion have to be built up before or during the learning event? Is there support for, or opposition to, any specific aspect of the learning event; its purpose, objectives, learners selected to attend, proposed media or methods, and so on? This factor, which I have loosely described as 'climate', is of great importance, since it often determines, out of a range of theoretically desirable and practically possible alternatives, what is actually feasible to aim for or design into a learning event.

An example of the importance of practical issues when designing a learning event can be given by continuing the case study which began in Chapter 12 (page 231).

## CASE STUDY: The Retail Store's Appraisal Project (Part 2)

Once the overall purpose and learning objectives had been agreed in outline, the Managing Director (MD), Personnel Officer and the consultant spent considerable time together deciding how to carry out Stage 1 of the project. Here, the discussion revolved around resources. The following points emerged:

### PERSONNEL: Management and Staffing of the Project

The managing of the project was agreed without difficulty: the MD would approve the overall parameters of each stage of the project, leaving the Personnel Officer and the consultant to work on the details relating to staffing, materials and physical accommodation.

The consultant would determine the detailed behavioural objectives, both final and intermediate, of each workshop, and would be entirely responsible for its design and running. He would return six or so months later to carry out a one-day Review (Stage 3 of the project) with the workshop members, and the Personnel Officer would arrange pre- and post-workshop briefing/debriefing sessions for all members and their managers, with special reference to following up agreed action. The Personnel Officer would also organize longer-term evaluation, a year after the whole project had ended.

Staffing posed some problems. It was clearly impossible for the consultant to run a workshop for 15 people on his own, whether it was Stage 1 (designing an Appraisal Scheme) or Stage 2 (developing appraisal skills). The Stage 1 workshop required one other tutor, and the Stage 2 workshop, if carried out, would require two more tutors. It was eventually decided that the Personnel Officer would act as co-tutor on the first since the kind of observational work to be done there posed no problems for her in terms of skills, once the consultant had given her detailed briefing. It was agreed to leave the matter of staffing of Stage 2 until a decision had been made about whether or not that Stage would, in fact, go ahead.

Another resourcing problem was that for the Stage 1 workshop (on the assumption that one would be needed), there would have to be EITHER:

1   one workshop for all the course members, with the consultant and Personnel Officer there throughout the two or three days;

OR:

2   two workshops, with half the membership attending one, half attending the other, staffed by consultant and Personnel Officer throughout on both occasions.

The direct cost of running Option 1 was less than the cost of running Option 2 (because Option 1 would only involve one consultancy fee, and only one sustained period of absence for the Personnel Officer instead of two), but difficulties of releasing all 15 store staff at the same time, together with the indirect costs incurred were these key people all to be away from their departments for three days during a week, might make Option 2 necessary. Checking of dates when consultant and course members would all be available at one time made it clear that Option 1 could not take place within the 2-month period initially desired by the MD.

On the other hand, Option 2 would take longer to carry out than Option 1, and this again brought the planners up against the time factor. It would also split up the learning group, when keeping them together in order to build them up as a work team was an important objective. And if Option 1 could be carried out over a long weekend, then the problem of all the managers being away from the store together would not arise.

## Physical resources
Materials and equipment needed for the workshops were available, and these constituted a relatively cheap part of the programme. Accommodation proved more difficult; the store had conference accommodation, although of limited size, and at first the MD felt that, for obvious cost reasons, all workshops should be held there. The consultant, however, pointed out the psychological advantages of going to a local hotel for the duration of the workshops. The relationship between consultant and course members, so important to cement quickly, given the demanding task they jointly faced, should benefit greatly from such a location and the social as well as task mastery motivation of the course members should receive a strong and continued boost. Equally important, managers and supervisors would be together as a team for a sustained period, away from their usual work situation, and this would be a very positive way of starting to develop the managerial team identity that the MD saw as so crucially important. This strategy was subsequently agreed by the MD.

## Finance
A maximum budget for the entire 3-stage consultancy project was agreed, based on tentative costings produced by the consultant. The budget was tight but not absolutely inflexible; it did, for example, allow for the possibility of some increase in initial costings over the period of the three stages. However, financial considerations posed certain problems related to staffing the workshops, as will be seen in Chapter 14.

**Climate in the organization**
After discussion, it was agreed by MD and consultant that to proceed more slowly than originally hoped would be a better strategy, if a positive climate about appraisal were to be developed in the store. The MD also decided that the objective of building up a strong managerial team from the start'was more important than his wish for the whole project to be concluded quickly. It was therefore decided that Option 1 would be followed (one workshop, involving all 15 people, lasting over a long weekend), with a relaxation of his initial timescale, so that Stages 1 and 2 would be spread over a five-month instead of a two-month period. This timescale would have the final and important advantage of allowing time for a considered decision after Stage 1 on whether or not to proceed to Stage 2.

---

I hope that this case study has helped to demonstrate how the important practical issues — resources, management, and 'climate' — should interact with the learning task when deciding how the learning event should be approached.

## CONCLUSION

Having read this chapter and completed the various activities it contains, you should now:

1  Be able to apply to the design of a learning event eight practical guidelines related to principles of learning

2  Understand what sort of practical issues need to be considered in designing learning events and be able to analyse such issues in order to identify the constraints and opportunities they present to the designer.

The main learning points connected with these objectives are:

**1  Applying principles of learning to design tasks**
The main 'principles of learning' can be summarized under 4 headings:

• Drive

• Stimulus

- Response

- Reinforcement

Throughout the learning process there must be stimulation and reinforcement of learning. An 8-point checklist can be used for incorporating the main principles of learning into the design of a learning event:

- Design an appropriate structure and culture

- Stimulate the learners

- Help understanding

- Include appropriate learning activities

- Build on existing learning

- Guide the learners

- Ensure that learning is retained

- Ensure that learning is transferred

In trying to ensure that learning is retained, attention should be given to practice and the 'reward/punish' issue.

'Learning curves' can provide useful information when designing learning events. They should, however, be seen in the context of 3 key factors:

- Difficulty of task

- Learner characteristics

- Practice periods

Successful transfer of learning will depend on ensuring:

- Appropriateness of the purpose and objectives of the learning event

- Relevance of learning throughout the learning event

- Learning outcomes are achieved

- Learning will be used after the learning event

**2   Practical issues**
The training designer must analyse:

- Resources, opportunities and constraints

- Management of the learning event

- The organizational climate

---

## REVIEW ACTIVITY

Finally, here are some questions which you can either tackle as coursework (if you are a student); discuss with fellow-students or colleagues; or simply think about now that you have completed this chapter:

- Show how you would use the principles of learning to help you in designing a training programme for a specific type of work with which you are familiar.

- Illustrate from incidents in your own organization, or one with which you are familiar, how practical issues can affect the formulation of a learning task.

## CHAPTER 14

# Designing the learning event
# 3: Learning technology

## LEARNING OBJECTIVES

After reading this chapter and completing the various activities it contains, you should:

1  Understand what is mean by the terms 'the technology of training' and 'learning (or training) technology'

2  Be able to select media and methods for a learning event using a simple checklist.

### Learning technology

First, terminology. We can use 'technology' in two ways in connection with training. First, when we refer to 'the technology of training and development' we mean:

**The systems, procedures and methods whereby the entire training and development effort is organized, including those relating to assessing needs, and planning, implementing and evaluating training and development activities.**

Thus in one company a structured, systematic approach to planning training may be characteristic of its 'technology' whilst in another there may be quite a different way of doing things.

'Learning (or training) technology', on the other hand, means:

**The media and methods used to convey learning to the learner.**

To this we can add two further definitions:

**Media of learning are the routes, or channels, through which learning is transmitted to the learner.**

**Methods of learning are the ways in which that learning is transmitted.**

Learning technology in this sense leaves, in this country, much to be desired. For example, in the 1987 Institute of Training and Development (ITD) media awards the standard of entries proved to be too low to justify gold awards in any but one category. Announcing the winners at the presentation ceremony in April, the ITD treasurer Ken Gardner said that lack of adequate support material; unsuitable choice or use of the medium; and an inadequate statement of objectives, of the target audience and of methods of use were the main weaknesses. He added that in several cases expensive well-produced programmes, made by commercial companies, were aimed at such broad audiences that they were probably ineffective with any sector; a telling indictment, which indicates that lack of skill in crucial areas of training is far more widespread than many would suppose, and extends to a considerable number of external 'professionals' whose services would be a significant cost to any organization employing them. The more that training staff working within organizations develop expertise in the design of learning events, the less likely it will be that their organizations will have to bear the consequences of such expensive mistakes.

The opposite danger, perhaps, is to get so immersed in the pursuit of new training technology that the fundamentals which make for a successful learning event are forgotten. In the first of *Personnel Management*'s new section on 'Training and Technology' Nick Rushby, head of the Training Technologies unit at Sundridge Park Management Centre, wrote:

**I have an uneasy feeling that training technologists become too concerned for the glamorous technology — to the detriment of the training, and of the necessary process of innovation which involves much more than providing alternative ways of training.**

*(Personnel Management, January 1988)*

He then points to the need to concentrate on the technology of training rather than on training technology.

Having made these important preliminary points, let us now look at some of the most widely used media and methods. The following list shows some major media together with examples of the kind of methods most frequently associated with them:

| MEDIA | METHODS |
|---|---|
| Oral (spoken word) | Talk, lecture, discussion, seminar |
| Printed (written word) | Handouts, books, distance learning texts |
| Radio, TV, computers | Wide variety of methods |
| On the job | Learning from a supervisor or co-worker; picking up learning by trial and error; using a training manual or a self-administered training package; coaching; job rotation; any form of integrating learning and work |
| Off the job | Any learning event organized away from the place where the learner does his/her everyday work |
| Vestibule | Simulated work situation, in a training room or centre, or other premises near the workplace |

**Figure 7:  Some media and methods of learning**

Obviously a learning event can use several media and a great variety of methods. For example, an external management course would be, by definition, using the 'off the job' medium; however, it might contain a significant element of work-related project work, to be completed when the manager goes back to the workplace, and therefore would also be using the 'on the job' medium. Furthermore, it might rely heavily on the oral medium, an also make significant use of the medium of printed texts. Perhaps, on the other hand, virtually the entire programme might be off the job, but reliant on a mixture of radio, television, and printed texts, as with the Open University's 'Effective Manager' unit. So:

> **One learning event may use several media, as well as a number of different methods.**

It is not the purpose of this chapter to acquaint the reader with media and methods in any detail, but rather to explain what 'technology' means in relation to a learning event, and to discuss what criteria should be used in order to decide which medium or media and methods to include in a particular learning system. For a full discussion of media and methods, Torrington and Chapman (1983) have a most informative chapter, and Kenney and colleagues are, as usual, very helpful (1979; 1986). There are also many articles in personnel and training journals, a few of which are listed in the chapter references at the end of this book in order to demonstrate the topics which are at present of particular interest to designers of learning events. One of the clearest and most practical discussions I have read is in Gagne's book (1965), and again in what follows I have been influenced by his ideas.

It is important to be clear that:

> **There is no one best medium or method, whether for a particular kind of learning objective, or learner group, or learning event.**

Certain media and methods may enjoy current popularity. For example, computer-assisted learning methods are in vogue because of their increasing availability, cheapness, the stimulating interaction they offer between the learner and the learning material, and the fact that they are adaptable to the learner's needs in terms of time, place, pace and feedback. Open learning can be described as a generalized medium, to which maximum publicity was initially given by the many Manpower Services Commission-sponsored 'Open Tech' projects, and later by the 'Open College' initiative. Within the open learning medium, distance learning is a widely popularized method, which may be used through the specific media of television, radio, cassettes, printed texts or computerized instruction courses. In this connection it is interesting to note that part of the Open College scheme involves a national Distance Learning centre, to which all learners will have access through a great many local and regional access points.

However, no matter how popular a medium or method may be at a particular point in time, there is no evidence to support a general superiority of any one medium or method, so other criteria for selection must be found. In fact a simple 3-point checklist based upon the points made in our previous two chapters will act as an adequate guide to the designer:

## 1  Consider the learning task
A properly defined set of objectives will tell the designer about the situations to which the learner will have to respond after the learning event, and the specific behavioural outcomes that the event must help the learner to achieve. These situations and outcomes must therefore be built into the learning event in some way, and this will give the designer ideas about appropriate media and methods. Furthermore, the particular learners involved will have characteris-

tics and skills, knowledge and attitudes which will indicate that certain media and methods are more applicable than others.

### Example

A course on time management: it may have up to 20 members, and can last no more than a day; it is to be held off the job in the company's training centre; and the learning objective is that course members should, by the end of the day, know and be able to use six methods of time management in the organization of their daily workload.

Oral language could be used as a primary medium, with methods ranging from lectures to one-to-one tuition and guidance, and including large or small group work with or without tutors at particular points in the learning process. Or the oral medium could use methods like audio cassettes or a video to transmit information, depending on how effective these are likely to be given the particular group of learners concerned. Case study work based on real-life situations of the learners will be useful learning vehicles, but in-tray exercises are likely to be even more effective, since they offer exact simulations of everyday reality.

### 2   Consider the principles of learning and their practical application

Having considered a number of media and methods which suit the learning objectives and the learners, the next stage is to consider how well each of them will achieve the practical application of learning principles. Here we must remember the eight practical points made in Chapter 13:

Design an appropriate structure and culture

Stimulate the learners

Help understanding

Include appropriate learning activities

Build on existing learning

Guide the learners

Ensure that learning is retained

Ensure that learning is transferred

In point 1 above we ended up with the possibility of using either oral or printed language, or both, as media, and a variety of methods were seen as attractive. But which of these media and methods, given the need to help our particular group of learners to become efficient quickly in time management, would be most likely to result in effective learning, going down our eight points? One task is to learn six methods of time management: should we use oral or printed language for this task, or a mix of the two? Perhaps orally-guided instruction would achieve better stimulation and reinforcement of learning, because printed instructions alone may not be clear enough for some of the learners. Or perhaps a printed list could act as a back-up to the oral medium? If the learning has to be done quickly, but the results applied immediately in the work situation, then undoubtedly the learners will need some form of written record, and to ensure accuracy, a short printed list given out by the tutor will probably be of real value to all of them.

When thinking about whether to use case studies or an in-tray exercises, prior discussion with some of the learners may well reveal that they would prefer in-tray exercises, and would find case studies too artificial (no matter how carefully designed) and time-consuming, given that there are going to be 20 course members, and only a day to cover the course content. The in-tray exercise may take just as long, but offers absolutely transferable learning. Therefore it emerges as most satisfactory, because it is most likely to stimulate the learners, to help them achieve and reinforce correct responses.

So at this second stage we narrow the field of choice by selecting those media and methods that look as though they will best incorporate the main principles of learning.

## 3   Consider practical issues
We must look at what we can and cannot afford, in relation to our total budget and to the learning environment (physical, social, and organizational). Remember here the importance of the culture and structure of the organization, which may favour some media and methods. For example, some senior managers may not support external courses as a way of developing their subordinate managers, whilst others may see such courses as an essential part of the developmental process. We must also obtain data on past effectiveness of certain media and methods, and on their current effectiveness in other organizations using them for similar learning situations.

At this point we may discover, from previous experience with similar groups, that one of the best methods of starting our day on time management is to give the learners about an hour around the table to explain in turn briefly what they hope the day will achieve, and their own particular needs/problems in relation to time management. If group discussion is possible in terms of the available time for the workshop, and since it is an extremely cheap as well as obviously effective learning method, we will probably build it into the programme. In the same way all the other media and methods are looked at and final choices are made.

Thus, to summarize, when selecting media and methods of learning the designer should consider:

The learning task

Principles of learning

Practical issues

No medium or method is universally effective. All have advantages or disadvantages in the particular learning situation. They must therefore be chosen carefully, and they must be acceptable to the organization which is providing resources, financial and other, to use them. Usually learning events need a combination of different media and methods, and must be flexible enough to enable changes to be made if learning problems develop.

In order to bring together the major learning points contained in this and the two preceding chapters on the design of learning, I am including at this point a major exercise for you to attempt yourself. It will require you to use your learning on appraisal (in Chapter 11) and to apply all the learning points contained in this chapter, and in Chapters 12 and 13. I will summarize these points here, but you may wish to go back to the detail of some of them at various times whilst you are tackling the Activity.

**Summary of Key Points Relevant to Designing the Learning Event:**
There are 5 sets of factors to consider in the design of a structured learning event:

- The learning task

- Principles of learning

- Practical issues

- Learning technology

- Evaluation.

The learning task comprises 3 elements:

- The overall purpose of the learning event

- The learning objectives

- The learners.

There are 4 key principles of learning

- Drive

- Stimulus

- Response

- Reinforcement

Practical issues are of 3 major kinds:

- Resources, opportunities and constraints

- Management of the learning event

- The organizational climate

---

## ACTIVITY

## CASE STUDY: The Retail Store's Appraisal Project (Part 3)

In previous chapters there have been descriptions of a consultancy assignment relating to the development of an appraisal scheme for a major departmental store. Please now re-read those descriptions (pages 231 to 237, and pages 251 to 253) before proceeding further with this exercise.

The outcome of the final discussion between the consultant and the Managing Director (MD) of the store was agreement to run a weekend workshop for the 15 managers and supervisors in six weeks' time.

Given the following additional information, please design a programme for the workshop, showing what will happen each day, session by session, throughout the weekend, (the length of each session should also be shown) with reference to the structure, culture, and learning media and methods that will be used. An example of the kind of format to follow for the programme is:

## DAY 1

10.00-10.45 am    INTRODUCTION
                  Explanation of the workshop objectives, struc-
                  ture and content, and discussion of these with
                  workshop members.

                                                *(Consultant)*

**Additional information**
*The learning task*
The 15 managers and supervisors, only four of whom know anything at all about appraisal (each having previously worked in an organization that had annual appraisal interviews), are to design their own appraisal scheme for their organization. The learning objectives are shown on page 265.

In the group of 15, 11 are managers and four are supervisors (two female). It has been agreed between the MD, Personnel Officer and the consultant that in all documentation about the appraisal project, all 15 will be referred to as 'managers', since a major aim of the project is to build up amongst all of them a managerial group identity. They come from a variety of different functions in the store: for example, one of the women is a supervisor of canteen staff, and the other of clerical staff; one of the male supervisors is responsible for the transport section, and the other for the packing department. Most have worked either at that store or another branch of it since leaving school or (in the case of three of the 'career' managers, university). None have any managerial qualifications, although several have professional or other qualifications related to the work they do. From an initial intense suspicion of the appraisal project (which they believed at first to be connected with redundancy or assessment for pay review or promotion) they are now looking forward to the workshop. All have had quite lengthy discussions with the consultant about the aims and desired outcomes of the workshop, and as a result most see appraisal as likely to be of real value in their jobs in future. The position of the supervisors is not quite so clearcut: they still think in terms of the shopfloor, rather than as members of the management team, and the women in particular have said very little to the consultant, and do not display any enthusiasm for the workshop — but neither have they indicated any opposition to it.

## Purpose of the workshop on appraisal

The overall purpose of the workshop is that the course members should design a simple pilot scheme for the appraisal of management performance at the store, and that proposals for the scheme and its operation should be prepared for submission to the Board of Directors.

The scheme that workshop members design will have the following aims:

1    to act as a vehicle for the review of the current work performance of store managers;

2    to lead to agreement between each appraiser and appraisee on the appraisee's work objectives, expressed in an Action Plan to cover an agreed future period (eg 6 months or a year);

3    to lead to the diagnosis of learning needs of each appraisee, primarily in their present work, but also in their continuous development; and to agreement on proposals for meeting those needs.

## Final behavioural objectives of the workshop

By the end of the workshop members will:

1    know about the major practices and problems in appraisal systems that are being experienced in a wide range of British organizations;

2    understand the major factors that explain performance of an individual in the work situation;

3    understand some of the principal systems and methods of appraisal which are relevant for assessing and improving managers' existing performance in their jobs.

4    have had practice in analysing and evaluating specific appraisal schemes;

5    have undertaken an evaluation of the ways in which performance is currently appraised at the store and have helped to design a simple pilot scheme for the appraisal of managerial performance in the store.

## Resources

The workshop will be held in a local hotel, from 10.00 am on Friday to about 2.00 pm on the Sunday. The consultant will be accommodated at the hotel throughout the weekend, but workshop members will not stay there overnight, unless they have a long distance to travel from home (none do). The workshop can go on until any time in the evening, and the MD has arranged for dinner at the hotel for all members on the Friday and Saturday nights. The usual equipment can be available for the consultant, should he wish to use it: overhead projector and screen; closed circuit television, film and video equipment, and so on.

The workshop should be timed to last for approximately 20 hours (excluding time for refreshments and meal breaks).

---

## FEEDBACK NOTES

It would be pointless to give any structured 'feedback' for this exercise, since there are a great many different ways in which this workshop can be planned. Ideas can be exchanged with fellow students with tutors, or with colleagues.

No matter what kind of design has been selected, it must be able to be justified by reference to:

The learning task

Principles of learning

Practical issues

Learning technology

Evaluation (in this connection, thought must be given to how evaluation will be done, when and by whom)

The programme should have a structure, culture, content and technology that are appropriate given the learning task, principles of learning, and resources available for the learning event.

The programme actually designed for the workshop was very participative and interactive in its structure, with a team-centred culture, and contained as wide a variety as possible of learning methods, bearing in mind the different learning styles and skills likely to be present in the learners, and the need to maintain continued stimulation in a group not accustomed to this kind of activity. The information content was conveyed in the first half of the workshop, with design activities taking up the second half, culminating in the team's presentation of an initial set of recommendations for an appraisal scheme to the Managing Director (who, on the advice of the consultant, had only come in at certain points during the weekend). Thereafter, when further work had been done on the recommendations, the Report would be submitted to the Board. Throughout the three days there were tasks of different kinds for members to do, in order to ensure that they were actively involved from the start.

At the end of the workshop each team member was given an evaluation questionnaire asking for comments on how far they felt the workshop had achieved the purpose and objectives set, and a number of other questions related to what they had liked best and least, found most and least useful, etc. The evaluations were highly favourable, and particularly commented on the way real teamwork and a team culture had built up during the workshop. Over the next few weeks groups of the members met again repeatedly to finish work on the report and get all the details of the pilot scheme and its operational procedures sorted out.

The report was finally submitted to and accepted by the Board, and after training in appraisal skills had been carried out the scheme was quickly established. There was a six-month and then an annual review of its operations, and two years later it is still running with the full commitment of all the management team, and has led to a sustained investment in training and continuous development in the store. Currently discussions are being held with a view to extending appraisal throughout the store, again on a collaborative basis.

---

I hope you have found this Activity useful, both as a design exercise in its own right, and as a way of revising the various learning points covered in Chapters 12, 13 and 14.

---

## CONCLUSION

Having read this chapter and completed the various activities it contains, you should now:

1   Understand what is meant by the terms 'technology of training' and 'learning (or training) technology'

2   Be able to select media and methods for a learning event using a simple checklist.

The main learning points connected with these objectives are:

### Learning technology
'The technology of training and development' means the systems, procedures and methods whereby the entire training and development effort is organized, including those relating to assessing needs, and planning, implementing and evaluating training and development activities.

'Learning technology' means the media and methods used to convey learning to the learner.

*Media* of learning are the routes, or channels, through which learning is transmitted to the learner.

*Methods* of learning are the ways in which that learning is transmitted.

One learning event may use several media, as well as a number of different methods.

There is no one best medium or method, whether for a particular kind of learning objective, or learner group, or learning event.

When selecting media and methods of learning, the designer can use a 3-point checklist:

- The learning task

- Principles of learning

- Practical issues

When designing a structured learning event or programme, it must finally be justifiable by reference to:

The learning task

Principles of learning

Practical issues

Learning technology

Evaluation

## REVIEW ACTIVITY

Finally, here are some questions which you can either tackle as essays (if you are a student); discuss with fellow-students or colleagues; or simply think about now that you have completed this chapter:

- Justify the training methods and media you would use in running an induction programme.

- As there is little empirical evidence about the relative effectiveness of training techniques such as the lecture or the group discussion, what factors should determine an instructor's choice of such techniques?

- What do you understand by computer-based training? What are its advantages and disadvantages?

- Distinguish between 'open learning' and 'distance learning'. Give reasons why training officers should be concerned with these approaches to learning.

- You are planning a new 'Introduction to Management' course for new supervisors in your organization, and you want to introduce a 2-day participative experience on 'leadership'. Draft and explain a suitable programme, giving reasons for your choice of methods.

CHAPTER 15

# Evaluation of the learning event

## LEARNING OBJECTIVES

After reading this chapter and completing the various activities it contains, you should:

1 Know the crucial questions to ask when faced with the task of evaluating a learning event

2 Know the criteria to apply when selecting the evaluator of a learning event

3 Be able to develop an evaluation strategy in a particular situation where evaluation needs to be carried out

4 Know what factors to consider when selecting evaluation techniques.

It is not the purpose of this chapter to review the literature about evaluation; nor to assess the merits of the various approaches that can be encountered there. For that kind of discussion the reader is referred to Kenney and Reid (1986); and for a detailed account of the two models on which I have mainly based my approach in this chapter, to Hamblin (1974), and to Warr, Bird and Rackham (1970). Neither does this chapter cover evaluation skills in any detail, being concerned rather with the criteria that should govern the selection of techniques, but see pages 123 to 135 on ways of measuring the training investment.

In this chapter the aim is to help you to develop a simple, practical approach to the key issues underlying the evaluation task, so that, when faced with the need to organize evaluation in a specific situation, you will (should it be necessary) be able to choose an appropriate evaluator, and also select effective strategy and techniques.

## Evaluation
Evaluation is an essential part of the learning process. Without it there can be no certainty that a learning event has achieved its objectives; or that, even if it has done so, those objectives were themselves worthwhile; or that, whatever the success and relevance of the learning event, it was carried out in the most cost-effective way. And without all that information, there cannot be valid planning of future learning events. Therefore we can say that:

**Evaluation looks at the total value of a learning event, not just at whether and how far it has achieved its learning objectives. It thereby puts the event in its wider context, and provides information essential to future planning.**

## Key Questions Related to Evaluation
Faced with the task of evaluation, the first step is to answer five crucial questions:

WHY is evaluation to be done?

WHAT will be evaluated?

HOW will evaluation be done?

WHO will do the evaluation?

WHEN is it to be done?

Let us look now at these questions in detail:

### Why evaluate?
We have already defined evaluation as the assessment of the total value of a learning event. *A Challenge to Complacency* (Coopers and Lybrand, 1985) emphasized the importance of evaluation as a means of changing attitudes to training, by showing in measurable ways the value to the organization of investing in training. It also reported a generally low level of skill in both cost-benefit analysis and a more general evaluation, notably amongst personnel practitioners. If training is to become a mainline business function, evaluation of it is a major need in most organizations today.

There are many reasons why evaluation may be required; perhaps to justify the cost of a particular learning event, or to establish its effects on the learners, or to measure the impact of the event on job performance, or on the profitability, performance, flexibility or survival of the organization as a whole. Each of these aims may involve the evaluator in a different set of activities, and will provide the frame of reference to all the remaining questions. The answer to this first question. 'Why?' will therefore also indicate the appropriate answers to the questions 'What, how, who and when?'

**What to evaluate?**
There are four sets of factors that should be evaluated, if learning is to be seen as an activity built into the system of the organization, and they form the basis of the CIRO model developed by Warr, Bird and Rackham (1970). I have produced a modification of that and of Hamblin's model (1974) for use in this chapter because I have found in consultancy work as well as in training sessions on evaluation that this seems to offer an easily-understandable theoretical framework, together with a simple yet comprehensive practical approach which can be applied to any evaluation task. However, for a full appreciation of the models on which I have based my ideas, it is important to read the two texts referred to above. They are particularly valuable for guidance on evaluation techniques and procedures.

The factors to be evaluated are:

The CONTEXT within which the learning event has taken place: how accurately needs were initially diagnosed, why this particular kind of learning was decided on as a solution, and how and what learning objectives were set. Examination of the organizational culture and structure is an important part of context evaluation.

The INPUTS to the learning event: the resources that were available for the event, and those that were actually used (personnel, physical and financial resources, time and natural learning resources); the learning structure and culture, content, media and methods; and the final cost of the learning event. Also the people who went through the learning event (the learners themselves) in terms of whether that membership and selection of the learners was valid.

The REACTIONS to the learning event by the various parties involved in it, especially in relation to the reactions that it was originally intended it should achieve.

The OUTCOMES of the learning event: the effects of that event by reference to the objectives set for it and the outcomes it has actually achieved.

**How to evaluate?**
This will depend on what is being evaluated. Using the same approach, evaluation can be carried out as follows:

*Context evaluation*
Look at the information that gave rise to the diagnosis of the original need for the learning event.

Then examine how that information was analysed and the learning needs established.

Then examine how learning objectives were set, how far they took into account the organizational context within which the learning would have to take place, and to which of the following levels they were mainly related:

*Level 1   Reactions*
Objectives concerned with the sort of reactions that the event is intended to achieve in the learners — for example, satisfaction with the media and methods used, or with the tutors or other mentors involved; commitment to the event itself, and/or to further learning events, etc.

*Level 2   Learning*
Objectives concerned with developing specific knowledge, skills and attitudes in the learner.

*Level 3   Job performance*
Objectives concerned with changing individuals' work behaviour and job performance.

*Level 4   Departments*
Objectives concerned with achieving improvements or changes at departmental level.

*Level 5   The organization*
Objectives concerned with achieving some overall organizational outcome; or with reinforcing or changing particular organizational values (for example, improving profitability, flexibility, or the organization's ability to survive, or the general morale and commitment of its workforce); or with changing the organization's culture and/or structure.

To achieve effective diagnosis of the context of a learning event, the evaluator should examine how far there has been:

**1   *The formulation of a philosophy and policies for human resource development in the organization.***
This may be expressed as a systematically-derived training purpose, policy and plan, using either 'total' or 'problem-centred' strategies to assess needs and draw up a training plan (see Chapter 6, and the 8 steps described there:

- The training need

- Possible solutions

- Select training events

- Create training plan

- Establish priorities

- Apply budgetary constraints

- Communicate results

- Evaluation).

Or it may be expressed in policies, allocation of roles and responsibilities, and identification of learning opportunities and needs relevant to a 'Continuous Development' approach (see Appendix 1)

Or there may simply be a general culture relating to human resource development in the organization, within which learning initiatives and specific training activities are generated.

Whatever the context, it must be analysed and understood, in order that the learning event is placed in its intended perspective when evaluation takes place.

**2   *Operational analysis***
Where people have to be trained to do particular jobs, has there been job training analysis (as described in Chapter 8) in order to arrive at a valid specification of the knowledge, skills and attitudes needed to the jobs for which training is to be provided?
   Where people are being continuously develped in the workplace, has there been identification of learning opportunities and needs, especially by reference to careful analysis of operational plans and

changes; job descriptions and specifications; and special reviews and audits of parts of the learning system? (See Appendix 1).

### 3 Assessment of individual needs

How were individual needs for learning assessed, and by whom? Were the appraisal processes and the decisions to which they gave rise likely to be valid and reliable? (See Chapters 9 to 11.) Where continuous development is a major learning approach, are appraisal forms, guidance notes, and interviews designed to focus on the integration of learning with work? (See Appendix 1.)

### Input Evaluation

Here, the evaluator should consider the relevance of inputs to the 3 factors examined in Chapters 12 to 14 of this book:

#### The learning task
The purpose and objectives of the learning event; and the learning group.

#### Principles of learning
How far these have been built into the learning event.

#### Practical issues
How far the inputs were cost-efficient, cost-effective and feasible given the resources available; how well, and at what costs, the learning event was managed; and how effectively the learning events were planned, designed and run with reference to the organizational climate.

### Reactions evaluation

Reactions of learners to the learning event can be obtained in many ways, the most obvious including questionnaires, interviews (especially appraisal interviews) and informal discussions. Hamblin (1974) particularly recommends the use of session assessments on training courses, where each session can be looked at in terms of any aspects in which the evaluator is interested; enjoyment, length of time given to discussion, level of presentation, informational content, relevance, length of the session; or to monitor the progress of a practical activity, perhaps with a view to establishing typical learning curves of different types of learners. Assessments can be done at the end of a session, or at the end of the whole programme, or at periods after the completion of the programme.

### Outcomes evaluation

Outcomes can be measured at the following levels:

### Immediate (Levels 1 and 2)
The reactions of the learners to the learning event (as described above).

Changes in the learner's knowledge, skills, attitudes measured at the completion of the training — for example by tests — compared to the level and type of knowledge, skills and attitudes at the start of that programme (as established by appraisal, or by tests, or by repertory grid, etc).

### Intermediate (Level 3)
Changes that subsequently take place in the trainee's job behaviour, as measured by appraisal, observation, discussion with the learner's superior/colleagues/staff, performance records, the views of the learners themselves and how far these are in accordance with the views of others (research quoted by Warr *et al*, 1970, indicates that there is usually quite a close correlation between the two sets of views).

### Ultimate (Levels 4 and 5)
Changes that take place in the entire department or organization at some stage after the completion of the training programme. This is the most difficult level of evaluation, and one that is too rarely attempted. However with careful thought, reasonable evaluation even here should be possible, providing that clear objectives have been set before training begins, and ways of measuring the achievement of those objectives have been agreed. The sort of changes involved might include alterations in departmental output, costs, scrap rates, turnover, accident frequency; or improvement in the overall profitability or the effectiveness in some other way of the total organization.

When it is continuous learning that is being evaluated, the kind of outcomes expected are contained in the Institute of Personnel Management's Code (see Appendix 1).

### Who should evaluate?
Choosing the evaluator is a key task in the evaluation process. Trainers, line managers, personnel function, top management, external consultant, will all bring their own viewpoints and aims to the task, so that none can be relied upon to be free of bias. Even the consultant may see evaluation as an opportunity to influence the organization to use their services in some other connection, or may take an approach to evaluation different from that of the organization, which could leave the organization very vulnerable to manipulation.

Finally, evaluation is a sensitive and technically difficult process, and the outcomes will only be as reliable and valid as the process that has produced them; for a formidable critique, for example, of the customary end-of-course evaluation run by trainers, see the article by Easterby-Smith and Tanton (1985).

Evaluators must therefore be carefully chosen. A practical checklist that can be applied to potential 'candidates' is as follows:

## Objectivity
How objective are they likely to be? What, if any, connection have they had with the design, running and outcomes of the learning event? Are they likely to cover up any weaknesses or strengths in the event — or to exaggerate them?

## Expertise
How skilled are they likely to be? Have they done any evaluation before? For whom? With what results? Can anyone give you an assessment of their abilities in the field? Does their explanation of how they will approach the task convince you of their knowledge, skill and professionalism?

## Interpersonal skills
Are they likely to obtain accurate and comprehensive information? What sort of relationship do they have, or can they be expected to form, with those whose views on the learning event they need to obtain? Can they expect to receive full trust and co-operation? What sort of relationship have they established with you, and what does that tell you about their interpersonal skills?

## Credibility
How credible are they likely to be with people in the organization? This will largely depend on the factors already examined above: their perceived objectivity, expertise and interpersonal skills. However, it will also, and crucially, depend on how quickly and well they establish an understanding of the 'world' of the organization: its tasks, structure and culture, technology, people, and environment. It is not necessary for an evaluator to have previous knowledge of the organization itself, but certainly previous knowledge of a similar organization, and the ability to demonstrate an awareness of its business and of its social, political, system is very important. Careful questioning and the requirement of a potential evaluator to explain in detail how they would approach and handle their task will be needed in order to assess their likely credibility.

## Cost

What will be the cost of using them? If, for example, you are considering using a consultant, will the fee be worth the end result? Could anyone else do the job more cheaply, and to an acceptable standard? If you were to use your own staff, how long would the task take them; could they be spared for that amount of time; would they have the expertise to do the task? If you use a consultant, what will happen when they leave? Will they have trained your staff to take over from them, especially in implementing any further stages of a lengthy project. Robinson (1985) observes that staff should be trained to give effect to consultants' recommendations, adding:

> **Incurring the cost of a resident consultant to carry out the implementation stage of the project is unnecessary, although it is advisable that the contract should allow for access to a consultant for advice.**
>
> *(Robinson, 1985)*

Thus a 5-point checklist to apply to the selection of an evaluator is:

Objectivity

Expertise

Interpersonal skills

Credibility

Cost.

Now, let us attempt an Activity which is based on a real-life consultancy assignment (only those details which would enable the firm in question to be identified have been altered) and involves choosing someone to evaluate a major development programme.

---

## ACTIVITY

### CASE STUDY: The Local Authority Evaluation Project (Part 1)

A Local Authority has, over the two years from 1982 to 1984, run a management and supervisory development programme in conjunction with the local polytechnic. There has been no clerical staff training, but 110 executive officers are due to be trained in the next stage of the programme, if it is decided to run one. So far, in Stage 1 of the programme, there have been six courses, with a total of 154 people attending, at a total cost of about £33,000. However, that figure only takes in the cost of holding the six courses at a local hotel, the fees and expenses of the three polytechnic staff who acted as tutors on the course, and consultancy fees related to the design and review of those courses. It does not take into account staff time involved in every stage of the programme, from the diagnosis of needs through to the running and review of the courses (the Authority has no training manager, so the Personnel Manager and her staff had to do this work on top of their normal workload; the Personnel Manager, an intelligent IPM-qualified woman of 39, has some experience of training, although none of evaluation, other than post-course review sessions). Nor does it take into account travel expenses of course members and personnel staff; the cost of course materials; overtime payments to supervisory staff, necessitated by absences on the courses; and the cost to the Authority in terms of non-availability for normal duties of staff who opted for flexitime instead of overtime payments. All of these costs came to a further total of £13,000.

The Authority now wants Stage 1 of the programme to be evaluated, with two aims:

1   to produce as accurate and comprehensive an assessment as possible (given the constraints of time and information sources) of the costs and value of the programme over the two years;

2   to produce recommendations arising from the evaluation, which may be helpful to the Authority in planning the future direction and organization of training and development, with special reference to whether to proceed with Stage 2 of the programme (in conjunction with the polytechnic), or to take some other approach to the training of the 110 executive officers.

Before the programme began, the Personnel Manager, with the help of a consultant, carried out a diagnosis of training and development needs of staff in the Authority, with special reference to needs related to a major computerization programme that began in 1981 and is still in progress. She drew up a Training Policy and Plan for the Authority, of which the programme forms the major part.

The Chief Executive of the Authority has now to decide who to use as evaluator. The choices are:

1   The Personnel Manager

2   Someone from the polytechnic (not necessarily from the tutors'
    department, as there is a unit in the polytechnic that specializes
    in course evaluation, albeit mainly concerned with evaluation of
    academic courses in the secondary and tertiary education sector)

3   An independent consultant

Using the 5-point checklist:

   Objectivity

   Expertise

   Interpersonal skills

   Credibility

   Cost

analyse who the Authority should choose, and why.

---

## FEEDBACK NOTES

Using the 5-point checklist we can arrive at a carefully considered
decision about who to select as evaluator:

**Objectivity**
It would be difficult for the Personnel Manager to be objective about
a programme that she herself did so much to produce, and
particularly difficult for her to have to admit to any significant
weaknesses in that programme. Equally, anyone from the
polytechnic might hesitate to be too critical when the programme's
tutors were polytechnic staff, and when a further large contract
hangs on the outcome of the evaluation.

**Expertise**
The Personnel Manager is not a professional training specialist, and
has already used a consultant to help with the design and review of
training. Whilst she clearly possesses a sound knowledge of how to
draw up a training policy and plan, and how to organize a training
event, it seems unlikely that she would possess the technical
knowledge and skills needed for this complicated exercise. The

polytechnic's special unit, on the other hand, may have expertise, but evaluation of courses in the educational sector is not fully comparable with evaluating the cost-effectiveness of this kind of managerial and supervisory programme. A consultant would probably have the most expertise, providing that some reliable reference can be produced on their work, and that they demonstrate a skilled approach in discussions about the project, together with a clear understanding of the organization, and the rationale for the programme.

**Interpersonal skills**
The Personnel Manager may well have the best interpersonal skills, if she already has good relationships with key parties in the Authority. However, getting this kind of information is not easy, and essentially she will be trying to find out what people think of a programme with which she has been very closely identified — so is it likely that people will be completely open with her? This latter point may hold true of polytechnic staff also, although if they come from a special unit rather than from the department that produced the programme's tutors, there may not be a problem.

Overall, an independent consultant may be the best choice, although knowledge of how they operate is essential to obtain, and the way in which they themselves explain how they would carry out the task of obtaining information should offer valuable insights here. They should be questioned, in particular, about how they would deal with difficult staff.

**Credibility**
Because of the Personnel Manager's heavy involvement in the programme, and her lack of training experience; and because of the polytechnic's involvement in the programme, together with the value to the polytechnic of securing the Stage 2 contract, both may be viewed by people in the organization as somewhat suspect. Of the three possibilities, a consultant would seem likely to have the highest level of credibility, providing that they are carefully chosen, have a good record of success with similar assignments, and/or can present a detailed and convincing explanation of how they will approach and handle the assignment.

**Cost**
The cost of the Personnel Manager tackling the evaluation task would be quite high, given that she has to carry out all training activities in addition to, or instead of some of, her normal workload. Can she spare the time to do the job? Or what personnel tasks would have to be put aside to enable her to do it? The polytechnic

will probably be cheaper than an independent consultant, but will the results be as good? The answers to the questions already asked would indicate that they probably would not be.

Use of the checklist therefore helps to show that, on all counts, an independent consultant would seem the wisest decision in this case, providing that they are carefully chosen, and that a close relationship is maintained with them by the Authority throughout the evaluation exercise.

---

### When to Evaluate

There are several choices possible here. Evaluation can be carried out:

BEFORE the learning event

DURING the learning event

at the END of the learning event

SOME TIME AFTER the learning event (short term)

LONGER TERM: perhaps a year after the learning event

The decision on when to evaluate should be made by reference to the purpose of the evaluation activity, and to what is to be evaluated.

If the purpose is to find out how valid the learning event was in helping the learners to reach certain levels of skills, knowledge and attitudes by the end of the event, then monitoring them before and at the end of the learning event may be sufficient. However, it would be advisable to evaluate at least once again, at a later date, in order to assess how far learning has been retained.

If the cost-efficiency of the inputs is to be evaluated, then evaluation using reactions of the learners during and at the end of the event, and pre- and post-tests of the learning they have acquired in relation to the event's objectives, would probably prove sufficient.

However, it may be that the cost-effectiveness of a programme needs to be evaluated, in order to decide whether the organization should invest again in such a programme. Then, depending on the objectives set for the programme initially, it may prove necessary to evaluate by reference to job performance in the short term, and then the long-term impact on both job performance and overall organizational trends, in profitability, morale, flexibility, etc.

Finally, what is ideal in theory is rarely feasible in practice, so the timing of evaluation must also take practical considerations into account; to evaluate on five different occasions, for example, would require a high expenditure of resources, and this may not be possible or justifiable given the benefits which can be expected to come from the evaluation effort.

We can therefore conclude this section with the statement:

**The decision on when to evaluate depends on the purpose of the evaluation, on what is to be evaluated, and on practical considerations.**

## Choosing an Evaluation Strategy

'Evaluation strategy' simply means the ways in which the evaluator proposes to handle the task of evaluation. Choice of strategy is a matter of posing, and finding answers to, those five key questions we have been considering so far in this chapter:

WHY

WHAT

HOW

WHO

WHEN

In order to show how a strategy can be developed on the basis of answers to those questions, I am going to continue with the example of the Local Authority's evaluation task, introduced in the previous Activity.

---

## CASE STUDY: The Local Authority Evaluation Project (Part 2)

An independent consultant was approached by the Authority's Personnel Manager. He was known to the Personnel Manager as a specialist in training and development, with considerable knowledge of evaluation, although he had not carried out a project of this kind before. He had done a lot of work with local authorities, and was familiar with their typical systems and procedures. He had not worked with this particular Authority before.

At an initial, exploratory meeting, the consultant and the Personnel Manager discussed the basic parameters of the project. It was at this meeting that the consultant obtained the information contained in Part 1 of this case study (pages 278 to 279).

The meeting ended with agreement that the consultant would prepare written proposals showing how he would carry out the evaluation project, were he to be appointed to do so, and that in the following week he would have a meeting with the Personnel Manager and the Chief Executive of the Authority, in order to present and discuss those proposals.

Knowing that he had both to give the Chief Executive an understanding of the basic parameters of evaluation and also show that he himself had expertise in the area, he produced the following proposals:

........................................................................................................

## EVALUATION PROPOSALS — 'Y' Local Authority Management and Supervisory Training Programme

### The Purpose of the Evaluation Project

I understand that the purpose of the evaluation project is twofold:

1  to enable the value of the first stage of the training programme to be assessed;

2  to provide information which may result in modifications to the next stage of the programme to be made, including the integration of an evaluation system into the design of that programme.

I have based my proposals on this perceived purpose.

### What Will Be Evaluated?

I propose that the evaluation will cover examination of the following:

### Context

This will involve collecting information about the initial work situation and assessing the information that was used to establish training needs. It will also involve examining how training objectives were formulated. This could mean looking at five levels of objectives:

#### Level 1

Desired reactions of the trainees

### Level 2
Learning objectives that were set during the programme

### Level 3
Job behaviour changes that were desired when the trainees were back at work

### Level 4
Departmental improvements/changes that were hoped for as an end result of the whole training programme

### Level 5
Organizational improvements/changes, if any, that were hoped for as an end result of the whole training programme; for example, the overall contributions to be made by the training programme to profitability.

## Inputs
Here, evaluation will be concerned with looking at the resources that were available for training, and those that were used; staff, materials, media and methods, training time, etc. It will also look at the kind of course structure and content that was put into the programme, and at the number and kinds of trainees and why they were selected. An examination then needs to be made of the cost of these inputs, and how effective and efficient they were in helping the managers and supervisors achieve their learning objectives; also how far they were justified by reference to the context and eventual outcomes of the training programme.

## Outcomes
These are the effects of training, and will need to be related back to the objectives that were set at the 'Context' stage. If imprecise objectives were set in relation to outcomes which it is agreed should form the focus of evaluation, then that evaluation will have to be by trial and error.

In part, the decision on which outcomes to examine will therefore depend on how far training objectives were set initially in relation to those outcomes. It will also, however, depend on what the Authority sees as most cost-beneficial and helpful to the organization. Evaluation at level 4 or 5, for instance, can be very time-consuming and in the end may be unproductive, if no clear-cut objectives were set in these areas before training began. On the other hand, obtaining any information in an area of major importance which up to now has been imprecisely defined could help in defining objectives more clearly for the next programme.

## How it is Proposed That Evaluation Should be Carried Out

I would propose that the evaluation of the Authority's Stage 1 management and supervisory training programme be carried out as follows:

### Context evaluation

*Information sources:*

Personnel Manager and programme consultant; trainees (by survey and discussions); other managers (ie who have not yet been through the programme); documentation relating to training needs and plan.

### Input evaluation

*Information sources:*

Personnel Manager and programme consultant; trainees and trainers (by survey and discussions); other managers; documentation relating to training needs and plan, and to types and effectiveness of resources.

### Outcomes evaluation

**Levels 4 and 5 (Departmental and Organizational levels), Information sources:**

Chief Executive and Personnel Manager; managers and a sample of staff who have not been through the programme; trainees (by survey and discussions); documentation on the Authority's training needs and plan.

*Level 3 (Job level), Information sources:*

As for Levels 4 and 5, plus managers of trainees; performance records and/or any other relevant indices of performance. This level will be one of the two main focuses of the evaluation exercise.

*Level 2 (Learning level), Information sources:*

Personnel Manager; trainers and trainees (by survey and discussions); any pre—training, interim or post-training documentation relating to learning possessed by trainees before the programme, and learning developed by that programme. This level will be the other main focus of the evaluation exercise.

*Level 1 (Reactions level), Information sources:*

Personnel Manager; trainers and trainees (by survey and discussions); any documentation on trainees' reactions to the training programme.

Information gained at each level will be used for two purposes:

1  to assess the value of the past training programme;

2  to produce information which will aid decisions to be made on the context, input and desired outcomes of the future training programme.

## Outline Strategy Proposed

It is not within the scope of these proposals to attempt a detailed cost-benefit analysis of the Authority's training programme, but rather to offer an assessment of the general programme at the 5 levels shown, in order to achieve the two purposes outlined above to a significant degree. Because of the short timescale for the project, it will not be possible to do a detailed evaluation at each of the 5 levels outlined above; instead, I have suggested concentrating the evaluation on levels 2 and 3, since they are likely to yield the most valid and reliable information about the value of the programme. From this it should be possible to give quite detailed recommendations about the future direction of training and development in the Authority.

Although it would, of course, be desirable to do a major evaluation of the organizational and departmental outcomes (levels 4 and 5) of the programme, this is an innately difficult task: many other factors could intervene between the learning event and any ultimate changes or improvements at those two levels. It is made more difficult in this particular case because I understand that no clearcut organizational or departmental objectives were set for the programme, nor were any ways of measuring achievement of those objectives through the programme agreed. Therefore I do not feel, with the information I currently possess, that spending time on an attempt to carry out detailed evaluation of organizational or departmental outcomes would be at all as productive (given the purpose of the Project) as focusing on Levels 2 and 3.

## Cost of the Evaluation Project

£X, excluding consultant's travel and subsistence expenses (if any) made up as follows:

**FEES:**       £Y per day

**PROJECT:**   Design of structure of project, and of
                       forms, interview check-lists, etc          5 days

                       Data collection and collation               10 days

                       Analysis of data and production of report    20 days

TOTAL DAYS                                   35 days

FEE                                          £X

EXPENSES                          To be inserted

**Timescale for the project**
If work on the project commences during the first week of May, the evaluation report could be produced by the end of June.

Signed:                                      Date:

...............................................................................................

(**Comment:**   In this document the consultant set out as clearly as he could WHY he understood the evaluation was to be done; and therefore WHAT should be evaluated and HOW evaluation should be carried out. He outlined the evaluation strategy he thought appropriate and feasible, and ended with an indication of the timescale within which the project could be completed, thus answering the question 'WHEN'. When evaluation strategy is being developed, it is essential that both parties have a clear understanding of one another's views on these crucial questions, and as we shall see, by setting out his own views in detail, the consultant was able to elicit from the Chief Executive new information that at this very early stage changed the consultant's understanding of how the project should be directed.)
    Having received these proposals, the Chief Executive then held a meeting with the consultant, at which his Deputy and the Personnel Manager were both present. The consultant's file notes on this meeting are reproduced below.

...............................................................................................

MEMORANDUM

*To:*    File                    *Date:*      21.4.84.
*From:*  Self                    *Reference:* LA Project

*Subject:* Meeting at Local Authority, 21.4.84.

I had a one and a half hour meeting with John White (Chief Executive); Philip Pierce (his Deputy), and Sandra Birtle (Personnel Manager), at which we discussed my proposals for the evaluation project.

## Aims of Evaluation

White said that he agreed with the need to evaluate the context and outcomes of the programme. However, the level of outcomes that he wanted the evaluation to focus on in most detail was Level 5 — the overall impact of the training programme on the organization. He also regarded evaluation at Level 4 (impact of the programme on departments) as essential. Levels 1, 2 and 3 need only be examined in so far as information on them would contribute to the evaluation of Levels 4 and 5. His reasons for his wish for evaluation to focus on Levels 4 and 5 became evident when he gave a detailed explanation of the aims that he wanted the evaluation to serve. These differed significantly in their emphasis from those initially described to me by Birtle (White had obviously only now really begun to think them through), and they do put a different complexion on the evaluation exercise.

The purpose of the evaluation of the management and supervisory Programme is in fact:

1  To determine whether training has contributed to the ultimate aim of improving the motivation and commitment of managers and supervisors to their work. For the Authority this is crucial, because some of the staff are very departmentalized, both in their work and in their attitudes, and the real value and meaning of their work is not always easy to measure or for other departments to appreciate. Staff have also had to adapt to many changes, primary amongst them the computerization programme and an increased push for cost-efficiency; so the commitment of all managers to whatever may be asked of them in their jobs is crucial to the success of the organization.

2  To give Council Members information on which to judge the value of the training programme, which is the first of its kind ever to be mounted in the Authority, and as such has represented a considerable act of faith and investment of money by the Authority. The Members' main concern, again, is not so much with whether learning objectives have been achieved, or with benefits at individual levels, but with the overall impact of the programme on departmental and organizational performance.

3  To enable the Council Members to decide whether training is an important investment to pursue in the future; and, specifically, whether to continue to support the programme through into a stage 2.

We discussed the implications of these aims, and agreed that what would therefore need to be evaluated would be:

The **CONTEXT** of the entire programme; that remains essential, for obvious reasons.

**INPUTS** to the programme only in so far as such evaluation would provide essential information regarding the overall value of the programme. Attention will therefore be given mainly to the membership, management, staffing and overall design of the programme, and to the financial investment in the programme. Evaluation will not be concerned in any significant way with the detail of the programme (course design, media and methods, content, etc).

**OUTCOMES** of the programme at departmental and organizational levels. Outcomes at other levels will only be examined in so far as they give important information about the impact of the programme in that wider context.

**REACTIONS** of trainees, trainers, and others involved in the programme will be the main source of information to be used in the evaluation of context, inputs and outcomes, since no detailed objectives were set at organizational or departmental level for the programme; there is little if any objective information about either individual, job or organizational behaviour and performance before the programme; and apart from some fairly informal 'reactions' discussions, no immediate evaluation of the effects of the programme on individual learning, on job performance, or on departments or organization was carried out once each of the six courses had finished. (The programme as a whole ends this month.)

### Intervening Factors Relating to Organizational Performance at the Authority

It having become clear that evaluation would have to focus on Levels 4 and 5, I explained to White that I needed to know what other factors, apart from the programme, might have caused departmental or organizational changes over the past two years.

We agreed that evaluation at Level 5 was the most difficult, and likely to be the most imprecise, form of evaluation, because of the number of factors that could have intervened between training and ultimate performance. White said that the main intervening factors here were:

When the training programme began, the computerization programme was already a year old. Thus some of the training would
have been affected by the anticipation of computerization, and
some by the introduction of it.

Computerization itself had changed people's jobs and roles in
many ways, and this had only been substantially built into training
in 1983/4.

Computerization had been introduced in April 1981, and before
that staff were told that in future their work would be evaluated
and measured much more stringently than ever before, and
costing would be tightened up. They were thus already aware at
that point of the critical importance and meaning of their
managerial roles. This itself could account for much organizational
improvement that may now be observed.

Sandra Birtle observed that one further factor was very important:

White himself had only taken up his post with the Authority three
years ago, and his Deputy had joined at the same time. White's
style — open, team-centred and dynamic — was in marked
contrast to the style of his long-serving predecessor, who had
retired. Under that Chief Executive and those before him the
Authority had been bureaucratic and complacent, controlled in a
paternalistic and authoritarian way. White and his Deputy, both of
whom had come in from industry, had done an enormous
amount very quickly to change the culture of the Authority, and
this in itself had had many positive effects on people's attitudes,
motivation, behaviour and, undoubtedly, performance. The
training programme, although proposed by Birtle, had only been
possible because of the active support of White and Pierce, who
had pushed it through the Council and were fully identified with it
in the eyes of the Authority's staff.

The same factors have affected the departments of the Authority.

## Timescale for the Evaluation Project
White would like the final report ready to send out on 1 July, for a
Council Meeting on 15 July. If it is delayed, the next occasion on
which the report could be presented would be September, which
does not fit in so well with his timescale. He would like some kind of
interim report on 3 June.

## Action Agreed

1  I will consider whether I can meet the above deadlines, and notify the Authority this week.

2  They will send me a letter of appointment by this Friday.

3  We will have an informal meeting to discuss progress with the Project on 3 June at 10.30 am.

.......................................................................................

(**Comment:**  As can be seen from the above memorandum, it was at this meeting that important additional information was obtained from the Chief Executive, relating to his precise aims in relation to evaluation ('WHY'): to the level at which he wished evaluation to take place ('WHAT'), and to his desired timescale ('WHEN'): he and the Personnel Manager also gave crucial contextual information about which the consultant had been unaware.)

Soon after this meeting, the consultant received a letter offering him the project. The final stage in the setting up of the project was his reply, accepting the offer and clarifying certain issues, especially the detail of HOW the evaluation would be carried out. This letter is reproduced below:

.......................................................................................

*Your ref:*  JW/JIC/MP                                    5 May, 1984.


Dear John,

*Re:Training Evaluation Project*

Thank you for your letter of 28 April, offering me an appointment as Consultant to carry out the above project.

I am very happy to accept this appointment, on the basis of costs as laid out in your letter, with the following provisos:

### Inevitable imprecision of the evaluation
As we agreed at our meeting on 21 April, evaluation at level 5 (in relation to overall organizational objectives) is the most difficult and necessarily an imprecise kind of evaluation. However, I am prepared to make the attempt in the belief that something of value will come out of it, in relation to establishing how far in general

terms the training was effective; whether in any major ways, it should be changed; and whether or not continued investment in this kind of training should be recommended to the Authority. The evaluation cannot, however, be in any way as precise as it would have been, had we been mainly concerned with the levels relating to reactions or learning.

### Limitations in existing data

In order to carry out evaluation at the level of job performance, and at the departmental and wider organizational levels, there should initially have been detailed objectives established, stating what changes were required in knowledge, skills, attitudes, behaviour and performance at each of those levels through the training programme. There should also have been data about pre-programme behaviour and performance in relation to these objectives, since if there is no such data, it becomes extremely difficult to be sure about the level and kind of changes that the programme itself has produced.

If it should be the case (and I understand that it is) that with your own training programme there is some imprecision in training objectives, and little detailed data on pre-training behaviour and performance, then that would by no means be unusual, and I do not see it as a matter for great pessimism: I am simply trying to establish at the start what expectations we should have about the project, and the necessary limits to its validity.

### Data to be obtained, and information sources to be used

To carry out evaluation at levels 4 and 5 I will need to:

a)  establish whether the context of the entire programme was valid. I will therefore need to speak at length to yourself, to Philip Pierce, and to Sandra Birtle, in order to look at the context of the training programme; at the inputs to it; at the expectations and objectives you had about its outcomes; and at your perceptions of those outcomes. I would think that initially about two hours with yourself, two hours with Philip, and a day with Sandra would give me the information I need for the interim report on 3 June. However, this is only an estimate. I would hope to be able to arrange a meeting with Sandra either this week or next, and I will then know more clearly how much time I would like to spend with yourself, and how much with Philip.

b)  depend for most of the rest of the information on the reactions to the programme both of those who have been through it and a sample of those who have not — since we do not have any more objective data available. I will therefore have to:

- send out short questionnaires to all the past trainees, getting their general views on the objectives and outcomes of the training as far as they personally are concerned. I would propose to follow these up with interviews with a sample of the trainees, in which more detailed questions will be asked, but that stage will probably come after our meeting on 3 June.

- send out short questionnaires to the supervisors/managers of all the past trainees, to get their views on the objectives and outcomes of the training, as far as job behaviour of the trainees and impact on the organization are concerned. Again, I would like to follow these up with selective interviews, after 3 June.

- interview a few people who have not been through the programme, to find out whether they feel that their own behaviour or performance and that of their staff has undergone similar changes during the period of the programme (if it has, this would cast some doubt on training being the cause of those changes); also to obtain their views on the overall impact of the programme. Effectively what I am trying to do here is to refer to some kind of 'control' group, albeit a very small one, and compare their reactions and views with those of the group who went through the programme. It will be an imperfect assessment, but still, I feel, one that should be attempted.

I am currently drafting both sets of questionnaires, together with interview schedules, and would propose that I discuss and agree them with Sandra at our meeting in the next few days. I would further propose that they should go out under my name and from my own address, so that the recipients can see that this is an independent evaluation, rather than one controlled by personnel within the Authority, who may therefore read their responses. However, the questionnaires will need to be printed by the Authority, since my costings, whilst allowing for printing of the two reports to which your letter refers, do not include any other copying or printing costs, or mailing costs.

### Evaluation restricted at levels 1, 2 and 3
Given the amount of time that will be involved in doing the work outlined above, and the deadlines set out in your letter, evaluation at levels 1, 2 and 3 will be restricted to that which is necessary in order to obtain data about the effects of training on departments and

organization. This, too, is consistent with your own views, express-ed in our recent meeting and in your subsequent letter.

I hope that the content of this letter gives you the information you need about the direction I now feel should be taken with the project. I hope, too, that my amended proposals still seem likely to meet your requirements. If you would like to discuss any of the points with me, or if there is anything which, at this stage, gives you concern, please do not hesitate to let me know.

I will telephone Sandra on 6 May to arrange a meeting as soon as possible to discuss the various points covered in this letter, and in particular to get the questionnaire survey started. I am looking forward to carrying out the project, and to working with the Authority in what is a very challenging undertaking. Thank you, once again, for offering me the appointment.

Yours sincerely,

......................................................................................................

(*Final comment:* The evaluation project went ahead exactly as agreed, and proved to be extremely successful. A wide range of positive results at departmental and organizational level were identified, notably in the area of teamwork, motivation and commitment, and improved flexibility of managers and supervisors. In consequence, Stage 2 of the programme took place, and the consultant's recommendation that a new post of Training Manager, responsible for a training budget, be established in the Authority was agreed by the Chief Executive, and approved by Council. That new post was advertised and filled in the following year.

The consultant also made a number of observations in his final report about the wider manpower issues to which the training programme related, and which reactions to it had brought into sharp relief. Some of these issues related to manpower planning, recruitment and selection; staff appraisal; career development and planning; and reward systems. They put training in the Authority into a wider context of personnel management and organizational development, and as such became the focus of scrutiny in the Authority, and their implications were carefully analysed.)

In this case study we can see various important points to which attention has already been drawn in this chapter.

**Evaluation looks at the total value of a learning event, not just at whether and how far it achieves its learning objectives. It thereby puts the event in its wider context and provides information essential to future planning.**

In this instance, it was convincing evidence of that total value that resulted in a commitment not only to a future training programme, but to the establishment of a professional training function in the organization, and re-examination of the relationship that should exist in future between training, personnel and wider organizational policies and systems.

**Faced with the task of evaluation, an appropriate strategy needs to be developed, and this can be done on the basis of answers to the questions why, what, how, who and when.**

We can also add the further important point:

**Evaluation strategy must be agreed between evaluator and client, although the evaluator must decide how far to try to lead the client, and how far to adapt to the client's demands. Strategy must always, however, be kept flexible, able to meet any contingency.**

It is notable in our case study that evaluator and client interacted throughout in the process of determining an appropriate strategy. The evaluator 'educated' the client in what evaluation involved, and then proposed a particular approach. In response, the client, now clearer in his own mind as to what he really wanted, produced further information and a rather different set of proposals. These were carefully considered, and the final agreement gave rise to an evaluation strategy which was in line with the client's aims, but which, at the same time, could not promise a totally valid or reliable end result, because of the inbuilt problems involved in the exercise. Note, in particular, how the evaluator in his final letter clarified exactly what kind of problems and uncertainties were bound to occur if he pursued the strategy that the client wanted. The client was therefore made aware from the start of imperfections which would reduce the validity of evaluation. At the same time, the consultant was willing to pursue the strategy, rather than attempt to persuade the client to change his mind, because on balance he agreed that it was the most appropriate in the circumstances.

This informed, negotiated agreement between the evaluator and the client explained the subsequent success of the whole enterprise, and laid the foundations of an enduring relationship between the organization and the consultant. It is an example of that fundamentally important collaborative relationship that all who are responsible for training and development should build between themselves and their many 'clients' in the organization.

## Selection of Evaluation Techniques

The choice of what techniques to use in evaluation is again largely determined by the answers to our five basic questions; why, what, how, who and when.

In our case study, for example, the kind of information the evaluator needed made it obvious that he would have to contact those who had been through the programme (a small enough number to make it possible to contact all of them; had the number been greater, then a sample would have had to be chosen); he would also have to get the views of managers of trainees (where those managers had not themselves been through the programme — most, as it turned out, had been); and the views of at least some of those who had not been involved in the programme as trainees or as managers. This is the technique of the 'experimental' and the 'control' group, adapted albeit imperfectly to fit the particular situation faced by the evaluator.

The most obvious techniques to use were informal discussions, questionnaires and interviews; and analysis of any documentation available on the organization's training policy, plan, and programme. These techniques were relevant because of the lack of other, more objective, information and the short time available in which to carry out evaluation. They were also relatively cheap, whilst promising an acceptable level of effectiveness. In the event, the questionnaire survey brought an exceptionally high response rate of 75 per cent, whilst responses to discussions, survey and interviews proved to be extremely open and productive. Clearly, the techniques chosen were justified, given the circumstances prevailing in this particular evaluation exercise.

An important factor in explaining the very positive responses obtained by the evaluator was that the simple techniques he used were acceptable to those whose views about the programme were being sought. More sophisticated techniques, even had they been relevant and feasible, would have been too unfamiliar and therefore threatening to the respondents. This factor of acceptability is as important as the cost-effectiveness factor.

We can therefore conclude this short section on techniques by stating:

**The choice of evaluation techniques should be determined by the purpose of evaluation, what is to be evaluated and how,**

**who is to evaluate, and the time available for evaluation. Techniques must also be cost-effective, and acceptable to those involved in the evaluation exercise.**

For detailed information about evaluation techniques, there are a number of useful books (see Bibliography and Further Useful Reading). For guidelines on measuring training activities and on cost-benefit analysis, see pages 123 to 135 of this book.

## CONCLUSION

Having read this chapter and completed the various activities it contains, you should now:

1  Know the crucial questions to ask when faced with the task of evaluating a learning event

2  Know the criteria to apply when selecting the evaluator of a learning event

3  Be able to develop an evaluation strategy in a particular situation where evaluation needs to be carried out

4  Know what factors to consider when selecting evaluation techniques.

The main learning points connected with these objectives are:

**1  Evaluation**
Evaluation looks at the total value of a learning event, not just at whether and how far it has achieved its learning objectives. It thereby puts the event in its wider context, and provides information essential to future planning.

**2  Key questions related to evaluation**
Before starting to evaluate a learning event, 5 questions must be answered:
WHY, WHAT, HOW, WHO AND WHEN?

*Why evaluate?*
It is essential to be clear about the purpose of evaluation, as this will determine the answers to the remaining 4 questions.

*What to evaluate?*
There are 4 sets of factors that can be evaluated:

- Context

- Inputs

- Reactions

- Outcomes

### How to evaluate?
This will depend on what is being evaluated. Using the same CIRO approach, evaluation can be carried out as follows:

#### Context evaluation
Examine the diagnosis of the original learning needs, and the plans and objectives to which it gave rise.

Training objectives can be at 5 levels:

- Reactions level

- Learning level

- Job level

- Department level

- The organization level

To achieve effective evaluation of the context of a learning event, the evaluator should examine how far there has been:

- Formulation of a philosophy and policies for human resource development in the organization

- Operational analysis

- Assessment of inidividual needs

#### Input evaluation
Examine the cost, relevancy and effectiveness of inputs to 3 factors:

- The learning task

- Principles of learning

- Practical issues

**Reactions evaluation**
These can be obtained from questionnaires, interviews, discussions, etc.

**Outcomes evaluation**
Outcomes can be measured at 3 levels:

- Immediate

- Intermediate

- Ultimate

**Who should evaluate?**
When choosing an evaluator, the following check-list should be used:

- Objectivity

- Expertise

- Interpersonal skills

- Credibility

- Cost

**When to evaluate?**
Evaluation can be carried out:

- BEFORE the learning event

- DURING the learning event

- AT THE END of the learning event

- SOME TIME AFTER the learning event

- LONGER TERM after the learning event

The decision on when to evaluate depends on:

- Purpose of evaluation

- What is to be evaluated

- Practical considerations

## 3 Evaluation strategy
Evaluation strategy can be developed on the basis of answers to the 5 questions:

- WHY, WHAT, HOW, WHO, WHEN?

Evaluation strategy must be agreed between evaluator and client, although the evaluator must decide how far to try to lead the client, and how far to adapt to the client's demands. Strategy must always, however, be kept flexible, able to meet any contingency.

## 4 Selection of evaluation techniques
The choice of evaluation techniques should be determined by answers to the 5 questions:

- WHY, WHAT, HOW, WHO and WHEN?

Techniques must also be cost-effective, and acceptable to those involved in the evaluation exercise.

---

## REVIEW ACTIVITY

Finally, here are some questions which you can either tackle as coursework (if you are a student); discuss with fellow-students or colleagues; or carry out on your own now that you have completed this chapter.

- 'The sole criterion for measuring the effectiveness of a training programme is the number of learning objectives successfully achieved in a motivated manner' (I K Davies). Discuss.

- 'The important factor in the evaluation of training is who does it.' Comment on this statement with reference to training programmes with which you are familiar.

# The IPM Code of Continuous Development: People and Work

## Introduction and Aims

'Continuous Development' is self-directed, lifelong learning. Continuous development policies are policies first to allow and then to facilitate such learning at work, through work itself.

An organization's success depends upon its people. If the organization is to grow (become more effective and efficient), its people must be nurtured in order that they can grow (learn). Thus, employee learning should be managed continuously — not specially and separately but constantly in relation to all work activities. Continuous development focuses on results.

The Code, *Continuous Development: People and Work*, was drawn up to help senior managers, not just personnel professionals, to broaden their views about learning and training, to help them firmly to anchor their learning activity in the organization's business activities, and most important of all, to emphasize that learning within the organization must be managed on a continuous basis. The IPM considered that such a Code was necessary because, in the UK, training is not thought of as a continuous process, rather as a series of short term expedients.

If learning activity in an organization is to be fully beneficial both to the organization and its employees, **the following conditions must be met:**

- the organization must have some form of strategic business plan. It is desirable that the implications of the strategic plan, in terms of skills and knowledge of the employees who will achieve it, should be spelled out

- managers must be ready and willing (and able) to define and meet needs as they appear; all learning needs cannot be anticipated; organizations must foster a philosophy of continuous development

- as far as practicable, learning and work must be integrated. This means that encouragement must be given to all employees to learn from the problems, challenges and successes inherent in their day-to-day activities

- the impetus for continuous development must come from the chief executive and other members of the top management team (the board of directors, for example). The top management team must regularly and formally review the way the competence of its management and workforce is being developed. It is important too that one senior executive is charged with responsibility for ensuring that continuous development activity is being effectively undertaken

- investment in continuous development must be regarded by the top management team as being as important as investment in research, new product development or capital equipment. It is not a luxury which can be afforded only in the 'good times'. Indeed, the more severe the problems an organization faces the greater the need for learning on the part of its employees and the more pressing the need for investment in learning. Money spent within the organization on research and development into human resource development itself is money well spent. An evaluation of current human resource development procedures can confirm the effectiveness of current practice or point the way towards necessary change. Such research is as valuable as technical research.

**Successful continuous development demands:**

- rapid and effective communication of priority operational needs

- the availability of appropriate learning facilities and resources as a normal part of working life

- recognition by each employee that he or she is able to create some personal development plan

- all strategic and tactical operational plans fully take into account the learning implications for the employees affected

- clear understanding, by everyone, of their responsibilities.

These issues are covered in greater detail in the Code under seven key headings:

Policies

Responsibilities and roles

The identification of learning opportunities and needs

Learner involvement

The provision of learning resources

Benefits

Results

## Policies

Most organizations find written statements of policy useful. **Any statement of general policy relating to the management of people should indicate:**

- a firm corporate commitment to continuous development

- that self development is a responsibility of every individual within the organization

- the need for all employees, clients and customers to understand as much as possible about how individuals and groups of people learn, and why it is important

- the organization's commitment to acknowledge improved performance, to use enhanced skills operationally and to provide appropriate rewards

- 'who carries responsibility for what?' in the identification of learning aims and the promotion of learning activity

- ways in which operational aims and objectives are communicated to employees

- agreed procedures and methods for performance appraisal and assessment

- avenues, procedures and processes for career development and progression

- facilities provided for learning during work time, including any policy on paid or unpaid leave for this purpose

- the organization's policy on employee involvement, especially that relating to involvement in reviewing education and training facilities and resources.

**If the statement of general policy is not to be a sterile document of mere good intentions:**

- the Board and chief executive must be committed to it and demand periodic activity reports

- senior executives and middle and junior level managers must be given the opportunity to suggest amendments to the statement in line with what they regard as 'current operational reality'

- the document must regularly be discussed with trade union representatives and/or other representatives of the workforce

- the organization must satisfy itself that it is making best use of the latest information relating to research and development findings in the human resource development field (and perhaps get involved with such research activity).

## Responsibilities and roles

All members in the organization should be able to view the operational life of the organization as a continuous learning process — and one in which they all carry responsibilities.

*Senior executives* have the responsibility to ensure that policy statements and practices promote continuous development (as set out elsewhere in this Code) and that forward plans incorporate future management needs, particularly to improve performance, taking into account the impact of key changes in legal requirements, technology, work patterns and (not least) ideas. They must encourage managers to plan learning activities to facilitate the process of change.

*Managers* as part of their responsibilities for getting the best out of their staff, must give regular and ongoing attention to subordinates' continuous development, that is, discussing needs, creating plans, coaching, introducing changes which make learning easier and/or more effective. Managers must promote their own 'learning about learning'.

**Personnel professionals** have various responsibilities. They should provide an ongoing information service on resources and continuously monitor the extent and quality of learning activity in the organization. If they feel the learning activity is inadequate to support the operational needs of the business, they should take the initiative in generating strategic and/or tactical discussions, recommending appropriate action as necessary. They should ensure that review discussions happen at least once a year within the senior executive group and within any consultative groups. Internal personnel department review discussions should take place frequently.

**All learners** (including the three groups above) should appreciate that they are responsible for clarifying their own learning goals within the framework established by forward plans and discussions with management. They should raise their problems with management; seek new information without waiting for it to be delivered; and demonstrate new learning whenever possible. The ultimate aim is for continuous development to become fully integrated into work, with learners managing most of the activity for themselves and everyone contributing to the identification of learning opportunities.

## Identification of Learning Opportunities and Needs

It is worth repeating that everyone needs to contribute to the identification of learning opportunities. But some sources are stronger than others, for example:

**Operational plans:** every proposal for a new operational element or instrument, that is, a new product, a new item of plant, a new procedure, a new department, a new member of staff, a new accounting convention, a new **anything**, should be accompanied by an estimate of:

which employees need to learn something

what needs to be learned

how the learning can happen.

If these things cannot be defined with confidence, the proposal should include a plan which allows this to be completed later. Some needs are indirectly related; new technical systems, for example, may demand not merely instruction in the system itself, but also new levels and types of maintenance. Removing existing resources (machines, materials, or perhaps people) may also demand a learning plan.

*Job descriptions and specifications:* documents outlining management responsibilities should normally include references to:

the roles of appraisor, counsellor, tutor

the responsibility to develop understanding of learning processes

the manager's inclusion of learning elements in operational plans.

Separately, all job descriptions and specifications (regardless of level or type) should emphasize the job holder's responsibilities for self development on a continuous basis.

*Appraisal:* appraisal forms and guidance notes should explicitly demand reports on improved performance goals and hence learning needs. Appraisal interviews should normally include joint appraisor/ appraisee discussions on the extent to which self development takes place, and again on the frequency of management-inspired learning plans. Ideally informal appraisal discussions will happen continuously; a standard question on these occasions should be 'how long is it since we/you/I learned something new at work?'

*Special reviews and audits:* parts of the learning system should be specially reviewed from time to time. Diagonal-slice (that is, various employees from various departments) working parties, joint consultative committees, trainee groups and, not least, particular individuals, can be charged with collecting data, analysing it and reporting to senior executives or to personnel management. These reviews are particularly useful in those parts of the learning system where knowledge or awareness needs to be renewed from time to time, as for example, in health and safety.

## Learner Involvement

Learners need to be motivated to want to learn. This motivation may be lacking if they feel that learning activities are imposed, especially if they seem unrelated to personal aspirations. It is necessary therefore to encourage learners' involvement in the creation of any training plans that will involve them.

**To that end:**

- joint appraisor/appraisee decisions should aim at joint definition of objectives and the means to achieve them

- standing committees should include in their agenda, at regular, periodic intervals, an item demanding review of their achievements and future aims.

- special organizational groupings (eg quality circles, briefing groups) should explicitly contain 'improved performance' and 'management of change' aims, and should devote time to discussing the learning aspects of any proposals for future activity

- when new plant or equipment is introduced, contracts with suppliers should explicitly contain reference to the early involvement of staff during the commissioning process. It is normally desirable that suppliers should provide more than written manuals; active dialogue between them and those who are to operate and maintain the new equipment (including contract maintenance staff where appropriate) is needed

- work teams should encourage a 'multi-skills' approach to their future operations, minimizing divisions between jobs and maximizing the flexibility that goes with increased versatility

- where unionized and/or joint consultative arrangements exist, policies relating to training should regularly be discussed with employee representatives at all levels

- reference should be made to training policies, and to any current learning priorities, in progress reports, house magazines and through other available communication channels. Incentives towards self development are as useful in this area as in others.

## The Provision of Learning Resources

Self development, team learning, and continuous operation development, all require resource material and facilities. **The organization should clarify its policies and practices on the following:**

- training/learning budgets

- authorities to approve training/learning plans and expenditure

- facilities for study during standard working hours, including paid/unpaid leave

- financial assistance with travel, books, tapes, and other facilities

- awards and/or scholarships

- coaching and tutorial resources

- management's responsibility to create an environment in which continuous development can prosper.

All employees, and especially management, should have access to documents detailing these policies.

## Benefits

Strategic plans, or research and development expenditure, are not expected directly to yield precisely quantifiable benefits. They are means to ends. In the same way, expenditure on education, training and development should be regarded as a necessary and calculated investment yielding consequent pay off in terms of enhanced business performance. **The following benefits can be expected:**

- strategic plans are more likely to be achieved

- ideas can be expected to be generated, in a form which relates to operational needs

- everyone in the organization will recognize the need for learning effort on their part if the organization is to survive and their jobs made more secure

- and, in general, fewer mistakes, fewer accidents, less waste, higher productivity, higher morale, lower staff turnover, better industrial relations, better customer service, and **hence, greater returns to the organization.**

*The major benefits are, first, improved operational performance, and second, the joint development of people and work.*

## Results

How do you spot the 'continuous development' team? Its characteristics are many and varied, but **here is a list of the key ones:**

- all members, management and non-management, appear to
  understand and share ownership of operational goals

- immediate objectives exist and are understood by all

- new developments are promoted; change is constructive and
  welcomed and enjoyed, not forced and resisted

- managers are frequently to be heard discussing learning
  methods with their subordinates and colleagues

- managers frequently ask subordinates what they have learned
  recently

- time is found by all the team to work on individual members'
  problems

- reference documents (manuals, dictionaries, specification
  sheets and the like) are available to all without difficulty, and are
  **used**

- members use other members as resources

- members do not just swap information; they tackle problems
  and create opportunities

- all members share responsibility for success or failure; they are
  not dependent upon one or more leaders

- members appear to learn while they work, and to enjoy both.

# Job Description and Job Training Specification: Key Task Analysis

*(Reproduced by permission of C Gray and the North Eastern Electricity Board)*

## JOB DESCRIPTION

### 1 Organizational Context

#### 1.1 Organization
The North Eastern Electricity Board (5000 employees, comprising approximately 500 professional electrical engineers, 500 professional and administrative staff, 1000 clerical staff and 3000 industrial staff at Headquarters, 5 District Offices, 47 Electricity showrooms and various other small locations.)

#### 1.2 Unit
Cleveland District (540 employees, split proportionately as above, located at District Headquarters and 2 Depots.)

#### 1.3 Nature of Business
Electricity Distribution.

#### 1.4 Job
Head of District Personnel Section, based at District Headquarters.

### 2 Job Context

#### 2.1 Job Title
Principal Assistant (Personnel and Training)

#### 2.2. Department
Manager's Department (Cleveland District)

#### 2.3 Section
Personnel and Training

**2.4  Responsible to**
Senior Executive Officer (Administration)

**2.5  Subordinates**
One Senior Clerical Assistant
One Clerical Assistant

**2.6  Purpose of job**
   a   To assist the SEO (Administration) in the supervision and control of the Personnel function throughout the District.

   b   To plan, control and coordinate the work of the staff under his control and to ensure that their efforts are continually directed towards the improvements of work standards and methods.

## 3  Duties and Responsibilities

**3.1  Industrial Relations**
*KEY TASKS
The implementation and control of National Agreements

The implementation and control of Statutory Instruments and Board Instructions as they relate to the Personnel function

To give advice on the above, insofar as they govern Pay and Conditions of Service

*OTHER TASKS
Act in the absence of the SEO (Administration) as Board Side Secretary of all Negotiating and Local Joint Coordinating Council (including Health & Safety) Committees

**3.2  Training**
*KEY TASK
Prepare annual Training Budget

*OTHER TASKS
To advise line management on a quarterly basis of training courses planned in the future, and to assist in the nomination of appropriate staff

To control and coordinate the District's involvement in a Work Experience Programme involving local schools and colleges

To ensure that the Industry's requirements and obligations are met in respect of Apprentice and Clerical Training in the District

## 3.3 Recruitment
*KEY TASKS

To assist in the recruitment and selection of clerical staff throughout the District, and represent the Personnel Section at selection interviews

To carry out craft apprentice and clerical trainee selection tests

*OTHER TASKS

To advise line management on various sources of recruitment available for clerical and industrial staff

## 3.4 Welfare
*KEY TASKS

On matters of sickness/staff welfare to carry out visits and demonstrate the interest the Board has in the well-being of its staff

To liaise closely with the Board's Nursing Officer in cases of long-term sickness or serious injury involving any District employee

*OTHER TASKS

To discuss with employees concerned, and to ensure that they fully understand, the provisions of the Industry's Pension Scheme in cases of ill-health retirement, and the financial terms applicable in cases of redundancy

## 3.5 Manpower
*KEY TASK

To assist as required in the preparation of manpower proposals and manpower budgets

## 3.6 General
*KEY TASKS

To give advice and information as requested to all staff on all matters covered by the Personnel function

## Reasons for Choosing Key Task Analysis

The job under analysis is a Junior Managerial/Supervisory job and a KTA approach has been adopted. A variety of separate tasks are involved under several headings, covering a wide range of Personnel specialisms, and I feel the best way to analyse the job is by establishing the **key** tasks (those tasks which are crucial to overall effectiveness) and identifying the knowledge, skills and attitudes required to fulfil those tasks, together with measures of performance. The level of the job would suggest that the job-holder does not require training in minor tasks, but that his training needs and priorities would be best isolated by establishing and analysing **key** tasks.

## KEY TASK ANALYSIS (Extract)

| Task | Knowledge | Skills |
|------|-----------|--------|
| INDUSTRIAL RELATIONS *The Implementation and Control of National Agreements* | a  Range, scope and content of each Agreement.<br>b  Constitutions of the Negotiating Bodies.<br>c  Local custom and practice.<br>d  I.R. Theory. | a  Ability to recognise **principles** in Agreements, rather than adopting an over-literal approach.<br>b  Judgemental skill in anticipating I.R. implications of changes or new interpretations of Agreements.<br>c  Verbal skill in drafting staff information sheets on I.R. matters.<br>d  Ability to think logically so that all relevant factors are taken into account (eg precedent, custom and practice, local circumstances etc) in implementing Agreements.<br>e  Apply I.R. Theory within context of Agreements and NEEB policy. |
| *The Implementation and Control of Statutory Instruments and Board Instructions as they relate to the Personnel function* | a  Range, scope and content of S.I.'s, especially those parts affecting the Board in relation to its employees and vice-versa.<br>b  Range, scope and content of all Personnel Instructions. | a  As above. |

| Attitude | Measures of Performance |
|---|---|
| a  Firm, but not legalistic. | a  Agreed terms and conditions applied consistently and fairly throughout District. |
| a  As above, but always aware of **legal** requirements. | a  NEEB's statutory obligations in the Employment field fully met throughout District.<br>b  Spirit and intentions of Personnel Instructions fulfilled in District. |

# Example of a Problem-Centred
# Job Training Analysis

## A Job Information

*Designation:* Management-Services Assistant

*Department:* Personnel and Management Services, M.B.C.

*Accountable to:* Team Leader in charge of 2-3 assistants.

*Liaising with:* Middle/Senior management of administrative departments.
Middle/Line management of craft departments.
Other support services staff, eg Finance, Legal, Computers.

## B Notes of Guidance

(i) I have tried, as far as possible, to follow the same methodology as Warr and Bird, but obviously without a large sample this is difficult to achieve.

(ii) Without going into great detail one cannot 'group' problems as Warr and Bird did, so the problems listed on the anlaysis sheets relate to specific instances. However, these could just as easily be classified under headings such as 'relationships with subordinates' etc. (See Warr and Bird).

(iii) The frequencies used in the examples relate more to the type of problem rather than to the specific examples quoted — eg in example 1B it is likely that the practitioner would experience interpersonal problems almost constantly.

(iv) The 'organizational factors' column indicates where problems can become endemic to the organization, although the link between the specific problem quoted and the general problem intimated may not appear to be very clear.

(v) Even under the job specific problems, an attempt has been made to indicate the type of person to be or not to be at risk.

(vi) The biographical information could be culled using a form very similar to Warr and Bird's with one or two amendments or additions, and therefore it was not felt necessary to include an example as such.

The examples are given on page 320 overleaf.

**Examples of Critical Incident Forms**

## 1A

### DAY 1
*What was the most difficult job or situation that you had to deal with today?*

'Joe Bloggs the Foreman at — Depot phoned me to ask if I would have a word with one of his chargehands who was having difficulty completing his paperwork and in particular his bonus and time sheets. I had already been out to see this chap when he started 3 weeks ago and I didn't see it as my job to interfere in a situation where I had no direct control or authority. Nevertheless I did it because we are supposed to be providing a service to management - aren't we?'

*Approximately how often do you have to deal with a difficulty of this kind?*

a   Daily

b   Weekly

c   Monthly

d   Every 3 months   ✓

e   Yearly

f   Other (please specify)

## DAY 2

'I had to go out this morning to study a tarmac gang laying a new type of material. When I arrived on site I was not happy about the number of men on the job nor the type of roller they were going to use to consolidate the tarmac. I informed the chargehand concerned in no uncertain manner about my misgivings and threatened to report the whole gang to senior management for trying to 'con' me. At this point the men laid down their tools and refused to be studied by me. I returned to the office and informed my team leader of what had happened.'

*Frequency:* weekly-monthly.

1C

## DAY 3

'I had a meeting this afternoon with senior management of the — Department, ie the Deputy Director, the Assistant Director (Admin:) and the ——— ——— ——— to discuss my report and recommendations on my investigation into the organization, structure and practices of the ——— Section of the ——— Department. I came back seething because although they agreed in principle with my recommendations and could not dispute my figures they could not agree to the implementation of my report due to 'external' factors which had recently arisen and which could not be discussed at this stage. When I protested vehemently I was told quite clearly by the Deputy that it was his department and he would organize it the way he liked. What's the point, I ask myself?'

*Frequency:* whenever the recommendations are in any way controversial or liable to cause departmental management too many headaches.

## PROBLEM CENTRED ANALYSIS

| Problem | Type of Person *Likely* to be at Risk | Type of Person *Unlikely* to be at Risk |
|---|---|---|
| 1  Tendency for one's concept of standard performance to err far away from the ideal and thus affect the accuracy of any resulting data particularly when using techniques such as time study and activity sampling. | b,c,d,e | a |
| 2  Dissatisfaction with the level and quality of work being given by the Team leader — generally boring, routine and mundane. | a,b | d,e |
| 3  Lack of clarity of role/function in relation to line supervision | b,c | |

| Type of Problem *ie Job Specific or Job General* | Possible Training Solutions | Organizational Factor |
|---|---|---|
| Job General — a technical problem of skill liable to affect almost all practitioners at some time. | a Regular (monthly) in-house 'rating' clinics' using bought-in films so that individual's performance can be measured.<br><br>b give those whose concept of standard is off beam more experience in the field to sharpen up their rating skill. | |
| Job Specific — liable to lead to low motivation and therefore poor performance. Problem probably stems from individual's lack of success/initiative in previous assignments. | a Course in creative/lateral thinking techniques to try to increase ingenuity and initiative.<br><br>b Secondment to other teams engaged in different types of projects for a certain period to give the individual a 'wider' experience. | The problem may be made more complex by the fact that the Team leader may need some training in leadership styles and motivational techniques. |
| Job Specific — | Awareness of organizational structures and relationships within the Authority. | Problems tend to indicate a need for a closer look at supervisory training or at least 'sideways' training to bring people in different departments doing similar level work together. |

| Problem | Type of Person *Likely* to be at Risk | Type of Person *Unlikely* to be at Risk |
|---|---|---|
| 4  Lack of knowledge of health and safety regulations in general and in particular with regard to the type of work carried out by local authority DLO's ie maintenance and minor works. | b,c,d | a,e |
| 5  Relationships with people from other departments involved in studies/investigations. | b,c,d | e |
| 6  Frustration at not having these recommendations accepted by departmental management. | b,c,d | e |

**Biographical information (see analysis)**

a  =   ex-tradesman
b  =   younger practitioners
c  =   graduates with little/no work experience
d  =   practiioners from outside industry with no local government experience
e  =   experienced practitioners/administrators

| Type of Problem *ie Job Specific or Job General* | Possible Training Solutions | Organizational Factor |
|---|---|---|
| Job General | In house training course for all management services assistants on the HASAWA and its provisions followed by more detailed analysis of type of safety problems likely to be encountered in local authority work eg eye protection, abrasive wheel regulations, ladder work etc. | Would be useful to involve the men's representatives/ chargehands and line and middle management of the Public Works Department. |
| Job Specific — maybe an attitude problem which is difficult to remedy and should perhaps have been noticed at the selection stage. | Interpersonal skills training either by attendance at a course and/or close supervision on the job. | Again perhaps a need to look at training information throughout the organization as a whole on the purpose/ role of a management services investigation. |
| Job General | Greater emphasis on negotiating skills and ways of implementation of schemes — probably in-house but could benefit from an IR Course in such skills. | The problem may not have a training solution *per se* but requires a clarification of function/ role/power by the Management Team or Committee. Again a lateral and vertical problem. |

# Personnel Specification

**Principal Assistant (Personnel Dept), North Eastern Electricity Board**
*(Reproduced by permission of C Gray and the North Eastern Electricity Board)*

| PERSONAL QUALITIES | ESSENTIAL |
|---|---|
| **IMPACT ON OTHERS** | |
| APPEARANCE | Clean and well-dressed; must be acceptable to others both within an outside NEEB. |
| SPEECH | Clear speech. |
| MANNER | Friendly, pleasant but also busines like when appropriate. |
| SELF-CONFIDENCE | Sufficient to deal face to face with a levels of staff, and to take initiative where appropriate in dealing with Senior Management. |
| COMPETENCE IN DEALING WITH SITUATIONS INVOLVING OTHER PEOPLE | Good interpersonal skills. Must be tactful and discreet where necessar |
| **QUALIFICATIONS** | |
| GENERAL EDUCATION | 4 'O' levels or equivalent, including Maths and English Language. |

| DESIRABLE |
|---|
| Very well-presented, certain to create good impression. |
| Good fluency in speech. Voice sufficiently powerful to address group, meeting or audience on public occasions. |
| Very good social skills and manner, able to mix well and communicate with all types of people. |
| Sufficient to make own decisions within sphere of competence and responsibility without always seeking approval.<br><br>Self-confidence necessary in exercising purposeful leadership of section. |
| High degree of tact and discretion required in dealing with matters of a confidential nature.<br><br>Able to demonstrate authoritative approach where dealing with others.<br><br>Persuasive skills to gain agreement of others to various courses of action. |
| Degree or equivalent. Evidence of ability to carry out a course of study successfully.<br><br>Potential for gaining further qualifications (IPM or ICSA). |

| PERSONAL QUALITIES | ESSENTIAL |
|---|---|
| OCCUPATIONAL TRAINING | None |
| OCCUPATIONAL EXPERIENCE | At least 18 months within ESI, preferab NEEB, including at least 6 months in Personnel work. |
| **ABILITIES**<br><br>APTITUDES | Numerate, good written and oral skills. Able to apply information intelligently. Must be potentially good Supervisor. Ability to meet deadlines. |
| I.Q. | Above average intelligence. |
| **MOTIVATION**<br><br>ABILITY TO ORGANIZE OWN WORK AND WORK OF SUBORDINATES | Ability to plan ahead and assess priorities. |
| ABILITY TO SET SELF GOALS AND SET SUBORDINATES' GOALS | Must recognize main purpose of own jc and of subordinates in order that realist and appropriate goals may be set. |
| ABILITY TO WORK ALONE OR IN A TEAM | Ability to work alone or in a team as appropriate. |

| DESIRABLE |
|---|
| NEEB Clerical Supervisory Skills Course (1 week). ESI Introduction to Management Course (3 weeks). |
| At least 1-2 years experience of Personnel work within NEEB.<br><br>Some District experience.<br><br>Some supervisory experience. |
| Excellent written style — skill in drafting and minute-writing.<br><br>Ability to plan ahead and control and organize work of section.<br><br>Public speaking skill. |
| High I.Q. Quick, perceptive thinker. Ability to absorb and analyse large amounts of written information. |
| Ability to relate all tasks within section to each other and establish efficient working practices. |
| Ability to identify priorities and delegate duties where necessary to concentrate on own priorities and goals and aid development of subordinates.<br><br>Ability to gain agreement of staff to goals set. |
| Ability to work effectively in role of team leader of section and to ensure team work of section is good.<br><br>Ability to work as part of team in Working Parties, Project Groups etc.<br><br>Ability to work alone where necessary and to motivate self to meet time and standard targets. |

| PERSONAL QUALITIES | ESSENTIAL |
|---|---|
| **ADJUSTMENT** | |
| RESPONSIBILITY AND RELIABILITY | Responsible, mature approach.<br><br>Reliable in handling confidential matte meeting important dealines and providing information to Senior Management. |
| LEADERSHIP | Must be potentially a good supervisor/leader. |
| ACCEPTABILITY | Appearance and manner should be acceptable to all levels of staff, and to people from outside NEEB. |

*(Using 5-Point Plan format, Fraser J M, 1971)*

**DESIRABLE**

High degree of responsibility required to work increasingly without supervision, and occasionally as stand-in for SEO (Admin).

Very responsible and reliable in dealing with all Personnel matters, especially own Key tasks.

Good leadership skills. Some supervisory experience.

Appearance and manner should at all times create a good impression.

Should be able to communicate effectively in a friendly, open way with all staff and outsiders.

# Self-Assessment Exercise

*(Reproduced by permission of the Institute of Personnel Management)*

## Self-Assessment Sheet for Continuous Development

### Current work performance

(i)   Professional knowledge of present job

A

Inadequate
Tendency to A
Tendency to B

B

Thorough knowledge of job

(ii)  Quantity of work (speed and consistency in producing required results)

A

Fair
Tendency to A
Tendency to B

B

Unusually high output

(iii) Quality of work (extent to which results meet requirements of accuracy, thoroughness and neatness)

A

Passable
Tendency to A
Tendency to B

B

High quality

(iv)  Attitude towards job

A [                    ]  Not always interested/enthusiastic
      [                    ]  Tendency to A
      [                    ]  Tendency to B
B [                    ]  High willingness and enthusiasm

(v)  Judgement and Analytical Ability (extent to which decisions or actions based on a sound appraisal of the situation and reached by logical reasoning)

A [                    ]  Conclusions sometimes inaccurate
      [                    ]  Tendency to A
      [                    ]  Tendency to B
B [                    ]  Sound judgement

## Personal characteristics in relation to the job

(i)  Personality and acceptability

A [                    ]  Impact and effect on others not always favourable
      [                    ]  Tendency to A
      [                    ]  Tendency to B
B [                    ]  Make a very good impression

(ii)  Ability to communicate

(a)  Verbal (At meetings, discussions, interviews)

A [                    ]  Verbal communication not always effective
      [                    ]  Tendency to A
      [                    ]  Tendency to B
B [                    ]  High standard of presentation

(b)   Written (Reports, memoranda, letters)

A   [        ]   Limited basic writing skills
    [        ]   Tendency to A
    [        ]   Tendency to B
B   [        ]   Writes very well

(iii)   Mental alertness and initiative (Initiative, grasp of new ideas, with problem solving, etc.)

A   [        ]   Tend to follow precedent
    [        ]   Tendency to A
    [        ]   Tendency to B
B   [        ]   Constructive and creative thinker

## Only Complete this Section if Responsibility is Held for Planning and Organizing the Work of Subordinates

(i)   Planning and organizing (Devising programmes, budgets, schedules, as required)

A   [        ]   Need some assistance
    [        ]   Tendency to A
    [        ]   Tendency to B
B   [        ]   Above average organizing ability

(ii)   Delegating (Assigning and monitoring responsibility for work)

A   [        ]   Find difficulty in delegating work
    [        ]   Tendency to A
    [        ]   Tendency to B
B   [        ]   Highly successful in delegating

(iii)  Controlling and co-ordinating (Keeping group working toward objectives, measure performance, interpreting results, initiating correcting action)

A ▢ Finding difficulty in controlling work
    ▢ Tendency to A
    ▢ Tendency to B
B ▢ Very successful in controlling work

(iv)  Leadership (Securing full and willing response from subordinates, both individually and as a team)

A ▢ Ineffectual
    ▢ Tendency to A
    ▢ Tendency to B
B ▢ Effective leader

(v)  Development of subordinates (Recognition and development of ability)

A ▢ Somewhat lacking
    ▢ Tendency to A
    ▢ Tendency to B
B ▢ Competent developing talent

**Assessment of learning needs/objectives for continuous development**

| Rate your ability in: | High | Low | Learning Needs (tick as appropriate) |
|---|---|---|---|
| Assessing other people's capabilities | ☐ | | ☐ |
| Decision making | ☐ | | ☐ |
| Delegating | ☐ | | ☐ |
| Giving instructions | ☐ | | ☐ |
| Problem solving | ☐ | | ☐ |
| Judgement | ☐ | | ☐ |
| Leadership/initiative | ☐ | | ☐ |
| Listening | ☐ | | ☐ |
| Planning | ☐ | | ☐ |
| Public speaking | ☐ | | ☐ |
| Running meetings | ☐ | | ☐ |
| Self discipline/coping with stress | ☐ | | ☐ |
| Selling ideas | ☐ | | ☐ |
| Thinking/creativity | ☐ | | ☐ |
| Understanding other people | ☐ | | ☐ |
| Use of time | ☐ | | ☐ |
| OTHER AREAS | | | |
| _____ | ☐ | | ☐ |

**Action Plan No. Continuous Development**
*(A separate sheet should be completed for each action plan)*

**1  Objective**

_____

**2  Factors helping**                                    Actions

_____

**3  Factors hindering**                                  Actions

_____

**4  Itemized plan of action**                            Timetable

_____

**5  Others to be involved**

_____

**Some Suggested Sources of Learning/Information for
Continuous Development**

1  **Professional**
   Journals/publications — (eg IPM Journal, Employment Gazette)
   Technical information services (IPM Library, Industrial Society,
   etc.)
   Colleges of Further and Higher Education
   Courses/Seminars
   The media
   'Others'
   Job rotation
   Job exchange
   Development of new aspects of one's own job
   Work-related projects

2  **Social**
   Evening classes — non-professional subjects
   Committee membership
   Community work

Date: _____

## ANCHOR HOUSING ASSOCIATION

### Appraisal Interview Record

Name: _____     Office: _____

Position: _____     Grade: _____

Date of joining Anchor: _____

Date of appointment to current position: _____

The purpose of this form is to help you and your manager obtain the most benefit from the appraisal interview. Areas for discussion have been laid down to provide talking points during the interview — but this should not prevent informal discussion about other aspects of your job.

Please prepare for the appraisal interview by completing this form within ten days of receiving it and pass a copy to your manager (to give time to consider your comments).

If the space for answering the questions is insufficient please use additional sheets of paper, numbering them accordingly.

You will be given the opportunity to read the completed Appraisal Interview Record and countersign it.

The appraisal interview will be held with: ......................................

The form will be countersigned by: ...............................................

| 1  Job Content | Manager's Comments |
|---|---|
| a   Under no more than five headings set down the key tasks or responsibilities in your job. | |
| b   Has the content of your job changed appreciably during the last year? If so please list the changes. | |

**2  The past year's work**

|  |  |
|---|---|
| a   In which areas of your work do you think you have done well during the past year? | |
| b   Do you think that your job has sufficiently involved and stretched you during the year; have any areas of the job been particularly difficult? If so, state the problem and the reasons for the difficulty. | |

**3  Improvements**

Can you suggest any ways of improving your own or your department's performance?

**4  Education and Training**              **Manager's Comments**

Can you suggest any training
that would improve your
performance?

---

**5  Career Prospects**
How do you see your career
developing

a   within the next 2 years

---

b   long-term

---

c   would you be prepared
to transfer to another
location within Anchor?

---

d   Would you consider
transferring to another
function within Anchor?
If so, which?

---

**6  Objectives for next year**

What are your main work
targets for next year?

---

# The Training and Development problem

## Brief for the Head of the Engineering Department

You have been appraising the performance of your Quality Assurance (QA) Manager, and have reached the stage of discussing his skills in appraising and developing his staff (seven inspectors). You both work in a small light engineering group which is part of a national engineering company. The group is virtually autonomous, with a young and very able Managing Director who, over the past five years, has built up a strong task culture and team-based structure, taking the group into a leading market position. There are 23 managers (including supervisors of shop floor workers) and about 100 other employees. (See Appendix 8 for the organization chart for your Department).

Three and a half years ago the company brought in a consultant who worked with the management team to design a simple appraisal scheme, with a self-appraisal strategy and focussing on key result areas and targets of performance. It aims to help with the appraisal of current work performance, work planning, and the diagnosis of training and development needs leading to individual development plans. The scheme has been running successfully for three years, and covers the whole group, not just the management team. The team chose the design themselves, and piloted the scheme for a year, before it was extended to the rest of the organization in the second and third years.

The QA Manager is 43, married, with one son who is an apprentice in the company. He has been in his present job for ten years (you yourself have only been here for 3 years, and are 34, a graduate recruit from another engineering firm and have — you have been led to believe here — top management potential). He has been with the company since himself being an apprentice. At the personal level you don't particularly care for him, and feel that he has no real liking for you either. You have never had an outright dispute with him, but find him unresponsive to views that do not coincide with his own, and unlikely to admit easily to weaknesses. Generally his performance in his job is good although without signs of any real potential which could take him higher in the organization. He achieves his technical targets, and is meticulous in carrying out his duties. His staff seem effective too, although not achieving much above adequate performance (judging from his own appraisal of them).

The problem with the QA Manager is, you feel, his poor record in appraising and developing his inspector team. Although he holds annual appraisal interviews, and appropriate forms are completed and action plans carried out relating to training and development, nevertheless his staff have spent less time on training and development activities than most others in the group — on average, about two days each per year compared with an overall average of eight days per person in the rest of the group. Furthermore, the training that they have been given is entirely technical, yet you would expect some developmental activities which would enable them to show potential for promotion, and generally to aid their longer-term development.

You have also noticed (because there is a space on the appraisal form which asks the appraiser to note how long the appraisal interview lasted) that his appraisal interviews last on average no more than an hour, whereas the overall average in the group is two hours. Furthermore, on at least two of the forms completed last year the Inspector concerned registered failure to agree with the QA Manager on matters related to areas which the QA Manager saw as weaknesses. The comments made by the appraisees showed that they had not been convinced by the QA Manager's reasons when he judged their performance as inadequate; they had put forward counter-arguments, which they felt he had dismissed without adequate discussion, and stalemate had been reached. In neither case had a final Appeal been made, but clearly this could come if such clashes were to recur and you wish to ensure that such an outcome does not occur.

It is difficult to know whether the QA Manager could be helped by skills training related to all the above issues or not. He did go through a two-day Appraisal Skills Workshop three years ago, run by the same consultant who worked with the management team in the design of the appraisal scheme, but perhaps some form of short course which would give him help specifically related to the weaknesses you believe he has would be appropriate now. Or is there some other form of training or development that might work? Or is some other solution altogether more likely to succeed? You intend to go into the whole matter at some length with him, since the basic issues of appraisal, training and development of his team are so crucial to the longer-term effectiveness of his unit.

You are not looking forward to this part of the interview, and therefore have planned it particularly carefully in order to try to achieve positive outcomes.

# Engineering Department Organization Chart

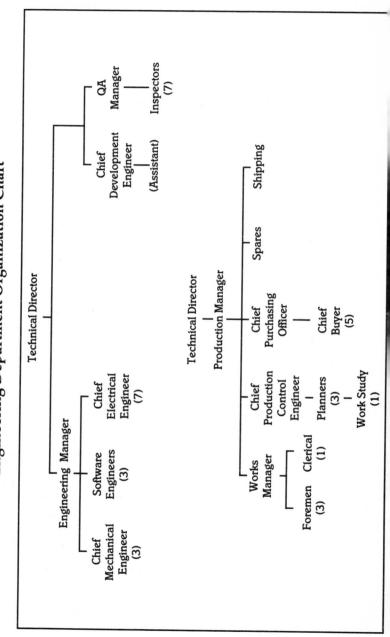

# The Training and Development Problem

## Brief for the Quality Assurance Manager

You are nearing the end of the 'appraisal of performance' part of your annual appraisal interview, carried out by your manager, the Head of the Engineering Department. You are pleased with the outcome of the discussion so far, but hope that it will soon be over as there is the usual build up of work over in your area, and you need to get back as soon as possible.

You both work in a small light engineering group which is part of a national engineering company. The group is virtually autonomous, with a young and very able Managing Director who, over the past five years, has built up a strong task culture and team-based structure, taking the group into a leading market position. There are 23 managers (including supervisors of shop floor workers) and about 100 other employees. (The organization chart for your department precedes this brief, Appendix 8.)

You are 43, married, with one son who is an apprentice in the company. You have been in your present job for ten years. You have been with the company since being an apprentice, and feel considerable loyalty to it. Although you would like to be at least one step higher up the management ladder than you are now, you are prepared to take things steadily and wait, confident in the belief that promotion will come before too long. Your manager is 34, a graduate recruit from another engineering firm, and has been in this company for three years as Head of Department. He is very bright, and is talked of as a future top manager. Personally you don't like him, and sense that the feeling is mutual. You work together well enough — you have never actually had an outright dispute with him — but find him unresponsive to views that do not coincide with his own, and unlikely to admit easily to weaknesses. You therefore avoid him as much as possible, and try to do your job in such a way as to make sure that you cannot be criticized for anything.

Three and a half years ago the company brought in a consultant who worked with the management team (including yourself) to design a simple appraisal scheme, with a self-appraisal strategy and focussing on key result areas and targets of performance. It aims to help with the appraisal of current work performance, work planning, and the diagnosis of training and development needs leading to individual development plans. The scheme has been running successfully for three years, and covers the whole group, not just the management team. The team chose the design themselves, and piloted the scheme for a year, before it was extended to the rest of the organization in the second and third years. In that first, pilot, year, you and the rest of the management team attended a two-day Appraisal Skills Workshop specially designed and run by the consultant, and you found it very useful. You have tried hard to apply the skills of appraisal to your own task of appraising your seven Inspectors annually. You have done that task twice now — once last year, and once this. You know that your performance in your job is generally rated as good, even though you never seem to get particularly enthusiastic comments from your manager. You achieve all your technical targets, and are acknowledged as being meticulous in carrying out your duties. As to your Inspectors, they're pretty good men, if with no obvious potential to get any higher. They do what they are told and never cause any real problems, and that is as much as you can hope for in work where everything has to be done so accurately and under so many pressures.

You never need to spend more than an hour on their appraisal interviews (you remember that, because you have to write on each appraisal interview form how long the discussion has taken) which is all the time you and they can ever spare to spend on this task. You always see that the appraisal forms are very carefully completed, and that any action plans relating to training and development are carried out exactly as agreed — you are conscientious in this, as in all your duties. Your staff actually do well on training and development, spending about two days each per year in some kind of formal refresher training activities (since all are adequate performers, they never need more than that), and coming to you for discussions whenever they hit problems in their jobs; in other words, you try to develop them in their daily work as well as you can, using their mistakes as learning points. They can always ask you if they want anything more (initiative, you feel, is very important in these matters) but so far they never have. It was a pity that on two of the forms completed last year the Inspectors concerned registered failure to agree with you on matters related to areas where they clearly had weaknesses (although neither ended up making any formal Appeal). The comments they made showed that they did not accept that their performance was inadequate; they had put forward counter-arguments, which they said you had dismissed without sufficient discussion, and stalemate had been reached. However, in both cases the problem was their poor interpersonal skills, which had caused difficulties, minor but repeated, with a small group of shop floor workers. It's always difficult to get anyone to accept that they are not good at dealing with people, and these two Inspectors, both into their fifties, are never going to change their ways; lengthy discussion would have only made matters worse, so in the end you had to simply instruct them in a few procedures to use in such situations, and warn them about the need to observe these if problems with the Union were to be avoided. They didn't like it, but at least there had been no further outbreaks and in every other respect their performance was quite satisfactory. Afterwards you had wondered whether training or development of any kind could have made any difference to this area of their work, but had come to the conclusion that even to have suggested it would have got their backs up; both are steady, reliable men, looking forward to their retirement, and very set in their ways — procedures are something they understand, but some form of 'interpersonal skills' training would be just seen as a threat, and would cause more problems than it would resolve.

# Bibliography

ANDERSON G, HULME D and YOUNG E. 'Appraisal without form-filling'. *Personnel Management*. February, 1987

ANNETT J, DUNCAN K D, STAMMERS R B, and GRAY M J. *Task analysis*, DEP Training Information Paper, No 6. London, HMSO. (Reprinted Sheffield, Training Division, Manpower Services Commission, 1979)

ARGYLE M. *The psychology of interpersonal behaviour.* Harmondsworth, Middlesex, Penguin, 1970 (reprinted 1983)

BARRINGTON H A. 'Continuous development: theory and reality'. *Personnel Review*, Vol.15, No 1, 1986

BASS B M and VAUGHAN J A *Training in industry; the management of learning.* London, Tavistock Publications, 1967. (Behavioural Science in Industry Series)

BELBIN E and R M. *Problems in adult retraining.* London, Heinemann, 1972

BENSON J, *et al.* 'Nabisco's winning strategy'. *Personnel Management.* May, 1987

BERLINER W. 'Success of a liberal curriculum'. *Independent.* 8 October 1987

BURGOYNE J and GERMAIN C. 'Self-development and career planning: an exercise in mutual benefit'. *Personnel Management,* April, 1984

CARBY K and THAKUR M. *Transactional analysis at work.* Information Report No 23. London, Institute of Personnel Management, 1977

CARRIER J. 'Maintaining excellence in a tight stretch'. *Personnel Management.* April, 1986

CHILD J. *Organization: a guide to problems and practice.* 2nd ed. London, Harper and Row, 1984

CONSTABLE J and McCORMICK R. *The making of British managers.*

A report to the British Institute of Management and the Confederation of British Industry, Corby, Northants, BIM, 1987

COOPERS AND LYBRAND ASSOCIATES. *A challenge to complacency; Changing attitudes to training.* A Report to the Manpower Services Commission and the National Economic Development Office, Sheffield, MSC, November, 1985

COWIE A. 'Art of training for life' (Ed. JUDD J.) *Observer,* 24 January, 1988

COWLING A and GRIPTON J. 'Evaluating selection tests'. *Training Officer,* August, 1986

CUTHBERT D. 'Why working together means training together'. *Personnel Management.* October, 1984

DEPARTMENT OF EMPLOYMENT. *Glossary of training terms.* 2nd ed. London, HMSO, 1971

DOWNS S. 'Trainability testing', *Personnel Management,* October, 1984. ('Selection Tests' section)

EASTERBY-SMITH M and TANTON M. 'Turning course evaluation from an end to a means'. *Personnel Management.* April, 1985

FELLBOM E. 'Swedish stamp on the customer service message'. *Personnel Management,* June, 1987

FLANAGAN J C. 'The critical incident technique'. *Psychological Bulletin,* Vol 52, 1954

FOWLER A. *Personnel management in local government.* 2nd ed. London, Institute of Personnel Management, 1980

FRASER J M *Introduction to personnel management.* London, Nelson, 1971

FRENCH J R P and RAVEN B H. 'The bases of social power' in CARTWRIGHT D, *ed Studies in social power.* University of Michigan Press, Ann Arbor, Michigan, 1959

FRENCH W L and BELL C H *Organization development: behavioural science interventions for organization improvement.* 2nd ed. Prentice Hall International Inc, 1978

GAGNE R M *Conditions of learning.* Eastbourne, Holt, Rhinehart and Winston, 1965

GANE C. *Managing the training function.* London, George Allen & Unwin, 1972

GENTLES E M *Training the operator.* London, Institute of Personnel Management, 1969

HAMBLIN A C *Evaluation and control of training.* Maidenhead, McGraw Hill, 1974

HANDY C B *Understanding organizations.* 3rd ed. Harmondsworth, Middlesex, Penguin Books, 1985. (Penguin Business Library)

HANDY C B *The making of managers: a report on management education, training and development in the USA, West Germany, France, Japan and the UK.* National Economic Development Office/Manpower Services Commission/British Institute of Management, 1987

HARRISON Roger. 'How to describe your organization'. *Harvard Business Review,* September—October, 1972

HARRISON Rosemary. *Equality at work.* Oxford, Pergamon Press, 1986. (Super Series No. 506; Open Learning for Supervisory Management, published for The National Examinations Board for Supervisory Studies in conjunction with The Northern Regional Management Centre)

HARRISON Rosemary. 'Nick Barton, special agent of change'. *Personnel Management.* February, 1988

HMSO, White Paper: 'Training for employment'. London, HMSO, 1988.

HMSO, White Paper: 'A new training initiative — a programme for action'. London, HMSO, 1981

HONEY P and MUMFORD A. *The manual of learning styles.* 2nd ed. Maidenhead, Peter Honey, 1986

INSTITUTE OF MANPOWER STUDIES, *Competence and competition: training and education in the Republic of Germany, the United States and Japan.* London, National Economic Development Office, 1984

INSTITUTE OF PERSONNEL MANAGEMENT. *Code of continuous development: people and work.* 2nd ed. London, IPM (NCTD Dept.), 1987

INSTITUTE OF PERSONNEL MANAGEMENT/MANPOWER SERVICES COMMISSION. *Helping young people to learn.* Sheffield, MSC, 1983

KENNEY J, DONNELLY E and REID M. *Manpower training and development.* 2nd ed. London, Institute of Personnel Management, 1979

KENNEY J and REID M. *Training interventions.* London, Institute of Personnel Management 1986

KILCOURSE R. 'Trainability testing as an aid to selection. *Personnel Management.* May, 1978

KING D. *Training within the organization.* London, Tavistock Publications, 1968 (Social Science Paperback)

KOLB D A, RUBIN I M and McINTYRE J M. *Organizational Psychology — an experiential approach*. Englewood Cliffs, NJ, Prentice Hall International, 1974

LATHROPE K. 'A clear demonstration of the pay-off from training', in 'Comment', *Personnel Management*, March 1988
LEIGH A. *20 ways to manage better*. London, Institute of Personnel Management, 1984
LONG P. *Performance appraisal revisited*. London, Institute of Personnel Management, 1986. (3rd IPM survey, Information and Advisory Services)

MACHIN J. 'Inter-manager communication; matching up to expectations?'. *Personnel Management*. January, 1981
MANN S. 'Why open learning can be a turn-off'. *Personnel Management*. January, 1988
MANPOWER SERVICES COMMISSION. *Direct trainers*. 2nd Report of the Training of Trainers Committee. London, HMSO, 1980
MANPOWER SERVICES COMMISSION. *Core skills in YTS: Part 1.* Sheffield, MSC, 1984
MANPOWER SERVICES COMMISSION. *Developing trainers: MSC support for training of trainers and staff development*. Sheffield, MSC, April, 1987
MANSFIELD B. 'Getting to the core of the job'. *Personnel Management*. August, 1985
McGREGOR D. *The human side of enterprise*. Maidenhead, McGraw Hill, 1960
MILLER R B. 'Task description and analysis', in GAGNE R M *ed. Psychological principles of system development*. Eastbourne, Holt, Rhinehart and Winston, 1962
MINTZBERG H. *The nature of managerial work*. London, Harper and Row, 1973
MUMFORD A. *The manager and training*. London, Times Management Library, 1971
MUMFORD A. 'What did you learn today?'. *Personnel Management*. August, 1981

OTTO C P and GLASER R O. *The management of training*. London, Addison-Wesley, 1972
OXFORD ILLUSTRATED DICTIONARY. COULSON J, CARR C T, HUTCHINSON L and EAGLE D, *eds*. 2nd ed. Oxford, Oxford University Press, 1975
OXFORD ENGLISH DICTIONARY. Oxford, Clarendon Press, 1978

PEDLER M, BURGOYNE J and BOYDELL T. *Manager's guide to*

354 *Training and development*

*self-development*. Maidenhead, McGraw Hill, 1978
PETTIGREW A M, JONES G R and REASON P W. *Organizational and behavioural aspects of the role of the training officer in the UK chemical industry: a research study in two phases*. Chemical and Allied Products Industry Training Board, 1981
PETTIGREW A M, JONES G R and REASON P W. *Training and development roles in their organizational setting*. Sheffield, Manpower Services Commission, 1982
PICKUP. *Paying for training*. Adult Training Promotions Unit Room 2/14, Department of Education and Science, Elizabeth House, York Road, London SE1 7PH, 1987
PIKE C *et al. Continuous development: a teaching pack for IPM course tutors*. London, Institute of Personnel Management, 1985

RACKHAM N, HONEY P and COLBERT M. *Developing interactive skills*. Northampton, Wellens Publishing, 1971
RODGER A. *The seven-point plan*. London, National Institute for Industrial Psychology, Paper No 1, 1952
RODGER D and MABEY C. 'BT's leap forward from assessment centres'. *Personnel Management*. July, 1987
ROSE D and NEWMAN P. 'Woolies shop around for excellence'. *Personnel Management*. May, 1987
ROTHWELL S. 'Integrating the elements of a company employment policy'. *Personnel Management*. November, 1984
RUSHBY N. 'How many psychotherapists are needed to change a light bulb?' in 'Training and Technology'. *Personnel Management*, January, 1988

SEYMOUR W D. *Industrial training for manual operatives*. London, Pitman, 1954
SEYMOUR W D. *Industrial skills*. London, Pitman, 1966
SEYMOUR W D. *Skills analysis training*. London, Pitman, 1966
SHEPHERD R. 'Off the line into management: an exercise in selection and training'. *Personnel Management*. December, 1980
SILLS P. *The behavioural sciences*. London, Institute of Personnel Management, 1973
SILVERMAN D. *The theory of organizations*. London, Heinemann Educational Books Ltd, 1970. (Heinemann Studies in Sociology)
SIMPSON B. 'T-groups, TA, NLP: what should we expect from human relations training?'. *Personnel Management*. November, 1984
SINGER E. *Training in industry and commerce*. London, Institute of Personnel Management, 1977
SINGER E. *Effective management coaching*. London, Institute of Personnel Management, 1979

STEVENS C. 'Assessment centres: the British experience'. *Personnel Management*. July, 1985

THOMAS M. 'Coming to terms with the customer'. *Personnel Management*. February, 1987
TORRINGTON D and CHAPMAN J. *Personnel management,* 2nd ed. London, Prentice Hall International Inc, 1983
TORRINGTON D and WEIGHTMAN J. *The business of management.* London, Prentice Hall International UK Ltd, 1985
TRAINING SERVICES AGENCY. *An approach to the training of staff with training officer roles.* Sheffield, TSA, 1977

UPTON R. 'The bottom line: Bejam's ingredients for success'. *Personnel Management*. March, 1987
UPTON R. 'Xerox copies the message on quality'. *Personnel Management*. April, 1987

WALDEN G. 'Leading lights in the battle against the new Dark Ages'. *Daily Telegraph*. 18 January, 1988
WARR P B, BIRD M and RACKHAM N. *Evaluation of management training.* Aldershot, Gower, 1970
WARR P B and BIRD M W. *Identifying supervisory training needs.* Training Information Paper No 2, HMSO, 1968
WOODCOCK M. *Team development manual.* Aldershot, Gower, 1979
WOODWARD J. *Industrial organization — theory and practice.* Oxford, Oxford University Press, 1965 (reprinted 1980).

# Further Useful Reading for Each Chapter

## CHAPTER 1
### An Introduction to Key Issues

HMSO, White Paper: 'Employment for the 1990's'. London, HMSO, 1988

INSTITUTE OF PERSONNEL MANAGEMENT. *A partnership in learning: how employers can and do use colleges for adult training.* A report produced by the IPM for the DES/PICKUP Programme. Oxford, Bocardo Press (for HMSO), September, 1986

INSTITUTE OF PERSONNEL MANAGEMENT DIGEST. 'IPM disappointed at MSC plans for training trainers'. No. 262, London, IPM, May, 1987

THE PLANNING EXCHANGE. *Paying for training.* The Planning Exchange (Helen Glass), 186 Bath Street, Glasgow, G2 4HG, Autumn, 1987

NATIONAL ECONOMIC DEVELOPMENT OFFICE. *People, the key to success.* London, NEDO, 1987

PETTIGREW AM, SPARROW P, and HENDRY C. 'The forces that trigger training'. *Personnel Management,* December, 1988

## CHAPTER 2
### The Politics of Training

BRAID J. 'Japanese culture in County Durham'. *Personnel Management,* March, 1982

BUCHANAN D and HUCZYNSKI A. *Organizational behaviour: an introductory text.* London, Prentice Hall International UK Ltd, 1985

BURNS T and STALKER G H. *The management of innovation.* London, Tavistock Publications, 1966

GALBRAITH J T. 'Matrix organization designs'. *Business Horizons,* February, 1971

HARRISON R. 'Nick Barton, special agent of change'. *Personnel Management.* February, 1988. (An account of the development of a 'Task' culture and matrix structure at a small private school)

HAYES C, ANDERSON A and FONDA N. 'International competition and the role of competence'. *Personnel Management.* September, 1984

LAWRENCE P R and LORSCH J W. *Organization and environment.* Division of Research, Harvard Business School, Boston, 1967

LEIGH A. *20 ways to manage better.* London, Institute of Personnel Management, 1984. (Chapter 6)

PETTIGREW A M. 'Some notes on power and political processes in organizations'. Paper presented to the British Psychological Society, London, 22 April, 1972

THOMAS M. 'In search of culture: holy grail or gravy train?'. *Personnel Management.* September, 1985

# CHAPTER 3
## Training and Development Responsibilities and Roles

BENNETT R. *Managing personnel and performance: an alternative approach.* London, Hutchinson, 1981. (Business Books Ltd)

BUCHANAN D and HUCZYNSKI A. *Organizational behaviour: an introductory text.* London, Prentice Hall International UK Ltd, 1985. (Parts 3 and 4)

BURNS T and STALKER G H. *The management of innovation.* London, Tavistock Publications, 1966

FRASER J M. *Introduction to personnel management.* London, Nelson, 1971

INSTITUTE OF PERSONNEL MANAGEMENT DIGEST. 'NCTD begins a very busy year'. IPM, January, 1988. (Explains current major training and development issues, including those relating to education)

LAWRENCE P R and LORSCH J W. *Organization and environment.* Division of Research, Harvard Business School, Boston, 1967

SILVERMAN D. *The theory of organizations.* London, Heinemann Educational Books, 1970. (Heinemann Studies in Sociology)

TRAINING SERVICES AGENCY. *An approach to the training of staff with training officer roles.* Sheffield, Training Services Agency, 1977

## CHAPTER 4
## The Integration of Learning and Work
## 1: The organization as a learning system

BARRINGTON H A. *ABCD: a boost for continuous development.* Focus on Adult Training, Dec/Jan, 1985/86

BARRINGTON H A. *Learning about management.* Maidenhead, McGraw Hill, 1984

BARRINGTON H A. 'Teaching managers their ABCD'. *Transition.* October, 1985

INSTITUTE OF PERSONNEL MANAGEMENT. *A boost for continuous development* Pack containing information about the campaign; articles; references; design for a CD Workshop. London, IPM (NCTD Department), 1983

INSTITUTE OF PERSONNEL MANAGEMENT. *A positive policy for training and development.* Policy statement prepared by the IPM National Committee for Training and Development. London, IPM, September, 1983

KENNEY J and REID M. *Training interventions.* London, Institute of Personnel Management, 1986. (Chapter 5)

NORD W R. 'Beyond the teaching machine: the neglected area of operant conditioning in the theory and practice of management'. *Organizational behaviour and human performance.* Vol 4, 1969

RICHARDSON J and BENNETT B. 'Applying learning techniques to on-the-job development.' Part 2, *Journal of European Industrial Training*, Vol 8, No 3, 1984

SKINNER B F. *Science and human behaviour*. New York, Free Press, 1965

## CHAPTER 5
## The Integration of Learning and Work
## 2: Auditing learning and developing effective learners

BARRINGTON H A. *Learning about management*. Maidenhead, McGraw Hill, 1984

BARRINGTON H A. 'Teaching managers their ABCD'. *Transition*, October, 1985

HONEY P. 'Learning styles and self-development'. *Training and Development*. January, 1984

INSTITUTE OF PERSONNEL MANAGEMENT. *A boost for continuous development*. Pack containing information about the campaign; articles; reference; design for a CD Workshop, London, IPM (NCTD Department), 1983

MUMFORD A. *Making experience pay*. Maidenhead, McGraw Hill, 1980

PASK G. 'Styles and strategies of learning'. *British Journal of Educational Psychology*. 46, 1976

PIKE C. *et al*. *Continuous development: a teaching pack for IPM course tutors*. London, Institute of Personnel Management (NCTD Department), 1985

REVANS R W. *Developing effective managers*. Essex, Longmans, 1971

## CHAPTER 6
## Establishing the Training Purpose, Policy and Plan at Organizational Level

ASHTON D, BRAIDEN E and EASTERBY-SMITH M. *Auditing management development*. Aldershot, Gower, 1980

BOYDELL T H. *A guide to the identification of training needs.* 3rd ed. London, British Association for Commercial and Industrial Education, 1987

HAYES C and FONDA N. 'Is more training really necessary?' *Personnel Management,* May, 1986

INSTITUTE OF PERSONNEL MANAGEMENT. *Identification of training needs.* Bibliography 102. London, IPM, July, 1986. (Information and Advisory Services)

MOORBY E. 'The case for the company training plan'. *Personnel Management.* November, 1982

MUMFORD A. *The manager and training.* London, Times Management Library, 1971. (Pages 18 to 25 give a detailed explanation of how to derive training needs from a manpower inventory and plan)

OLIVER S. 'The personnel role in technological change'. *Personnel Management,* July, 1984. (Explains how a requirement for technological change in an organization needs to be reflected in its training policy and plan)

ROBINSON K R. *A handbook of training management,* 2nd ed. London, Kogan Page, 1985

ROTHWELL S. 'Integrating the elements of a company employment policy.' *Personnel Management,* November, 1984. (Illustrates how training strategy and policy must and can be integrated with overall employment policy in an organization)

## CHAPTER 7
## Organizing and Managing the Training Function

BENNETT R and LEDUCHOWICZ T. 'What makes for an effective trainer?' *Journal of European Industrial Training,* Vol 7, No 2, Bradford, MCB, 1983

CASEY D. 'When is a team not a team?'. *Personnel Management,* January, 1985. (Argues persuasively that not every group of staff needs to be organized as a 'team' in the fullest sense of the word)

DAVIES J and DEIGHAN Y. 'The managerial menopause'. *Personnel Management,* March, 1986. (Emphasizes the importance of taking a positive attitude to the development of all staff in a department or function, not just the motivated and the high fliers)

GARBUTT D. *Training costs with reference to the Industrial Training Act.* London, Gee and Company Ltd, 1969

HANDY C B. *Understanding organizations.* 3rd ed. Harmondsworth, Middlesex, Penguin Books, 1985. (Penguin Business Library) (Part 2)

HARLEY J. 'How to assess your training costs'. *British Industry Week,* 22 November, 1968

INDUSTRIAL SOCIETY. *Personnel systems and records.* 3rd ed. London, Gower Press, 1979

INSTITUTE OF PERSONNEL MANAGEMENT. 'IPM disappointed at MSC plans for training trainers'. *IPM Digest,* No 262. London, IPM, May, 1987

INSTITUTE OF PERSONNEL MANAGEMENT. *Training.* Bibliography 21. London, IPM, June, 1986. (Information and Advisory Services)

KING D. *Training within the organization.* London, Tavistock Publications, 1968. (Social Science Paperback) (Chapters 9 and 14, dealing with the organization of the training function, and the selection and training of training staff)

KENNEY J AND REID M. *Training interventions.* London, Institute of Personnel Management,' 1986. (Chapter 2, on organizing the training function and training staff.)

KENRICK P. *Costing, budgeting and evaluating training.* Luton, Local Government Training Board, 1984. (Open-learning programme)

MUMFORD A. *The manager and training.* London, Times Management Library, 1971

PAGE D and JONES L H. *Maximising the pay off on investment in training.* London, Castlevale Ltd, 1983

PEPPER A D. *Managing the training and development function.* Aldershot, Gower, 1984

ROBINSON K. *A handbook of training management.* 2nd ed. London, Kogan Page, 1985

SINGER E J. *Training in industry and commerce.* London, Institute of Personnel Management, 1977. (Chapters 2 and 10, on organizing the training function)

TALBOT J R and ELLIS C D. *Analysis and costing of company training.* Aldershot, Gower, 1969

TORRINGTON D and CHAPMAN J. *Personnel Management.* 2nd ed. London, Prentice Hall International UK Ltd, 1983. (Chapter 32)

TORRINGTON D and WEIGHTMAN J. *The business of management.* London, Prentice Hall International UK Ltd, 1985. (Chapter 20)

TRAINING SERVICES AGENCY. *An approach to the training of staff with training officer roles.* Sheffield, TSA, 1977

WILLIAMS R. 'What's new in career development'. *Personnel Management,* March, 1984. (Explaining why career development must be planned for all, not just for the high fliers)

WILLIAMSON B, ed. *Directory of trainer support services.* London, Kogan Page and Institute of Training and Development, 1985

WOODCOCK M. *Team development manual.* Aldershot, Gower, 1979. (Full of diagnostic questionnaires and practical exercises)

WRIGHT P L and TAYLOR D S. *Improving leadership performance: a practical new approach to leadership.* London, Prentice Hall International (UK) Ltd, 1984. (Like Woodcock, very useful because full of practical exercises, checklists, and other diagnostic activities)

WRIGHT P L and TAYLOR D S. 'The interpersonal skills of leadership; their analysis and training'. Part 1 and 2. *Leadership and Organizational Development Journal.* 2,2 and 2,3, 1981

## CHAPTER 8
### Assessing Needs at Operational Level: job training analysis

BASS B and VAUGHAN J. *Training in industry: the management of learning.* London, Tavistock Publications, 1967. (Behavioural Science in Industry Series)

TALBOT J R and ELLIS C D. *Analysis and costing of company training.* Aldershot, Gower, 1969

TORRINGTON D and CHAPMAN J. *Personnel management.* 2nd ed. London, Prentice Hall International (UK) Ltd, 1983. (Chapter 27)

YOUNGMAN M B *et al. Analysing jobs.* Aldershot, Gower, 1978

## CHAPTER 9
### Assessing Needs at Individual Level.
### 1: Personnel specifications and records of performance

BENNETT R. *Managing personnel and peformance: an alternative approach.* London, Hutchinson Group, 1981. (Business Books Ltd)

TORRINGTON D and CHAPMAN J. *Personnel management.* 2nd ed. London, Prentice Hall International (UK) Ltd, 1983. (Chapter 28 gives an excellent discussion on the design and use of personnel specifications)

## CHAPTER 10
### Assessing Needs at Individual Level.
### 2: Trainability tests, assessment centres and self-assessment

BARRINGTON H A. 'Continuous development: theory and reality'. *Personnel Review.* Vol 15, No 1, 1986

BARRINGTON H A. *Learning about management.* Maidenhead, McGraw Hill, 1984

BOEHM V. 'Using assessment centres for management development: five applications'. *Journal of Management Development.* 4.4, 1985

BYHAM B. 'Assessing employees without resorting to a 'centre''. *Personnel Management,* October, 1984

INDUSTRIAL TRAINING RESEARCH UNIT. 'Trainability tests: a practitioner's guide'. Cambridge, ITRU Research Paper, June, 1977

LEWIS R and MARGERISON C. 'Working and learning — identifying your preferred ways of doing things'. *Personnel Review.* Vol 8, No 2, Spring, 1979

MACKINNON D W. *An overview of assessment centres.* Technical Report No 1, Centre for Creative Leadership, May, 1975

MEGGINSON D F and BOYDELL T H. *A guide to management coaching*. London, British Association for Commercial and Industrial Education, 1979

MUMFORD A. *Making experience pay*. Maidenhead, McGraw Hill, 1980

HONEY P. 'Learning styles and self-development'. *Training and Development*. January, 1984

POVAH N. 'Using assessment centres as a means for self-development'. *Industrial and Commercial Training*. March/April, 1986

STEWART A and STEWART V. *Tomorrow's men today; the identification and development of management potential*. London, Institute of Personnel Management; and Brighton, Institute of Manpower Studies (University of Sussex), 1976

STUART R. 'Using others to learn'. *Personnel Review*. Vol 4, 1984

THOMAS L. 'Learning to learn in practice'. *Personnel Management*. June, 1976

TRAINING SERVICES AGENCY. *Coaching for results*. Millbank Films Ltd. (Package of two films and instructor's notes)

## CHAPTER 11
### Assessing Needs at Individual Level.
### 3: Appraisal of performance

CANN P. 'Whitehall rewrites the appraisal form-book'. *Personnel Management*. March, 1986

DAVIES J and DEIGHAN Y. 'The managerial menopause'. *Personnel Management*. March, 1986

FARNSWORTH T. 'Appraising the appraisals'. *Personnel Management*. July, 1973

FLETCHER C. 'What's new in performance appraisal'. *Personnel Management*. February, 1984

FLETCHER C and WILLIAMS R. *Performance appraisal and career development.* London, Hutchinson Group, 1985. (Personnel Management series)

GEORGE J. 'Appraisal in the public sector: dispensing with the big stick'. *Personnel Management,* May, 1986

MEYER H H. 'Self-appraisal of job performance'. *Personnel Psychology.* 33, 1980

RANDELL G A, PACKARD P M A and SLATER A J. *Staff appraisal: a first step to effective leadership.* 2nd ed. London, Institute of Personnel Management, 1984

ROBINSON K. *Effective performance review interviews — a self-help guide.* London, Institute of Personnel Management, 1983. (A brief but excellent guide for practitioners, particularly helpful for its ideas about what to do during and after the development discussion)

# CHAPTER 12
## Designing the Learning Event.
## 1: The learning task

BASS B M and VAUGHAN J A. *Training in industry; the management of learning.* London, Tavistock Publications, 1967. (Behavioural Science in Industry Series)

BLOOM B S. *Taxonomy of educational objectives — cognitive domain.* Essex, Longmans, 1956

HARRISON R. 'A new look at the retraining of unemployed executives'. *Journal of European Industrial Training,* 1978

KENNEY J, DONNELLY E and REID M. *Manpower training and development.* 2nd ed. London, Institute of Personnel Management, 1979. (Chapter 6, pages 95 to 96, 'The age factor')

KENNEY J and REID M. *Training interventions.* London, Institute of Personnel Management, 1986. (Chapter 5, page 136, 'The age factor')

KRATHWOHL D R. *Taxonomy of educational objectives — affective domain.* Essex, Longmans, 1964

OTTO C P and GLASER R O. *The management of training.* London, Addison-Wesley, 1972

SIMPSON E J. *Taxonomy of educational objectives — psychomotor domain.* University of Illinois, 1966

# CHAPTER 13
## Designing the Learning Event.
## 2: Applying 'principles of learning' to design tasks: practical issues affecting design

BASS B M and VAUGHAN J A. *Training in industry: the management of learning.* London, Tavistock Publications, 1967. (Behavioural Science in Industry Series)

DUNCAN K D and KELLEY C J. *Task analysis, learning and the nature of transfer.* Sheffield, Manpower Services Commission, 1983

HILDGARD E R and BOWER G H. *Theories of learning.* 3rd ed. London, Appleton-Century-Crofts, 1966

HOLDING D H. *Principles of training: research in applied learning.* Oxford, Pergamon Press, 1965

JAMES R. 'The use of learning curves'. *Journal of European Industrial Training.* Vol 8, No 7, 1984

KENNEY J and REID M. *Training interventions.* London, Institute of Personnel Management, 1986. (Chapter 5)

OTTO C P and GLASER R O. *The management of training.* London, Addison-Wesley, 1970

SKINNER B F. *Science and human behaviour.* New York, Free Press, 1965

STAMMERS R and PATRICK H. *Psychology of training.* London, Methuen, 1975. (Essential Psychology Series)

WELFORD A T. 'On changes in performance with age'. *Lancet,* Part 1, 1962

## CHAPTER 14
## Designing the Learning Event.
## 3: Learning technology

BASS B M and VAUGHAN J A. *Training in industry; the management of learning.* London, Tavistock Publications, 1967. (Behavioural Science in Industry Series)

COOPER C L, ed. *Improving interpersonal relations — some approaches to social skill training.* Aldershot, Gower, 1979

CROFTS P. 'Distance learning's broader horizons'. *Personnel Management.* March, 1985

DOWNS S and PERRY P. 'Can trainers learn to take a back seat?' *Personnel Management.* March, 1986

INSTITUTE OF PERSONNEL MANAGEMENT. *Training.* Bibliography 21. London, IPM, 1986. (Information and Advisory Services)

GRANT D. 'A better way of learning from Nellie'. *Personnel Management.* December, 1984

PATRICK J. 'What's new in training'. *Personnel Management.* September 1984

PATRICK J and STAMMERS R B. 'Computer assisted learning and occupational training'. *British Journal of Educational Technology.* 3.8, pp 253-267, 1977

ROBINSON K R. *A handbook of training management.* 2nd ed. London, Kogan Page, 1985

ROBERTS K. 'The slide to video'. *Personnel Management.* April, 1984

RYNN B. 'Taking stock of computer based training'. *Personnel Management.* June, 1984

WRIGHT D. 'Keeping up with computer based training'. *Personnel Management.* October, 1981

## CHAPTER 15
## Evaluation of the Learning Event

DEMING B S. *Evaluating job-related training.* Washington D.C. American Society for Training and Development and Englewood Cliffs, New Jersey, Prentice Hall, 1982

INSTITUTE OF PERSONNEL MANAGEMENT. *Attitude surveys in industry.* Information Report no 3. London, IPM, 1970

INSTITUTE OF PERSONNEL MANAGEMENT. *Evaluation of training.* Bibliography 103. London, IPM, July, 1986. (Information and Advisory Services)

INSTITUTE OF PERSONNEL MANAGEMENT. *Training.* Bibliography 21. London, IPM, June, 1986. (Information and Advisory Services)

KENRICK P. *Costing, budgeting and evaluating training.* Luton, Local Government Training Board, 1984. (Open learning programme)

NEAGLE J J. 'Practical methods of evaluating and validating training'. Parts 1 and 2, *Training and Development.* Vol 2, Nos 5 and 6, September and October, 1983

PEPPER A D. *Managing the training and development function.* Aldershot, Gower, 1984

SINGER E J. *Training in industry and commerce.* London, Institute of Personnel Management, 1977

SMITH M. 'Using repertory grids to evaluate training'. *Personnel Management.* February, 1978

# INDEX